Issue 1	Date	14.01.97	Time	08.30	Location	Title
	Contact	Anna Guerrier	Telephone Fax	+44(0) 1483 711390 +44(0) 1483 720157	McLaren International Woking Business Park Albert Drive Woking Surrey GU21 5JY England Tel: +44(0) 1483 728211 Fax: +44(0) 1483 720157	**MP4-12**
	Contact	Wolfgang Schattling	Telephone Fax	0049 711 1784008 0049 711 1749010		
Details	NOTICE All information contained in this release is correct at time of going to print					Sneak Preview
	© 1997 McLaren International Limited	Designed and produced by TAG McLaren Marketing Services				

The science of
Speed

As part of our ongoing market research, we are always pleased to receive comments about our books, suggestions for new titles, or requests for catalogues. Please write to: The Editorial Director, Patrick Stephens Limited, Sparkford, Nr Yeovil, Somerset, BA22 7JJ.

The science of
Speed

Today's fascinating high-tech world of Formula 1

David Tremayne

PSL

Patrick Stephens Limited

First published in 1997

British Library Cataloguing-in-Publication Data
A catalogue record for this book is
available from the British Library

ISBN 1 85260 589 8

Library of Congress catalog card no. 97-61075

Patrick Stephens Limited is an imprint of Haynes Publishing,
Sparkford, Nr Yeovil, Somerset, BA22 7JJ.

Tel: 01963 440635 Fax: 01963 440001
Int. tel: +44 1963 440635 Fax: +44 1963 440001

E-mail: sales@haynes-manuals.co.uk
Web site: http://www.haynes.com

Haynes North America, Inc., 861 Lawrence Drive,
Newbury Park, California 91320 USA.

Designed & typeset by G&M, Raunds, Northamptonshire.
Printed and bound in France by Imprimerie Pollina s.a.,
Luçon, France n° 72408

Contents

Introduction

YOU THINK OF RACING car designers as self-effacing back room chaps of high-brow mentality who go around staring at distant horizons with the pre-occupied expressions of men perpetually twiddling some sort of mental slide-rule. Yet the pensive exteriors cloak natures just like any other personality in the Formula 1 paddock – be it driver, team owner, official, sponsor, journalist, or hanger-on. Giant egos just waiting to be unleashed.

Fortunately they are real people. Very clever – far cleverer than most of the others put together – but real nonetheless. And creative and devious and cunning, and often wondrously capable of lateral thought that can take your breath away.

And brave too, in their own way. The drivers take the real risks, but these are the men upon whose shoulders rests the ultimate responsibility for their safety. The men whose waking hours have been spent perfecting, mentally at first, and then in tangible form on drawing-board or CAD screen, the vehicle which the drivers will be expected to race to its absolute maximum. It is not an occupation for the faint-hearted, though most are paid just the right side of the National Debt for their brilliance.

Though this book is about the science behind the modern Formula 1 car, it is very much the story of these fellows, for it takes human beings to provide the spark that creates the machinery, just as it takes human beings to bring out its best.

Some of the chapters occasionally go over similar ground, but if the design of a Formula 1 car is a complex tangle of interrelated parameters, many of which impinge directly on one another, then so is any book which seeks to provide an insight into some of the mysteries.

We may all have serious regrets about the politics. But with all the implacability of dear old Daniel Bernoulli's venturi theorem, the ever-present polemics shape the direction in which the science is led, and control the extent to which it is exploited. Many far smarter types than I have tried to divest the sport of this necessary evil, and they didn't succeed, either.

David Tremayne
Harrow and Stapleton
1997

Acknowledgements

A TECHNOLOGICAL TOME PRESENTS A stimulating challenge to a writer better versed in books about people. Nowhere is the old adage 'a little bit of knowledge is a dangerous thing' more menacingly apposite. But technology doesn't happen without people driving it along, thank God, and in Formula 1 the men responsible for doing that drive as well as the guys out on the track. Some better.

Formula 1 is a curious blend of second-rate human beings, opportunists, and disgruntled millionaires, characters with light-switch smiles and nano-second memories. But the mix is spiced up by some peerless fighters to whom the spirit of competition is oxygen. I count it my fortune to have enjoyed the support and advice of some of the latter individuals, and to have benefited from their willingness to share knowledge without restraint. My thanks and appreciation go to them: Gary Anderson, John Barnard, Gerhard Berger, Jean-Christophe Boullion, Ross Brawn, Antonio Conterno, David Coulthard, Ron Dennis, Frank Dernie, Bernie Ecclestone, Heinz-Harald Frentzen, Mike Gascoyne, Mika Hakkinen, Hirohide Hamashima, Nick Hayes, Patrick Head, Mike Hennell, Johnny Herbert, Damon Hill, Mario Illien, Eddie Irvine, Alan Jenkins, Eddie Jordan, John Judd, Leo Mehl, Max Mosley, Adrian Newey, Steve Nichols, Jackie Oliver, Mark Parrish, Harvey Postlethwaite, Andy Tilley, Jos Verstappen, Jacques Villeneuve, Tom Walkinshaw, Martyn Walters, Charlie Whiting, Nick Wirth, and Peter Wright.

Foreword

by Patrick Head
Technical Director, Williams Grand Prix Engineering Ltd

In this book, David Tremayne takes an inside look at the frenetic background to the technical aspects of the cars that compete in the global Formula 1 Championship. For this challenge, approximately 20 cars are built to conform to the same regulations which leads to them all looking superficially very similar, indeed they are most easily distinguishable by their gawdy colour schemes. Underneath the shell however, they are very different.

Each car is the expression of a team of designers, most of which are led by one or two senior, highly experienced people. It is their interpretation of the rule book that becomes ever thicker in an effort to restrict excessive leaps in performance and to enhance safety aspects, year by year.

To achieve their objectives the team is assisted by many tools including some that are analytical and predictive of performance. Computer programs can predict airflow and forces developed by the car while chassis dynamics programs help to achieve optimum suspension characteristics. These are all part of the weaponry which each team develops to try to maintain a lead or overcome the lead of their rivals.

David has included many transcripts of conversations with designers, as well as with Max Mosely, President of the FIA. He is regarded with deep suspicion by most of the designers who all tend to think that the FIA is trying to manipulate the regulations to their team's particular disadvantage, paranoia is a close attendant in this highly competitive environment. *The Science of Speed* gives a clear insight into the rapidly developing technical aspects of Formula 1!

Prologue

Drivers v Computers

'Actually, the car would have done it itself, but . . . the next thing would have been
a little computer to control the inputs, to simulate a lap, and off it would have
gone. And you could have driven it around all day long.'

Gary Anderson, Technical Director, Jordan

L ATE IN 1996 AN event took place in
heartland America that vindicated
in full the remarkable decision made
four years earlier by Max Mosley, the
President of the *Federation Internationale
de l'Automobile*, to ban a number of complex computer-controlled driving aids
on Formula 1 cars.

On the 'Smart Highway' section of
Chrysler's Automated Durability road
test facility near Michigan, endurance
testing was augmented by the use, for
the first time, of robots instead of drivers
to pound test vehicles round the track
via a system of inductive coils and a
guide wire. Not only did the robots pos-
sess greater stamina for the taxing and
tedious duties, but word had it they were
cheaper, complained less, and didn't
chase the daily help. Mosley might have
been tempted, after all, into thinking at
times that at least some of these unusual
characteristics could beneficially be
applied to motor sport, but he had done
everything within his power to prevent
racing drivers from suffering the embarrassment of such mechanized emascula-

tion. 'It is important,' he said at the time,
'that racing drivers should be seen to be
in charge of their machinery. We are not
far short of the time when, if development continues at its present rate, there
is a very real danger that cars could be
conducted around a track without needing a driver. They would simply become
high-speed computer operators.'

Amid much wailing and gnashing of
teeth from teams which had invested
millions of dollars in the development of
this high technology, there was also an
overriding scepticism for Mosley's point
of view. But then Formula 1 is renowned
for its insularity and occasional inability
to spot wood where trees grow.

During that 1993 season, Alain Prost
won his fourth and final World
Championship, exploiting to the full a
Williams–Renault that put at his disposal a plethora of technical goodies which
helped to speed him on his victorious
way. There were anti-lock brakes, to
minimize the risk of wheel locking; traction control, to maximize acceleration
out of corners by preventing the rear

wheels from spinning; and active ride suspension, to smooth away surface undulations and optimize the car's aerodynamic pitch. Additionally, should he so wish, he could decide when and where his car changed gear for him, by altering software programming to suit his own tastes.

Then, at a stroke it seemed, the FIA outlawed such 'gizmos'.

The axe fell on the weekend of the Canadian GP in June, on the Ile Notre Dame in Montreal, confirming the Formula 1 teams' worst fears and generally taking the rest of the world, which had been largely unaware of brewing undercurrents, by surprise. What made it all the more perplexing was that Mosley himself had, not six months earlier, pledged the FIA's whole-hearted support for pushing this complex new technology to its limits.

At the end of the 1992 season the newly-crowned World Champion, Nigel Mansell, had beaten a hasty and embarrassing retreat to America, quitting Williams in disgust at its insistence on employing Alain Prost and its refusal to agree financial terms for him to stay, and running headlong into the welcoming arms of IndyCar team owners Carl Haas and Paul Newman. It was embarrassing for Mansell, a proud man denied a season in which to savour his long-sought success and the likely chance of repeating it. And it was embarrassing for the Formula 1 community, and Williams in particular, to lose yet another World Champion at a time when IndyCar racing had established itself as a far better 'show' (albeit a technologically inferior one). That winter, unable to resist the opportunity to rub a little salt in the wounds and to denigrate what he described as a 'domestic' racing series of vastly inferior quality, Mosley defended the use of electronics with eloquent vigour:

'There are so many things on an F1 car,' he began, (before falling back on the barrister's ploy of ingenuous self deprecation to add, 'I'm not an engineer and I'm not an expert'), 'but there are many things that you'd like to be able to change from one point to another on the circuit. All sorts of aspects. At the same time electronics enables analysis of what's going on in the car to a much greater extent. Already they've got the

The start and the finish. As Alain Prost and Damon Hill led away at the start of the 1993 Canadian GP in Montreal in their high-tech Williams FW15s, the Stewards of the meeting had already deemed that the majority of the cars in the race contravened the regulations, and the FIA's move to ban the electronic 'gizmos' was well advanced. (LAT)

means of knowing everything that's happening. Then you've got all those sorts of systems like suspension, gearbox and so on. The engine. And the interesting thing, I think, is that all of these things have a parallel with ordinary cars. So you have all of those things going on in Formula 1, all of which, or most of which, have a benefit to ordinary cars.'

He warmed to his theme as the discussion meandered gently through the role of high technology in the sport's premier category:

'It's an important thing if the environmentalist lobby gets stronger, as it will. I think in the long-term that motor sport has to be sold on positive benefits to the environment because it speeds up research and development. So long as the regulations are directed in the right way, or push research in the right direction, that's okay on the one side. On the other side, it creates an atmosphere in which it's not the thing to go quickly on the roads. If you want to go out and go fast, you compete. That ethos will gradually start to come across. Those are the two planks on which we can continue to justify motor sport in an increasingly environmentally conscious society.'

The problem with dramatically increased use of electronics, somebody quietly pointed out, was its effect on good old-fashioned entertainment. Mosley appears to be at his best answering such questions. 'Well that comes by itself,' he responded, almost rubbing his hands with undisguised enthusiasm. 'What's a good example? It doesn't in any way detract from the excitement that we've got semi-automatic gearboxes, yet a Formula 1 semi-automatic gearbox is an enormous leap forward compared to a road automatic because there's no power loss, therefore it's more economical. If we bring in a stepped undertray so that the ride height becomes realistic and the electronic suspensions can be developed in a way that they are useful for road cars, that wouldn't affect the

entertainment factor at all. And in fact it would be doing some very useful work.'

But that was then, and this was now. And now there had been a dramatic change of heart that sent shock waves reverberating up and down the pit garages at the Circuit Gilles Villeneuve. All, that is, except for the habitually troubled Scuderia Italia garage where, in a glorious quirk of irony, its tardy and uncompetitive Lola–Ferraris, which lagged dreadfully behind their rivals in the development stakes, were declared the only legal cars.

Contrary to appearances, however – and, indeed, contrary to Mosley's own comments outlined previously – the axe had been poised to fall for quite some time. On 12 February, a Friday, what was then known as the FISA's Formula One Commission had met at the Hilton Hotel at Heathrow Airport's Terminal 4. The subject of the meeting was the very future of these electronic aberrations, and those in favour of banning them found a potent proponent in Ferrari. The Italian team had, courtesy of designer John Barnard, been the first to introduce the semi-automatic gearbox, which relied on electronics to operate its hydraulic systems to shift gears far faster and far more accurately than any human being and conventional clutch system could. But as 1993 in particular was to prove, Ferrari's attempts at creating an active ride system were to be both laughable and, in one race, downright dangerous. For when Gerhard Berger tried to rejoin the Portuguese Grand Prix at Estoril, his Ferrari took it into its mind to turn sharp left leaving the pits, when a gentler manoeuvre to the right was required. Riding a Prancing Horse that was now even less predictable than the wildest mustang, Berger could only sit it out as the red car shot across the track at 90 degrees to the flow of traffic, which included Derek Warwick's Footwork and J. J. Lehto's Sauber, which were approaching at maximum speed of around 180 mph. Only by the grace of God was a catastrophic accident avoided.

Ferrari, then, had little cause to thank the British teams for their technological strides, and early in February 1993 its chairman Luca Cordero di Montezemolo played one of those political jokers that the team habitually appears to hold up its sleeve for just such occasions. Without fundamental changes to the regulations, he threatened, Ferrari would quit Formula 1. Cleverly, he sought out the FISA's weak spot, with a thinly veiled threat to race in the IndyCar series.

Playing neatly into Mosley's hands was another factor. Back in November 1992, in a quite remarkable oversight, Frank Williams had submitted his team's application for the 1993 World Championship one day late. This was a sensitive time, for Frank's team had given its rivals a damned good kicking as Mansell ran amok to win nine of the 16 races in the 1992 series, and had clearly enjoyed a devastating technical advantage. Any means by which Williams might be slowed down, even if it was by engendering doubt over acceptance of its entry, was welcomed by his rivals.

At this time the sport was run on principles outlined in the Concorde Agreement which, as lawyer to the Formula One Constructors' Association (FOCA), Mosley himself had drafted back in 1981, the year when FOCA and FISA finally made peace after years of internecine warfare had come to a head with threats of a breakaway World Championship. Under the terms of the Concorde Agreement, any change to the technical regulations required unanimous agreement from all of the teams, but now Williams, the team least likely to agree to a ban on 'gizmos', had ill-advisedly put itself in a weak bargaining position. This unanimity would be a bone of contention right up until sweeping changes were introduced for 1997 when the agreement was next renewed, but it was at that time a cornerstone of Formula 1, and as such non-negotiable. But without Williams in the championship there was a greater chance that others, all of whom lagged behind, might decide against continuing along the high-tech route. Frank was over a barrel. And the man who was pushing hardest to hold him there and to bring about the demise of 'gizmos' was Flavio Briatore, the boss of Benetton.

Briatore broke the mould of racing drivers/entrants turned Formula 1 team owners, for his background encompassed no probationary spells in the lower echelons of the sport. Instead he was a businessman whose business now happened, on behalf of the Benetton clothing chain, to be Formula 1 motor racing. Briatore had been involved since the middle of 1989, and was now prepared to flex as much muscle as he could. He was steadfastly opposed to Williams being allowed to race, unless Frank capitulated.

'If Frank didn't change, then I was very strong in my position,' he said. 'He would not have got an entry if we had anything to do with it, unless he changed. Even if we had had to get all the Benetton lawyers in the world on it. If he had got an entry without change, it would have been no problem for Benetton to stop. Our new technical facility was suitable for any of our other activities, if we were to have pulled out of Formula 1 if it did not come to its senses.'

And he made other views very clear, too. 'Ferrari? Is vital to Formula 1. For sure, is a very important part of the future of motor sport. More important than Williams, McLaren and Benetton together.

'You know, Frank didn't seem to understand the need for the new proposals. How's it going to affect him any worse than any other team not to have spare cars, for example?

'We spend a fortune making the cars go fast, then a fortune to make them go slow. The difference goes in the rubbish bin. Is crazy. If this business hadn't changed in the next three or four years, it would have been finished. We don't just need Williams and McLaren; we need little teams too. Formula 1 must have technology, but not just to please the engineers. Honda pulled out, and Frank was saying that technology is the future. It's okay for Honda to leave after bringing in all the technology in the first place. But television wants something different. If you interview 3,000 people, none of them would be interested in traction control or whatever. They want it to be a sport, and a fight between drivers. People see a car on television, they don't know how fast it's going. They have no idea. You can slow the cars and the technology down, and nobody would worry.'

Mosley failed to get the unanimity that he sought when the meeting was held. However, despite this disappointment he did achieve compromises that were to have far-reaching effects, for, in order to be granted his entry, Williams was forced to agree to limitations on the use of the spare car, and on the number of tyres teams could use at race meetings. This was where such proposals were initially propounded and accepted. And it was here that Mosley pushed through his plan to ban 'gizmos' altogether from 1994 onwards, and to introduce stepped bottom chassis for 1995 in order to reduce aerodynamically generated undercar downforce by automatically mandating a higher ride height.

This was a stunning development for everyone concerned, and though Williams abstained during the vote (along with Ron Dennis of McLaren, which was also making massive investment in the new technology), the writing was on the wall.

Thus, with effect from the first race of 1993, the new rules regulated the timing of practice and qualifying (which would later be amended for 1996 so that there was only an hour of qualifying on a Saturday afternoon), and teams would

be allowed seven sets of tyres per car per event. Spare cars were permitted to be used only on race day, and while fuel companies were still allowed to research into exotic brews, some 'rocket fuels' of the past were outlawed.

Williams, of course, was duly 'allowed' back into the fold and went on to dominate 1993 just as it had 1992. However, Mosley's proposed ban on electronic aids was not proceeding at the pace he required, and, in a bit of thinly disguised collusion, the stewards in Canada made the 'sudden' discovery just before qualifying on Saturday afternoon that everything bar the Lola–Ferraris contravened the regulations. The news was kept a close guarded secret as the teams were circularized with an official statement, which read:

'The Stewards have received a report from the FISA Formula One Technical Delegate that the cars listed below do not comply with Article 3.7 of the FIA Formula One Technical Regulations in that each one has one or more specific parts which influence its aerodynamic performance but do not remain immobile in relation to the sprung part of the car.'

It then listed Williams, Tyrrell, Benetton, McLaren, Lotus, Minardi, and Ferrari. Mosley had found his loophole for an immediate ban: the cars' active suspension systems were effectively movable aerodynamic aids, which were specifically proscribed. He was not present in Canada, having only two days earlier added presidency of the FIA to that of the FISA (which at that time was the FIA's sporting arm but would later be brought back under the FIA title alone).

The stewards' statement continued: 'The report also states that the following cars do not comply with Articles 1.3 and 2.4 of the FIA Formula One Technical Regulations in that their propulsion systems are not under the control of the driver at all times.'

And they listed Williams, McLaren, Footwork, Jordan, Larrousse, Minardi,

Ligier, Ferrari and Sauber, because they all had traction control and most of them had fly-by-wire throttles.

The stewards concluded: 'We are of the view that the issues raised are very substantial and involve the entire championship. Consequently, the most appropriate course of action is for us to send a full report to the FISA under Article 152, paragraph 3 of the FIA Formula One Sporting Code, and to allow the above mentioned cars to participate in the 1993 Canadian Grand Prix.'

This lofty tome was signed by Roger Peart, J. Gordon Betz, and Roberto Causo (later to act as Williams's lawyer in the Senna case).

Those who recalled Mosley saying 12 months earlier: 'We've got to let technology have its head. Electronics enables analysis of what's going on to a much greater extent,' smiled wryly, but not for long. Along the pit lane there was widespread derision that technical delegate Charlie Whiting had suddenly made the 'discovery' after so many races, and a degree of sympathy with the position his absent boss was believed to have placed him in. And most of the team owners saw it as a warning shot across the bows of dissidents Frank Williams and Ron Dennis, who had been making noises about recourse to international law to stem what they saw as a breach of the Concorde Agreement. Generally, this latest move was seen as the FIA telling them that if they couldn't get them one way, they'd get them another, and not to bother doing anything so foolish.

Frank Williams and Patrick Head were in no mood for small talk, but issued a press statement which ran: 'We refer to the Stewards' Bulletin no 3 issued today following a report from the FISA Formula 1 technical delegate concerning the legality of certain teams' cars in the 1993 World Drivers' and Constructors' Championships.

'We consider this document to be regrettable in its contents and regrettable in its timing.

'We sincerely hope the validity of Nigel Mansell's World Drivers' Championship and the Williams–Renault World Constructors' Championship are not called into question by the contents of this document. The team's suspension system has been identical for the past 22 Grands Prix, and its conformity with the regulations has never been called into question until today.'

Alain Prost won the Canadian GP from Michael Schumacher, with Williams teammate Damon Hill third, and a week later, as the sport mourned the sudden death of the much-loved former champion James Hunt, a degree of sense was emerging as the FISA sought to clarify the report by outlining the difference between the Sporting Regulations and the Technical Regulations, something that would again be useful when the subject of grooved tyres was raised for the 1998 season.

'Under the Sporting Regulations if the proposed changes are voted by the Formula One Commission and the World Council and published before the 31st of October, the new rules are applicable as from 1st January of the following year, without any need for unanimous agreement from the Teams.

'Unanimous agreement of the Teams is needed only for changes at shorter notice than above.

'If the proposed changes are voted by the Formula One Commission and the World Council they are applicable, without the need for the unanimous agreement of the Teams, as from the second 1st January following the date on which they are voted (e.g. any change voted and published before 31st December 1993 will be applicable as from the 1st January 1995).

'The unanimous agreement of the Teams is needed only for changes relating to the engine, transmission, or minimum weight and for changes at less than the above notice.'

It then proceeded to discuss the 1994

changes which were in the process of being railroaded through:

'At its meeting on 12th February 1993, the Formula One Commission approved, by 10 votes in favour and three abstentions, the ban on automatic driver aids and confirmed that these changes affected the Sporting – and not the Technical – Regulations. Both the FISA World Motor Sport Council (18th March) and the FISA Plenary Conference (9th June) unanimously endorsed these proposals. The changes are therefore applicable as from 1st January 1994.'

The FISA also tackled the Canadian GP report, stressing that it was a report and not a decision. It stressed that it could not comment on the report until it had been examined by the World Council which, conveniently enough, was not due to meet until 13 October.

Though ostensibly similar in external appearance, the 1997 contenders from Williams and Stewart were very different machines to their 1993 forebears. Gone were the 3.5-litre engines, computer-controlled active suspension, anti-lock power brakes, and self-shifting gearboxes, while the chassis, though still of carbon composite manufacture, were stronger still and offered the drivers even greater protection. (ICN UK Bureau and Stewart GP)

Effectively this meant that the teams would be away in Japan and Australia, preparing for the final two events of the year. There was also a ridiculous chance that, as they did so, the Lola–Ferraris of Michele Alboreto and Luca Badoer might find themselves vying for the World Championship, although ironically this team had also tried traction control in Canada, removing it from the side of the righteous . . .

There were also grumbles that the basis of Whiting's assertion that leading cars such as the Williamses and Benettons were illegal, because their active suspension included a control (known as the 'low-drag' button, which allowed their drivers to alter the chassis rake along the straights), did not apply to other, less sophisticated cars. Yet everyone had been tarred with a similar brush.

Jackie Oliver, founder of the Footwork (Arrows) team, spoke for those in favour of the aids when he said: 'The banning of technology was firstly suggested to reduce cost, to keep people in Formula 1. I disagree with that; I don't think it does. People would stay in Formula 1 with only three wheels if they could save money.

'I thought active ride was very useful; it was a useful tool to sort things out. If it had been left in place it would have become as cheap as automatic gearboxes.'

Teams could sell their active systems to others, to defray the development costs, as McLaren TAG sold its system to Footwork. Yet Oliver remained opposed to suggestions that teams should be allowed to sell chassis technology as well. 'Who would they sell them to?' he asked. 'I disagree with the idea of selling to new teams, to keep down their entry costs. I think it would destroy the entire fabric of Formula 1.'

On that, at least, it seemed he was in agreement with the governing body.

In the end all the semantics mattered little, for Mosley had the perfect weapon to ensure that everyone agreed to drop the driver aids for 1994. If they didn't agree, they might just jeopardize their points scores not only in 1993, but in 1992 as well. And there was one more trump card to play, for Mosley and Vice-President of Marketing, Bernie Ecclestone, had also set their minds on the reintroduction of refuelling for 1994, to liven up the television spectacle. To nobody's great surprise, the FIA won the day. The 'gizmos' were dead.

Was Mosley right, after all, in his prediction that even Formula 1 cars might be capable of automatic guidance around a race track? In 1993 Jordan technical director Gary Anderson had voiced this opinion: 'More and more, the move is towards total electronic control. In five years electronics will control everything on the cars. They can do things so much better and so much quicker than the driver can. It's the way things are going.'

And in 1997 he had provided a comment that was all the more telling when put into its correct perspective, which was that at the time of the 'gizmo' ban Jordan was still a small team, and a long way behind the dominant Williams, which was the clear master of electronic aids. And yet . . .

'Where would it have been now if nothing had changed?' he mused. 'Well, we specified out some things when we were working with a hydraulics company at the time, and I'm really glad we never went ahead with them because in hindsight I don't think they would have worked. But it was a fully active car, really. The driver was just giving the inputs; he was going to tell the car when to turn right or left. Actually, the car would have done it itself, but . . . The next thing would have been a little computer to control the inputs, to simulate a lap, and off it would have gone. And you could have driven it around all day long. So, no, it wasn't far away. It was a long way away but it wasn't, if you know what I mean. With a little imagination and a lot of money . . .'

Chapter 1

How much technology do you need?

'I don't think there's much justification in having huge amounts of technology unless it actually gives you something, to be honest. But at the end of the day, what would make you think that you could actually catch up with Williams?'

Frank Dernie, former Technical Director, TWR Arrows

'WHEN I FIRST WENT from Leyton House to Williams, the thing that most impressed me was the organization, without doubt,' Adrian Newey said. 'The organization and the management. The range of machinery, all the floor space. The overriding thing was the calm, collected way in which the place was run.'

Like many a designer who had made his name with a small organization, Newey was appreciating one of the reasons why a top team is so successful, why moving to work for one can put a designer's work onto a completely different plane. Why the technology behind the modern Formula 1 car is so utterly crucial to its success.

'I think Leyton House always had a very weak management structure, and got away with it in the early days when there were only 50 people because there wasn't much to manage! The problem was that when it grew, the management didn't grow with it and it became more and more uncontrollable. Williams expanded much more slowly over the years, and Frank Williams and Patrick

Head have always done an exceptionally good job of making sure that they employ good managers. They've got the infrastructure, the strength in depth.'

The other point that came home to him fully as he took up the post of chief designer – which he would hold until leaving for technical directorship of McLaren in 1997 – was that the big teams can invest in sufficient people to conduct the research and development that is an essential part of a new design. Thirty years earlier, Ron Tauranac drew out his Brabham BT24, Robin Herd penned the McLaren M5A, Tony Rudd created the BRM P115, and Mauro Forghieri the Ferrari 312. Only Colin Chapman, as usual ahead of his time, really relied on other designers, such as the late Maurice Philippe, to flesh out his basic design concept. Today the picture has changed dramatically, for it is no longer possible, nor even desirable, for one man to design a complete car with all of its various high-tech systems.

'It hasn't been possible for one man, in the true sense, to design a car for a

This was but the tip of the Williams–Renault iceberg as Damon Hill and Jacques Villeneuve posed at Paul Ricard in 1996 with members of the race and test teams, and personnel from Renault Sport. In total, Frank Williams employed around 240 people at his new factory in Grove. (ICN UK Bureau)

very long time,' Newey confirmed. 'I think it's possible for one man to come up with a broad concept, but that's becoming increasingly difficult as the car becomes more and more a complex technical beast, if you like. Certainly, you never think of one person being responsible for the design of the Airbus, for example. It's just too big a project. I think Formula 1 car design is going that way, so what you do need is one or two people who are responsible for the overall concept, to make sure everybody is headed in the same direction.'

Nick Wirth took over as chief designer at Benetton for the 1997 season following the 'retirement' of chief designer Rory Byrne (who shortly afterwards changed his mind and accepted an offer to take up a similar position with Ferrari) and the switch to Ferrari of technical director Ross Brawn. Wirth was the man behind the short-lived Simtek team which raced in Formula 1 in 1994 and part of 1995 before succumbing to the financial pressures, and as he spelled out the new structure at Benetton he provided a graphic insight into why the top Formula 1 teams have such high staffing levels.

'Now that I have "moved up", Graham Herd has stepped forward to take charge of organization and decision-making in the design and drawing office. Then there are the section leaders, Andy Moss in composites design; Dave Wass (a former Arrows designer) in transmission design; Andy Wymer in stress analysis; and Martin Tolliday in mechanical design. I'm in overall charge of aerodynamics, too, with senior aerodynamicist James Allison running the programme and reporting directly to me. There is a strong group working within the drawing office, and we are also massively upgrading our computational facilities within the company. We've just put together a deal with Hewlett Packard that will take us, literally, a quantum leap forward.'

On the technological side today, the technical director is king, but the various roles can be confusing, as Ross Brawn explained:

'I would say I was a designer in the days when a designer did everything. I designed the Arrows A10s and A11s and the World Sportscar Championship Jaguar XJR-14. So I've done racing cars and so I have a pretty good insight into design and I can understand that side of it. And I've been going racing for a long time, so I have a lot of experience of it. It's that combination of things.

'These days, though, the roles are becoming so separate. You get a designer who stays at the office, you get somebody goes to the track. I was fortunate to be involved in motor racing when you tended to do all those things. I've spent time designing cars, and time at the race track, and it's going to be interesting because not many people are doing that now.'

This hands-on experience makes Brawn very strong in terms of overall technical organization. 'That's what I like to do,' he confirmed, 'though I'd love to design a car again, but I can't. If I get too heavily involved in that, something else would suffer so I have to try and keep a balance about the whole arena and devote my activities to whatever is the weakest area at the time.'

Frank Dernie's career spans back to his Hesketh 308E, which he designed in 1977, and encompasses spells as chief aerodynamicist at Williams, chief designer at Lotus, race engineer at Benetton, and technical director at Ligier and then Arrows (for whom he was responsible for the A18 which Damon Hill drove in the 1997 season), until he left mid-season as John Barnard took over.

'The most important thing the technical director has got to do is decide how to prioritize the design process,' he said. 'Which bits you carry over from last year's car because the reliability is worth more than trying to improve them; whether you should put more of your resources into aerodynamics or into a titanium upright or into a nine-speed gearbox or what have you. You have to make a decision where to put the emphasis, and some people obviously have different opinions to mine.'

Dernie worked for Benetton during Michael Schumacher's championship-winning years, and team chief Flavio Briatore admitted that he would spend £33 million in the 1997 season, over and above the cost of using Renault engines. By then, of course, his wage bill had fallen because Schumacher had gone to Ferrari and Gerhard Berger and Jean Alesi could command less, but the saving in salaries had been invested elsewhere, into technology. Historically, those teams which cannot afford or attract the best drivers always express the opinion that investment in technology – to build a car so good that it does not need the best driver – is preferable to forking out vast sums for somebody who will only be part of the organization for a short time before moving on or retiring. But what level of technology is desirable?

Dernie provided a typically forthright response to the question. 'I have no idea what is desirable. Desirable to whom? I mean, it's desirable to me, because it's fun. But whether the technology makes the motor racing more attractive to the spectators, I have no idea. To spectators like me, it perhaps does. But to people who just want to see cars going four abreast round corners, banging wheels, then it probably doesn't.'

And there is a suspicion today that technology embraces the 'bigger toys than the next boy' syndrome. 'Maybe,' Dernie conceded. 'I don't think there's much justification in having huge amounts of technology unless it actually gives you something, to be honest. But at the end of the day, what would make you think that you could actually catch up with Williams, never mind hope to overtake them, unless your technology is better than they are going to have? There's no point in having the ambition to match what Williams had in 1996, by the time you've built up to the level you want to

Viewed from any angle, the new TWR Arrows factory in Leafield, Oxford, is a highly impressive, self-contained facility. Small wonder that, having been persuaded to visit it in September 1996, World Champion elect Damon Hill decided to throw in his lot with Tom Walkinshaw's team. (TWR)

reach, because by then they'll be years ahead still. You've got to go to where you think the future lies, and you've got to hit it, too, because if you were to arrive at the point where you think the future lies and it doesn't lie there, and teams such as Williams are already well past that, you've not even caught them up never mind overtaken them.

'What would make anyone think that they could catch up with Williams, or McLaren for that matter, like that? Without the knowledge, without the equipment? You would be spectacularly lucky, wouldn't you? Like there are 10,000 to one odds against that sort of thing ever happening!'

For aspiring new Formula 1 teams,

the statistics can indeed be daunting. Taking the three statistically most successful teams, this is how Ferrari, McLaren, and Williams stacked up at the end of the 1996 season:

Ferrari employed 330 people at its Maranello base, where its factory occupied 60,000 sq ft, and a further 30 in the Ferrari Design & Development offshoot in Guildford run by designer John Barnard (which Barnard bought from Ferrari and renamed B3 Technologies early in 1997).

It also owned its own test track, Fiorano, which, recently modified, now measured just under three kilometres; it was often criticized because it lacked truly high-speed corners, but nevertheless provided a mixture of turns up to fourth gear, and, since the track was equipped with the very latest measurement telemetry all round its length, it allowed precise calculation of engineering improvements to be made on the cars.

In terms of its basic engineering facil-ities, Ferrari had everything a Formula 1 team could wish for, including five-axis cutting machinery, autoclaves, and four-poster test rigs, and its all-new 60 per cent wind-tunnel was due to become operational in the middle of 1997, in time to play its role in the design of the 1998 car.

McLaren International employed between 250 and 260 staff, broken down thus: design 35; management 10; race team 30; test team 20; research and development 20; marketing 25; production 110 to 120. There was a 75,000 sq ft factory in Boundary Road, Woking, for McLaren International, with another 40,000 for McLaren Cars and the research and development department. Once regarded as the Formula 1 factory par excellence, Boundary Road had become cramped for McLaren's burgeoning needs, and team owner Ron Dennis was working on a new facility which would occupy some 150,000 sq ft in a 40 acre green field site.

Clinical conditions prevail at Leafield, where TWR Arrows has two different sized autoclaves at its disposal for baking carbon fibre composite components. (TWR)

McLaren's engineering facilities were also state-of-the-art, with very high quality machining and fabrication capabilities, and it employed full CAD-CAM (computer-assisted design and computer-assisted manufacturing) equipment. Its 1996 contender, the MP4/11, was 100 per cent designed on a CAD system. McLaren also had a four-poster static test rig, and a five-axis cutting machine, but at that point did not have its own wind-tunnel. Instead it had a special use agreement at the 40 per cent facility owned by the Royal Ordnance Society in Teddington. It also had access to Cray computers so that it could complement its wind-tunnel aerodynamic research with the branch of mathematics known as computational fluid dynamics, which enable an operator to create mathematical models for prediction and comparison use.

In 1996 Williams moved from its cramped Didcot factory, which had occupied 90,000 sq ft of an 18 acre site, to a brand new facility in Grove, not far from Oxford. This occupied 150,000 sq ft within a 32 acre site which looked like a movie lot at Pinewood Studios, and accommodated between 230 and 240 staff. Management, administration and finance accounted for eight; design 30; research and development 20; the race team 25; the test team 18; marketing 12; and production 117 to 127.

More than anything else, Williams has always placed an emphasis on its engineering ability, and it too had all the state-of-the-art machining and fabrication facilities that one would expect of a major Formula 1 team, including full CAD-CAM equipment, and a five-axis cutting machine. At that time is was also the only team to own and utilize a 50 per cent scale wind-tunnel.

By contrast, when Eddie Jordan took his team into Formula 1 at the start of the 1991 season he employed around 30 people and was still operating from his old premises inside Silverstone circuit, which occupied 15,000 sq ft. At Christmas that year he moved into his new purpose-built 60,000 sq ft factory opposite the gates of the track. By the time he clocked up his 100th GP in Argentina, six years later, the staffing level had risen to 140, and he had also acquired a 45,000 sq ft technology centre in Brackley which housed a wind-tunnel. This race marked the first time that the team was in genuine contention for victory, as Ralf Schumacher fought it out with eventual winner Jacques Villeneuve and Eddie Irvine, but Jordan said of this milestone: 'If I tried to do today what we managed to achieve in 1991, it just would not be possible.'

Jordan sourced out much of the manufacture of its car, including the monocoque chassis (which is now made in-house), and relied on the use of proprietary engines leased from Ford. The team was able to graduate from Formula 3000, in which it had been highly successful, and to grow as its Formula 1 fortunes improved. But Jordan does not believe he could repeat that now. 'Today, if you are coming into Formula 1 with the view of challenging for the World Championship within three or five years, you simply cannot do it without a relationship with a major engine manufacturer, and access from the start to very high levels of technology, in-house. Things have moved on in the past six years, and it has become much, much harder for relatively small teams, as we were back then, to graduate in that manner.'

Dernie enlarged on the lurking difficulties that are all too ready to push back the schedule of expectations:

'When you are starting a team from scratch to be fully competitive in three to five years, the investment in technology is simply massive. And that takes a long time. For example, in March 1997 our five-axis machine was finally manufacturing the first thing that it had manufactured for a race car, and I started at

Arrows just after the Brazilian GP in 1996 and it had been ordered then . . . So a year later it was just in the process of making its first bit. So a piece of equipment that was ordered a year earlier hadn't been of benefit at all in the car we were then running.'

From this it's possible to appreciate not only that the time-scale for engineering can be very, very long, but also that teams need to make the investment a long time before they will begin to see it even start to repay. That's one of the principle reasons why graduation to Formula 1 can be such a difficult undertaking. Few newcomers have anything like the level of funding that they really need, and very often their budgetary calculations are guesstimates that prove to have erred on the low side once a project is fully up and running and reality places a hand on the tiller. Such teams either have to bite a high velocity bullet (which is most unlikely given the financial pressures) or else have to go to outside companies for the work to be done. Either way, compromise is inevitable.

'We did a massive upgrade to the instrumentation in the wind-tunnel in the winter of 1996,' Dernie continued, 'and we were able to start using the revised tunnel in March 1997, so that meant that there was absolutely nothing from that huge investment in the current car. That was a significant investment. It's a brilliant kit, but none of it was available for the design of that car.

'So while the time-scales at the race track are very short, like 1 min 19 sec or whatever a quick lap may take, behind that everything is incredibly long term.'

The need for a wind-tunnel, and for a composite facility and in-house machining and fabrication capacity, are self-evident, but less obvious at first sight is the need for a four-poster rig or, as the very best teams now have, a seven-poster. Gary Anderson, technical director of Jordan, explained just why this has become just another key element in the

technological armoury in recent years:

'The whole thing about the car running on the track is the aerodynamics, the roll and pitch and the air load. And every bump that you go over is important. If you're going at 300 kmh it's a very small bump because the thing has so much grip. It'll put a shock in the car but the grip will be there. And the sevenposter is just to put all these loads into it. A complete aero map, complete roll and pitch map, so that the car is actually doing the things on the rig that it does on the track. It has the same tyres it has on the track, so they're also giving an input. So it's very complex.'

A four-poster just pushes it up and down, moving the wheels against the mass. It's quite a sight as the frequencies and oscillations build up to the point where a 550 kg car is literally bouncing off its four pads, and you can appreciate just how stiff the suspension really is. A seven-poster does the same thing with the wheels and the mass, but also adds the aerodynamic responses too, the effect of all the attitude changes under braking, acceleration, and yaw.

Data acquired by a car's onboard telemetry can be downloaded directly into the seven-poster's system. Thus for the team's engineers it is just like running the real car, so they are able to monitor with great precision exactly what really happens when the car is in action on any given circuit, because on the rig they can duplicate a Grand Prix the same way that transient dynamometers can put engines through their paces exactly as if they were racing at, say Monte Carlo. For durability running a car can be put through GP distances at varying frequencies to monitor its responses and to enhance safety or reliability margins. It is very sophisticated research.

Williams and McLaren were probably the first teams to run a car on a rig at the factory while downloading empirical information from a practice or qualify-

The static four-poster test rig is an essential part of all top teams' armouries, since it can precisely duplicate the forces and loadings a car experiences on any given circuit, in any given set-up configuration. (Sporting Pictures [UK] Ltd)

ing session at a race track, thus creating immediate in-the-field feedback. The responses assessed there overnight allowed the operating engineers to advise the race engineers at the circuit on the best set-up for the following day's running.

'In Argentina on the Friday we were gathering together packets of data that would be running back at the Silverstone factory while we were sitting back after practice,' Anderson said early in 1997. 'Then we'd see what the car was doing and then work through Friday night and Saturday morning to try to work out three or four different set-ups.' Jordan had not long acquired its rig, and he estimated that it would take the team three or four races to become fully familiar with interpretation of the data.

'When we got back from Brazil, for example, we discovered that what we'd had there wasn't right. It takes time.' Yet by the next race, in Argentina 10 days later, his cars were much closer to the pace.

This is where manpower is so important, for there is a clear risk of information overload. 'Sure, that can be a problem,' Anderson agreed. 'Really, one of the biggest things is that the FIA has now done away with testing in the week before a Grand Prix, and there's no testing from the last race until 5 December, or whatever it is. All that is a good idea, and the theory was that it would save money. But teams will just simply spend what money they would have spent testing on test equipment instead. And if we'd just had a one-car test team, maybe we'd go for a two-car team or a four-car team and just pack more in. Or if the test rigs are going flat-out, you need twice the staff to do that. The more you limit it, the more expensive it's going to be.'

At 1997 prices a seven-poster rig cost around £300,000. But to that you then had to add the cost of a self-contained unit in which to house it, and a dedicated test car, and the staff to run it.

With wind-tunnels a great deal naturally depends on the scale and sheer size of the tunnel and the power of its motor, but teams now talk airily of £5 or £6 million pounds for a state-of-the-art facility. Even the smaller 40 per cent tunnels are around £2 to £3 million by the time the facility has been installed and calibrated. Wind tunnel testing is thus dramatically expensive, whether a team invests in its own equipment or uses a proprietary tunnel. With the level of investment required for the former, it takes many years to amortize the cost, regardless of the saving on the latter. Typically, a team will use its facility every other week, five days a week, testing for that duration and then spending the next week analysing the data and formulating further test ideas. That's a minimum of around 125 days of the year actually running in the tunnel, and the bigger teams will do even more than that.

★ ★ ★

In 1995 there were vague suggestions that one means of helping small teams to graduate to Formula 1 might be to waive the regulation demanding that all entrants must design and build their own chassis, and permit existing teams to sell their outdated chassis to the newcomers, just as in the past teams such as Lotus had sold the previous year's 'works' chassis to private entrants such as Rob Walker. In the end Bernie Ecclestone was against it, on the basis that it might devalue Formula 1, and that the requirement to design and man-ufacture its own chassis was an indication of a team's commitment. Jackie Oliver, the founder and part owner of the Arrows team (which raced for some years under the Footwork banner), explained why this was also particularly repugnant to the smaller teams, which were less successful but still prepared to create their own cars:

'There are many people who want to come into Formula 1. A lot of them don't do it because it's so difficult, because you've got to build your own car. That's the premise Formula 1 is built on. If you allow those teams at the top to sell their cars they would agree because they can get some extra money. So more money would flow into Formula 1 and go to those people up the front of the grid, and it's not them who need it. It's those down the back who do. That's the first premise.

'The second is that it would bring new teams into Formula 1, who had no infra-structure at all to build their own race car. They would hire 20 mechanics, and a young driver, 1,500 sq ft of empty floor space, start up a few months before the start of the season, with a Williams, and graft an engine to it. They can go to the sponsors and say, "We have the World Championship-winning car, this young driver, we can do what Hill did last year." In reality that wouldn't happen, but the sponsor would like that sales pitch and the money would not go to Arrows, Tyrrell or whomever, but to this new team. Economics being what they are, Arrows would collapse and this new structure would be formed based on engineering sold to it by Williams, which would then have no further interest. The team would not perform to the same standard that Hill did because there are so many factors involved, the sponsor would go away disappointed. Then Williams decides not to sell the technology any more, and the guy says: 'I'm not going to be dependent on them. I'm going to build my own car.' And he remembers that the Arrows factory has been on the market for a year, and he buys it . . .'

Oliver also denied that it would be cheaper for a team to start up buying somebody else's car rather than creating its own manufacturing base and designing and building its own car, even though the latter course requires an investment of around £5 million to produce the first chassis.

'Okay, start-up costs would be less, but you wouldn't be able to maintain the chassis. Say you crash it; and Williams won't make you another one. So you've got to borrow the moulds and have one built by a composite company. Outside suppliers, I can tell you, are more expensive because you've got to pay their profit and their overhead.

'Everybody thinks you could buy an F1 car like you do a Reynard or a Lola in IndyCars, but they are geared up with full service back-up. But Formula 1 teams selling their cars would not be, and that's where it would all fall down. People are idealistic; they don't understand what makes the business work.'

Oliver, it should be said, does. Though Arrows failed to win a single one of its 283 Grands Prix in his time as co-owner with Alan Rees, and though he did sell a sizeable shareholding to Tom Walkinshaw in 1996, the team survived. Only Ken Tyrrell knows more about that key element of Formula 1 than Jackie Oliver.

The message, then, is clear: Formula 1 is for big boys with big toys, and those who can't afford to play the game shouldn't even consider venturing into the playground. As recent history relates, however, there has been no shortage of hopefuls willing to chance their luck and, more often than not, someone else's money. Pacific, Simtek, Forti, and Lola all came and went in the effective space of three seasons, leaving trails of bills in their wake. In Lola's dreadfully misguided case the largest and most successful manufacturer of proprietary race cars allowed Formula 1's siren song to lure it on to the financial rocks. When founder Eric Broadley saw the chance to enter sooner than he had intended, thanks to the carrot of sponsorship from MasterCard, he pressed the green light a year earlier than intended. His bulky T97/00s thus rolled into Melbourne not just short on testing but without even having ventured into the wind-tunnel that Lola had used so successfully to shape the IndyCar that had won Michael Andretti five victories the previous season. The cars were hopelessly off the pace, failed to qualify, and were pushed into oblivion before they had even turned a wheel at the next race. If a team with all of Lola's experience could be drawn into such a catastrophic error of judgement, it was indeed a salutary lesson for anyone else with aspirations to venture on to Formula 1's yellow brick road.

Chapter 2

The design process

'There are good reasons why things have evolved the way they have, so we try to avoid change for change's sake. You can never fall shy of saying something isn't good enough, but we do things the way we know is going to work.'

Mike Gascoyne, deputy Technical Director, Tyrrell

E VEN AS LATE AS the 1970s, a racing car was designed from the inside out, chassis first and then bodywork. The former had to be sufficiently large to carry the driver and the fuel, and strong enough to offer maximum pro-

The shape of the modern F1 car evolved over the years, the principal differences between the Eighties and the Nineties being the move to raised noses and underslung front wings, smaller rear wings, and the use of 'barge boards' to smooth airflow behind the front wheels. This is Damon Hill at Monaco in 1995. (ICN UK Bureau)

tection in an accident. Once that basic structure had been determined, it was clothed in the smoothest bodywork possible.

The advent of the carbon fibre composite monocoque chassis in 1981, when John Barnard at McLaren and Colin Chapman at Lotus introduced their new models, opened up vast new vistas by enabling designers to mould complex curvatures into their chassis, where before the manufacturing shortcomings of sheet or honeycomb aluminium had restricted their licence. Carbon fibre composites also did away with the need for complex box section structures, facilitating the construction of narrower monocoques.

But it was when, in the mid- to late-1980s, aerodynamics really assumed the importance that they enjoy today, that an unseen revolution began to take place. From that point on the basic thinking changed. Instead of designing from the inside out, the concept became to design from the outside in. Aerodynamicists outlined the optimum shape they required, and it was then up to the designers to package all the necessary equipment within that smooth outer shell.

When he had designed his trend-setting McLaren TAG Porsche MP4 series of cars in the early 1980s, Barnard had liaised very closely with engine designer Hans Metzger at Porsche, with the result that the cars were harmoniously packaged to optimize their aerodynamics. With the trend towards sleeker cars with minimal aerodynamic compromises,

McLaren's MP4/12 was widely regarded as the most elegant and aesthetically integrated car of the 1997 season, though again it was evolved from its predecessor. When the trend was for high noses, the MP4/12 'broke' new ground by reverting to a droopier shape. (McLaren)

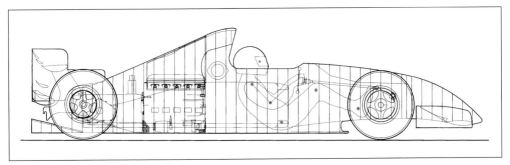

If the design of a Formula 1 car could be represented geometrically, it would be a circle, for the process has no beginning and no end, and designers chase integration from one end to another. This general arrangement drawing of Tyrrell's 1995 023 model nicely illustrates the way in which the various components – such as driver, wheels, engine and gearbox – are packaged within the overall shape. (Tyrrell)

packaging became ever more important, hence the rash of transverse gearboxes at one time to package the rear end more neatly, and then in turn the reversion to longitudinal transmissions when regulation changes favoured them more from the aerodynamic standpoint (see Chapter 11).

Perhaps the most extreme expression of this aerodynamically minimalist philosophy was seen in Adrian Newey's highly original 881 design for Leyton House March in 1988. This was a car of quite outstanding beauty, which appeared to set new standards for aerodynamic excellence; but there was a heavy price to be paid, and that price was driver comfort. Time and again either Ivan Capelli or Mauricio Gugelmin suffered leg cramps because the cockpits were so restricted, and more than once Capelli burned out the clutch because there was so little room for his left foot that he would inadvertently rest it on the clutch pedal. Jackie Stewart once tested one of the cars for a magazine series, and wrote: 'It's a wonderful car, but a lot of its attributes are completely wasted if the driver does not remain comfortable enough during the course of a race to be in a position to exploit them to the full.' Likewise, Ross Brawn's 1989 Arrows A11 was so minimalist that when he collided with Bernd Schneider's Zakspeed in the Brazilian GP at Rio de Janeiro, driver Eddie Cheever fell over as he climbed from the cockpit because his cramped left leg had gone numb.

Clearly, no matter what new philosophies were brought to bear in Grand Prix car design, there were no short cuts and no magic wands to obviate the need for good, old-fashioned common sense. Good Formula 1 design today remains fundamentally what it has always been, experience, knowledge, and flair mixed with the process of clear and logical thinking and intelligence. Where the differences lie are in some of the methodology, a lot of the materials, and the sheer number of people who are now an essential part of the design and production process. The days of the one-man band designers are as distant as the eras of front engines and high-mounted wings.

In 1996 the Tyrrell team was a relatively small entity nestling in a modest 20,000 sq ft site in Ockham in the woodlands of Surrey. It employed 110 personnel, of whom 15 were engaged in design work, 30 worked as mechanics/race engineers, 10 to 15 in administration, marketing and management, and the rest in production. The size of Tyrrell's workforce exerted an inevitable

The right working atmosphere is essential. This is the design office at Arrows's Leafield plant, where each work station has a CAD system. (TWR)

influence on its working practices. 'We haven't got the biggest budget in the world either,' said deputy technical director Mike Gascoyne, 'so over the past few years we have worked at creating a very structured method to how we approach the design process.'

Tyrrell, of course, is a long-established team, so inevitably its design process for a new car will begin with a ruthless assessment of its predecessor. Initially, around June in a current season, Gascoyne and Harvey Postlethwaite, Tyrrell's managing director of engineering, liaise very closely with production manager, Simon Barker, as they start to consider the initial specification for the new car in a series of design meetings. At this point only the three of them are involved.

'When we had our meetings for the 025, our 1997 car,' Gascoyne said, 'the two things we started with were (a) when we wanted to run the car; and (b) the specification of the car, what we actually wanted to do. With the first of those points we consulted Simon and worked backwards from the reference points he provided, and worked out our schedule that way.

'It was really a matter of going back over all of the basics and asking ourselves the obvious questions. What were we going to do with the gearbox? Were we going to keep the existing internals or go for something new? That sort of thing. In our situation we knew from the outset that we were really going to produce "Son of 024", our 1996 car, and that we were not looking to create anything revolutionary. I always get amused when somebody says of a new car:

"Everything is different". There are a lot of areas on a car where there is no performance; they can only go wrong. And the last thing you want to be doing is redesigning. Everyone redesigns a bit; you will redraw it and there will be small changes. But really with a lot of it you can say the concept is going to stay the same. The fuelling system, for example. You may have to redesign it slightly, but generally speaking the concept is going to stay the same.'

It's the old adage: if it ain't broke, don't fix it. And since time is money in Formula 1 there is very little point investing man hours and money into redesigning something if there isn't going to be a discernible performance gain.

'You are trying to evolve a car,' Gascoyne continued. 'The aerodynamics might be totally different because there might be areas you want to redress, but at that preliminary stage Harvey and I would be working on drawing up a detailed specification.' And that specification really is very detailed. The initial specification for Tyrrell 024, as an example, was more than 25 pages long.

At this early stage of the process nothing fundamental is fixed, and anything may be changed if circumstances later require it. And this is the point where a team's inherent discipline and structure, allied to careful planning, can later reap dividends not only in terms of funding saved, but also in efficiency gained. The watchword at Tyrrell is cut the haste, enhance the speed. 'You can save a month later on just by being a week ahead early in the process,' Gascoyne said.

The items with the longest lead times are the gearbox and the monocoque, and they are the most expensive, too. The former may be marginally more expensive because more of it usually has to be done out of house, though costing the manpower to make a tub can be difficult. But both cost around half a million pounds apiece.

Once the initial meetings have produced the detailed specification for the new car the net is widened, as it is sent to the senior designers for their comment. Once they have provided their feedback to Postlethwaite and Gascoyne the project begins to gather pace.

'We had the 025 briefing around June,' Gascoyne said, 'but you never actually have a day when you can say right, we've started, because of course you are constantly updating last year's car. But about the end of April, start of May, you think okay, we've run the car, done all the tests, done some races, we know how quick it is and we know what its problems are . . . And by then you should have in place a lot of the programme to improve the car, because you finished a lot of the aerodynamics the previous November or December, so you've had six months working on the aerodynamics, and the new components, such as undertrays and diffusors, what have you, should be coming through from the production department.'

As an example, the Tyrrell 024 was unveiled in February 1996, and by the San Marino GP at Imola in late April/early May a new undertray was ready. Later in May new wishbones and suspension were ready for the Spanish GP at Barcelona.

'Around May you ask yourself what it is too late to change on the existing car, and what shortcomings it has that you must fix. By that stage also you've most likely found some beneficial things in the wind-tunnel that you can't incorporate into the existing car because it's too big a job. You can't do all-new bodywork, for instance. So effectively that's going to be the basis of the new car.'

Such new investigative work at Tyrrell will probably have started in the wind-tunnel in June, after perhaps two months on the drawing board. Manufacturing lead times for full-scale parts can be up to three months, hence the early start.

By the end of June the design directors will issue the design specification for the new car, which will contain all its major parameters: wheelbase, dimensions and location of the rear bulkhead, engine length, gearbox type. Even if a team isn't absolutely sure what engine it will use the following year, it can still go a fair way down the line at this stage. Most likely it will use the same gearbox internals, but a change of engine make, or even just a lowering of something such as the crankshaft centreline, can require a new transmission casing, and that can require three months' lead time. That's because the new casing will require new casting patterns, which take between six to eight weeks, while the actual casting takes one to two weeks, and machining the raw casting ready to accept the internals can add up to another six weeks.

'By the time we get to this stage the only things we are thinking of are the chassis, the nosebox to a small extent, and the gearbox,' Gascoyne said. 'On our 1996 car we used a pneumatic gearshift, but we were investigating hydraulics for 1997. We were not worried so much where the suspension goes, and though we might be discussing concepts on it, what the geometry is going to be wasn't relevant.'

Suspension components are relatively easy to make, but the production process must nevertheless be structured carefully to avoid subsequent bottlenecks in the fabrication and machine shops.

By the end of June, then, in Tyrrell's case, the design document was ready, covering the architecture, bulkheads, predicted weight distribution, general concepts, the designers' aims for the car, and the concepts of suspension, steering, and stiffness, defining as much of the final specification as possible after the input from the senior designers. But even at this stage the specification can be modified, if necessary. Tyrrell lets its

small group of designers get on purely with designing. Rather like Colin Chapman used to, Postlethwaite and Gascoyne set the concepts and targets, and then give the designers the autonomy to turn those concepts into final production drawings and to justify any suggestions they might have for altering any aspects.

Even in a small team such as Tyrrell, design roles are well defined. Mark Tatham was responsible for the suspension; Gary Thomas the gearbox; Chris Radage the engine installation, which included fuel, oil, and cooling systems; and Chris White the increasingly important electronics, which must be integrated fully. Nigel Leaper was in charge of the composite department, and Paul Mason actually did the drawings for the chassis. Gascoyne headed the aerodynamics department, which was run day-to-day by Bonnie Lane, while simultaneously acting as Postlethwaite's filter by handling the day-to-day running of the technical side and the drawing office. All of the senior designers had the assistance of detail draughtsmen, and besides the obvious aims of efficiency, lightness, and reliability, the overriding objective in every instance was to optimize integration of all of the car's components. To that end, none of the designers worked in isolation, but liaised very closely with the others.

Once the decisions had been made on what parts of the 024 would be modified on the 025, they were ordered where necessary in areas such as the transmission, not only to give the supplier time to organize its production, but to help the team's own cashflow.

Gascoyne stressed that Tyrrell had developed its own in-house style for designing its cars, having learned the hard way after decades in the business. 'There are good reasons why things have evolved the way they have, so we try to avoid change for change's sake. You can never fall shy of saying something isn't good enough, but we do things the way we know is going to work.'

Tyrrell's aim by the start of July 1996 was to have provided its in-house pattern makers with information on the chassis for 025. They worked by hand then, but plans were already in the pipeline to conduct a lot more of the manufacturing work with the aid of computers. Most teams make significant use of computer-aided design technology, which allows them to create 3D images on the computer screen and to alter any part of the design and assess quite quickly its effect on other areas. Once mastered, this complex technique is inevitably more detailed and accurate than the old-fashioned method of drawing everything on paper, though some designers, notably John Barnard, like to do full-scale drawings as well, as it helps them better to visualize the new car.

Tyrrell invested heavily in upgrading the CAD facilities in its drawing office in the early part of 1996, with 10 new stations using the Pro Engineer software produced by technology partner Parametric. The longer term plan for 1997 was also to build up its CAM (computer-aided manufacturing) side for the future. The machine shop already has five computer-controlled machines. Most teams have relationships with the major computer hardware and software suppliers, and McLaren and Stewart in particular made much of the fact that their cars were 100 per cent designed by CAD.

When they received the cross-sectional datums for the chassis of Tyrrell 025 the pattern makers began creating its broad outline using a series of thick wooden blocks matching the various sections. As these were bonded together they began to form the shape for the buck of the new chassis. This would then be used in the composite shop to create the mould from which the first carbon

Computer-generated co-ordinates are duplicated by machine to create a series of cross-sections which the chassis department uses in the preparation of the buck, from which the monocoque chassis moulds are taken. (Sutton Motorsport)

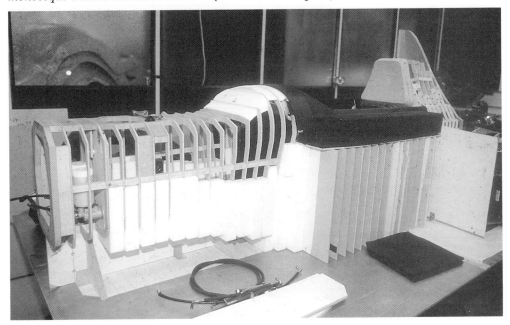

fibre composite chassis would be produced.

Even at this stage the facility existed to alter the shape of the buck, but by the end of July the pattern makers had all of the relevant information they needed to create the bucks for the chassis and the rear bodywork. Again, planning here was crucial to avoid bottle-necks in the carbon shop when the moulds were produced, and later in the trim shop. While that work was going on the design office had begun looking in earnest at sidepod, wing endplate, and undertray shapes, all simple enough components which nevertheless require numerous moulds and therefore present points of potential delay.

By August the patterns were finished, and the moulds of the chassis and the rear bodywork were ready by September. The composite department then began to lay up the first chassis. This was done by applying layers of carbon fibre, Kevlar, and, in places, honeycomb aluminium, in carefully stipulated directions, rather as if the craftsmen were laying up conventional glass fibre mouldings. The tub was then run through its essential cooking cycle in an autoclave to bond it together. This complete process took around six weeks, because it was the prototype, but subsequent monocoques take significantly less time.

Once cooked, the monocoques must have all of their suspension pick-up points and systems mounting points machined on a super-accurate jig, which ensures that the process can be repeated from chassis to chassis with 100 per cent accuracy and confidence. This is a three week job with the prototype, but subsequently takes a week per chassis.

A final polish is essential before this mould for a carbon fibre undertray is put to use, so that the surface is completely smooth and will release the finished component easily. (Fondmetal)

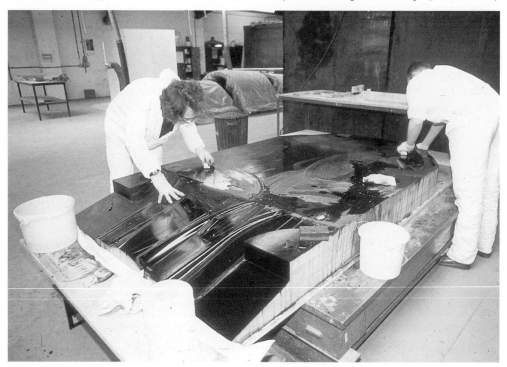

Tyrrell's first 025 'tub' reached the shop-floor early in December, so that final assembly and fitting out could be completed over the Christmas run-up. At this stage the fabrication shop, which had been working in parallel, had simultaneously finished production of the suspension components and suppliers such as Secam had provided radiators. After all that effort, the first chassis then usually goes through its mandatory crash test sequence at Cranford, prior to its first track test.

'Generally we aim to finish our new cars by the second week of January, and test by February,' Gascoyne said, 'but inevitably that all slips along the way. It's an ongoing system and we are trying to develop it all the time. You can't expect to be like Williams, without going through that process. You can't have a system where you keep changing things all the time. You need stability, and the right people.'

Consistency wins races, because it brings in its wake stability, reliability, and repeatability. Gascoyne added: 'If you look at the McLarens in the late 'eighties, they were all the same basic car. The Williams since the FW14 in 1991 was a similar concept. The car looked totally different by 1997, but I'm sure it was the same concept. That's what brings success.'

In that comment also lies the root of why motor sport dynasties come and go, why one team will dominate for a long period before another finally overtakes it for its own spell up front. If a team can gain an advantage and keep hold of it, it can stay one step ahead of the opposition, and this is precisely what McLaren managed in the late 1980s, and what Williams did for most of the 1990s. But the trick is to be able to spurt forward into that initial lead, let alone to maintain it.

Things don't always go to plan, as McLaren showed in 1995. Nigel Mansell was a late signing for the team,

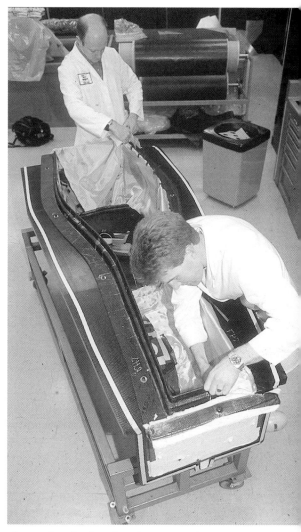

Once the basic chassis mould is ready, technicians can begin laying up the various weaves of carbon fibre, Nomex, and honeycomb composites. Most chassis bucks are split longitudinally for ease of manufacture of the chassis, the halves of which are then bonded together. (Sutton Motorsport)

following prolonged negotiations with Williams which had eventually proved fruitless, and by the time the deal with McLaren was done the MP4/10 design had been finalized and manufacture and construction were well under way. The car had been designed around the Finnish driver Mika Hakkinen, who was taller and much slimmer than the hefty British former World Champion. In his first test in the new car, it soon became apparent that Mansell, a driver who liked to put a lot of muscular effort and strength into his driving, had trouble getting comfortable in the cockpit.

Adrian Newey had also gone through a similar problem back in his Leyton House March days, when his smooth 881 set new records for cockpit tightness. He recalled: 'I'm more mature on things like that now! But what actually happened with the 881 was that we built the usual mock-up that the driver sat in. When the 881 was designed Mauricio Gugelmin hadn't been signed, so it was only Ivan Capelli at that stage. He sat in the mock-up and said it was okay. In the event it obviously wasn't, because it was too tight for Mauricio. It seems that drivers can sit in a mock-up and think it will be okay, and when they actually do have to drive it, they can't manage it.'

After lengthy discussion Mansell and McLaren managing director Ron Dennis decided that it would be best if he stood down for the first two races. The British driver Mark Blundell thus deputized, while McLaren began a frantic race to modify its existing chassis and to alter the moulds sufficiently to create new cars for Mansell's use. This entailed a massive logistical operation that McLaren carried out with military precision under the supervision of operations director Martin Whitmarsh.

'Our plan centred around changing the shape of some non-structural inner panels in the monocoque,' Whitmarsh explained. 'Instead of being slab-sided, they would be concave to realize an extra 50 mm in the mid-section. Nigel was not abnormally proportioned, it was just that the car was optimized around Mika and was in any case narrower than the previous year's MP4/9 at the point where the driver's backside was. It was also narrower in the hip area. When Nigel just sat in the car he felt the cockpit was tight, and as soon as he tried driving it hard he knew it was not on.

'The problem was that we could not simply knock up a new chassis to accommodate him. The process was just too complicated. First of all we initiated a packaging study, which took three days. Then we produced a mock-up, based on that. That accounted for another three days. Then we analysed Nigel's feedback for a day, before using computer-aided design to create the surface geometry. That was another three days' work. After that some of the programmes were carried out in parallel, as we investigated structure and lay-up, but this is how the rest of the programme ran:

'Making the model patterns took ten days; painting the chassis patterns five; making the new moulds four; manufacturing new components another ten; assembly two; five-axis machining six; final assembly of the new monocoque five; assembly of the internal chassis structure two; undergoing new FIA crash tests another two; painting three; and final car build and set-up six. That was a total of 65 days' work, but we actually started the project on March 16th, and completed it by April 18th, making it a little over 30 days. We worked 24-hour days, and were quite pleased with ourselves . . .'

Overall, that little project cost McLaren around £300,000, or around £12,000 per millimetre of space realized. Or £150,000 per race for the two races that Mansell finally did do for the team before deciding to quit Formula 1 for good at the Spanish GP.

Ron Dennis has frequently stressed that there is no magic in Formula 1, just a lot of hard work and common sense, and the Mansell saga underlined that. But as McLaren itself proved in its victory-less drought from Adelaide 1993 to Melbourne 1996, it doesn't require much to be amiss in the design for a team to fall from front-running status. The worst part of it all is not that there is a fundamental problem necessarily in any Formula 1 car that doesn't win a race; just that the car that does win is doing things just slightly better still. And that's why Formula 1 is such a complex, competitive sport, where everyone is working right on the limit of their abilities. Dennis summarized it best when he said at Imola in 1997: 'People fail to understand the complexity and performance of Formula 1 cars. And just how very hard it is to win. We have been invincible once, and I know how you can fall out of it. It's tough, but then if it was easy everyone would be doing it. If you look at the performance of the top three teams over the past 20 years, you can see their ups and downs and just how damned difficult it is. This is a business in which it is very, very tough to win.'

Chapter 3

Catching the wind

'Aerodynamics are one of the single most important performance parameters. Certainly, if the aerodynamics aren't any good then the car won't be any good.'

Adrian Newey, Technical Director, McLaren

M AX MOSLEY IS FOND of saying that trying to get rival designers to agree on anything is a thankless task. But if there is one thing about which none of them has to think twice, it is the importance of aerodynamics in Formula 1 design. Since the tyre war between Goodyear and Bridgestone the rubber has assumed prime importance as a means of reducing lap times, but aerodynamics remain a very close second. Some of the leading players gave their views:

'Aerodynamics are one of the single most important performance parameters,' said Adrian Newey, the former chief designer of Williams and now technical director at McLaren. 'You know, people try to put percentages on how much the driver contributes, and how much the engine does and all that sort of thing, but I think that's all rather meaningless, personally. Certainly, if the aerodynamics aren't any good then the car won't be any good.'

Ross Brawn, the technical director at Ferrari, was in no doubt which area he would concentrate on most if he were to start designing again: 'I like aerodynamics, and I started my career in the late 'seventies and early 'eighties working in the wind-tunnel at Williams, doing a lot of work on the ground effect cars. So that's something I enjoy. It was quite a spectacular period. But even that's becoming more technical now. We have computational fluid dynamics (cfd), we have new techniques for tunnel testing. It used to be a little bit of a black art, but we have four or five aerodynamicists now.'

Before the question about priority of design influences was even finished, Arrows's former technical director, Frank Dernie, said: 'Aerodynamics, by a country mile. We were in the tunnel all the time, every week, several days a week. And there was just so much data coming back, which is why you needed so many people. I didn't process it; somebody else processed it for me. I asked them what to look for, told them what I wanted, and I had to rely on their integrity and what they were doing. That was one of the hazards of moving further up the chain. I used to do that at

Wind-tunnel testing is the most detailed and expensive research that any Formula 1 team will conduct, but as Williams has proved time and again, it is investment that pays off. Talk to any designer, and it's the one area above all upon which they place the greatest emphasis. (Sporting Pictures [UK] Ltd)

Nothing is new in motor racing. Though Williams pioneered the droopy lower plane in its rear wing, the idea of the secondary wing mounted as an extension of the main wing was in general use by 1994, while the small strakes on either side of the FW16's nose were an echo of BRM's P133s of 1968. (ICN UK Bureau)

Williams, and then at Benetton, Ligier, and Arrows I had to rely on somebody else doing it for me.'

'Traditionally, if you improve the aerodynamics of a car, it responds very well in terms of lap times,' suggested Nick Wirth, who took over from Rory Byrne for 1997 as chief designer at Benetton. 'I think that the improvement in aerodynamics has come from packaging. We haven't changed our wind-tunnel yet, but we are going to. We are building something very special . . .'

* * *

Over the years the FIA has tried very hard to place a reasonable ceiling on lap speeds, by controlling aerodynamic excesses. Much of the move against active ride would spring from that. A year before the 1993 watershed it had reduced the width of the tyres in order to limit cornering speeds, but typically the disgruntled designers did not feel that trading off the reduction in grip against reduction in frontal area was sufficient compensation. They did not regard offsetting the advantage of drag reduction, by running more wing angle to compensate for the reduced cornering power, as progress, and progress is everything. 'In this game,' said Gary Anderson, 'you simply cannot afford to stand still. So what we have tried to do is to package our 1993 car to take advantage of the tyres but also to gain a proper increase in downforce, rather than just balancing the reduced drag from the smaller tyres by cranking on more wing.'

This is the sort of thinking that the FIA would constantly find itself up against as the two bodies pursued their mutually incompatible aims, one trying to speed the cars up, the other trying to slow them down.

The tyre changes for 1993 were important, but equally important were others to the front wings. At that time, and since 1983, all Formula 1 cars had to have a flat floor, and that floor was taken as one of the datum lines from which measurements for the official parameters were made. All aerodynamic concepts centred around this.

'Overall, I think the new regulations have lost us around five or six per cent of our 1992 downforce,' Anderson continued. 'In 1992 the regulations said that everything ahead of the centreline between the car's front wheels had to be at least 25 mm above the ground. Now that measurement is 40. Additionally, that area of measurement has now been extended further back, so for 1993 the area that must be 40 mm above the track is now measured from a line taken across the car from the back edge of the front tyres.

'What this means is that you won't see those sparks that you used to get from the special titanium skids fitted to the wing endplates. They were there because they helped the wings to channel air beneath the flat floor and feed it to the diffusor.'

The diffusor is the upsweep at the tail of the car's floor, which controls the undercar manifestation of what is called the Bernoulli Effect. This is the classic venturi theorem expounded by the Swiss physicist Daniel Bernoulli. When air passes beneath the car it becomes compressed. As this happens its flow speeds up and its pressure falls, and since the undercar pressure is now less than that acting on top of it, the result is the creation of undercar suction, or ground effect. The diffusor's purpose is to accelerate the compressed air and to control it as it is released. Over the years, the FIA's slow-down campaigns would frequently concentrate on this area. According to Dernie, at this time the diffusor could generate up to 70 per cent of a car's underfloor downforce. The modern Formula 1 car then weighed just over 1,100 lbs (500 kilos), and at 150 mph could generate some three times its own weight in downforce, at high speed on quick tracks such as Silverstone.

Small wonder that aerodynamics is such a critical factor.

1994 brought further changes, with the ban on active suspension (see Chapter 12) which placed fresh demands on the aerodynamicists who now had to rediscover mechanical and aerodynamic means of controlling factors such as pitch sensitivity (see Chapter 4) without recourse to computer technology. One of the most dramatic changes was the introduction of a 10 mm thick strip of wood to be mounted longitudinally in the middle of the underside of the car's floor. Made of a hard-wearing wood called Jabroc, this came to be known universally by the hi-tech name of 'the plank', and was aimed at discouraging teams from running their cars really low to the ground to generate maximum ground effect. There would be serious penalties for teams who incurred too much wear on the plank, as Schumacher and Benetton would discover later.

There had already been two nasty testing accidents, in which J.J. Lehto and Jean Alesi suffered neck injuries, when the San Marino GP that year sent shock waves reverberating through the sport. Rubens Barrichello had a serious accident on the Friday, Roland Ratzenberger was killed on the Saturday, and then Ayrton Senna died in the race itself. Then, less than two weeks later, Karl Wendlinger lay comatose in hospital after his relatively low-speed accident at Monaco. In what can now be seen as something of a knee-jerk reaction, resulting from the highly political atmosphere that prevailed in that dark period, the FIA moved quickly. The day after Wendlinger's accident, Mosley outlined new changes to the regulations which were to take immediate effect, the specific intention being to slow the cars fur-

Likewise, John Barnard's 1994 Ferrari 412T echoed the Italian team's famous 'shark-nose' car of 1961 around its radiator intakes, which were subsequently revised mid-way through the season. (Proaction)

ther. Among these the most critical was the effective chopping off of the diffusor section that extended beyond the rear axle line, thus cropping downforce immediately.

Eleven days later the Portuguese driver Pedro Lamy had a most fortunate escape at Silverstone when, during a test session, the modified rear wing fell off his Lotus. The car crashed heavily, and the monocoque section landed down a pedestrian tunnel. Lamy, still protected by it, nevertheless suffered serious leg injuries. It was thus amidst an atmosphere of rebellion that the Spanish GP went ahead days later, and that was when Mosley faced the strongest opposition to his leadership (see Chapter 14).

As they tend to, things settled down in what nevertheless remained a turbulent and acrimonious season, and it was at Spa, just after he had 'won' the Belgian

GP, that Schumacher's Benetton became the first car to be excluded from the results when it was found that his plank was excessively worn, indicating that the team had gambled too much on its aero set-up.

Schumacher had spun through 360° in the double left-handed corner, Pouhon, while leading the race on the 19th lap, and Benetton claimed that this had resulted in the wear, but the stewards weren't having that. At that time Formula 1 cars had 10 mm skidblocks, which were allowed a 10 per cent wear rate; this meant that planks could wear to 9 mm during the course of a race. But the FIA technical delegate Charlie Whiting had measured the depth of Schumacher's plank between 9 mm and 7.4, suggesting a contravention of as much as 1.6 mm, or 18 per cent. He pointed out that, in contradiction of the

Just visible at the base of the Benetton's chassis, behind the front wheel, is the tip of the under-car 'plank' – the decidedly non-technical term given to the strip of Jabroc that ran down the centre of the cars' undersides – which caused Michael Schumacher and the team so much grief a year earlier, at Spa in 1994. This device, which forced teams to run higher ride heights, was instrumental in reducing under-car downforce when first introduced for 1994. (ICN UK Bureau)

Benetton defence, most of the marks on the plank were longitudinal, with only some affecting the area which had gone over the kerb during Schumacher's spin.

As ever, views were divided, though everyone agreed that aerodynamic set-up at a circuit such as Spa was critical. As many designers could be found to suggest that the infringement would confer a significant advantage in grip and therefore lap time, as could be found saying that the benefit would be minimal. Cynics saw something ironic in the fact that a high-tech sport was in the headlines because of a bit of wood tacked on beneath a sophisticated carbon fibre composite monocoque chassis.

Perhaps Patrick Head, technical director at Williams, put it best when he said: 'It seems that anything below 9 mm after a race will be illegal, so set-up is going to be very critical. Remember that, for every pound per square inch less air in the tyres at maximum speed, the car runs 2 mm lower. So if the safety car came out, for example, there would be a pressure drop around three pounds per square inch, so on the straight the car would run 6 mm lower until the tyre comes back up to temperature. You've got to allow for that in your set-up.'

It was a harbinger of 1995, when the FIA's plan to run chassis with stepped bottoms came into effect. What this meant in effect was that a 60 mm plank had now been added along the centre-line of the underside of a car, hiking the sides even higher off the ground to limit undercar downforce even more (though in practice all teams made the extra 50 mm an integral part of the chassis, and just tacked the 10 mm plank on afterwards). At the same time refuelling was reintroduced, which meant that the bolder teams could build less compromised cars with smaller tanks, all of which had influences on the aerodynamics.

John Barnard, chief designer at Ferrari at that time, was one of many who complained bitterly about the lateness of the definitive regulations, which were finally released at the end of October. Bearing in mind the typical gestation period for a Formula 1 car (see Chapter 2), this was clearly going to bring in its wake the need for compromise.

'We were still arguing about engine covers even then,' Barnard said, 'whether to have them high or low, you know . . . And that really was quite naughty. It gave us a lot of struggle. You just don't change anything today on a Formula 1 car without it affecting the rest of the car.'

The FIA had considered the idea of low engine covers in order to outlaw the airbox, which created ram effect at high speed and thus helped to boost engine power, but this was soon dropped. Rumour had it that teams and engine manufacturers alike had pointed out quite forcefully that mandating low engine covers would do away with a prime advertising site at a stroke . . .

'It was all a compromise, for sure,' Barnard confirmed, 'because it all affected the airbox design and thus the aerodynamics. I'm sure if we'd started with the idea of a normal engine intake and snorkel in mind, instead of having to do one at very short notice, then a few things on the car might have been different.'

Early in 1995 Barnard summarized his elegant Ferrari 412T2, and with it the effects of the new regulations on Grand Prix car design. Uppermost in his mind had been aerodynamics, engine packaging and weight distribution.

'The smaller fuel tank made a lot of difference, to engine packaging and weight distribution. But the aerodynamics were paramount. We've moved into a new aerodynamic era, with stepped floors and low wings and all the rest of it. That's forced us to go and look at other areas and look in different ways.

'I think fundamentally that aerody-

The lateness with which the definitive 1995 regulations were finalized did not help designers, and Barnard in particular was critical of the delay, claiming that the engine cover on his Ferrari 412T2 was a compromise as a direct result of the designers expecting a ban on high covers and then finding that the FIA had relented. (ICN UK Bureau)

namics is the key at the moment. But the small fuel tank has allowed us to correct lots of things like weight distributions and make the cars very driveable. It's a whole combination of things that you do. Certainly, our car is very, very driveable this year.' Indeed it was, as Gerhard Berger and Jean Alesi showed on many opposite-lock occasions, but the end for the visibly oversteering Formula 1 car (and indeed for the glorious V12 engine) was drawing nigh.

The regulations allowed for the step to taper from 50 cm width to 30 in places. 'You could go between the two, or in and out,' said Barnard. 'Looking at it early on I said to the engine people that I wanted to be able to come in to 30 if I needed to, at the back. But as it turned out on the 412T2 we didn't think

it was necessary to come in to 30 after all, so we chose somewhere in between.'

Like others, he had made a discovery in the wind-tunnel. 'It does appear that the centre of the car isn't very sensitive now, is not very effective in terms of downforce,' he explained. 'I still think the real influence is from the sidepod area underneath, and the diffusor. But it's difficult to isolate these things. It's just fascinating how interactive everything on the car is.'

By 1997 Barnard's driveable Formula 1 car was fading into history, as Jordan designer Gary Anderson revealed. 'For a long time now racing cars have never been something that you could really slide. What used to happen was that you drove the tyre grip. The old cars had no aerodynamics at all and you drove them sideways because all you were really doing was driving the mass on the tyre grip. And then aerodynamics became involved so the thing became more and more like driving on rails, because the car's attitude and airflow was effective on the parts creating downforce, and hence getting more tyre grip.

'Since 1994, when they started to cut some of the parts that were giving you downforce, we have ended up with a situation where the cars are getting more and more critical to being kept in a straight line, because we've learned how to create more downforce.'

★ ★ ★

As is so often the case with Formula 1 equipment, the wind-tunnel game frequently sinks to a 'mine's bigger than yours' mentality. At the start of the 1997 season Williams was generally adjudged to have the best tunnel, which was located in a special area at its new factory site in Grove, near Wantage, and looked more like a film lot.

The richest teams would think nothing of making a vast investment in investigations into airflow, because aerodynamic stability is all about controlling and maximizing a car's behaviour at high speed, and about having the common sense to sort out the good and the bad from the copious data. To do this you need the best equipment and the best people to run it.

By the late 1990s aerodynamics was certainly no longer the black art that it had been 30 years earlier, when Formula 1 designers were just beginning to tack on bib spoilers to the noses of their cars, and rudimentary rear wings. Airflow exerted a massive influence on a car's stability and competitiveness, and research had become frighteningly detailed.

As much as it was a prerequisite in high-speed car handling, control was also a key element during the research process, which by now took two forms: wind-tunnel testing and computer pro-gramme modelling (called computational fluid dynamics). Williams had a 50 per cent tunnel, which meant that it could cater for test models of 50 per cent scale. Ferrari's bespoke new facility, meanwhile, was rumoured to be as big as 60 per cent, while others, such as TWR Arrows, had their own 40 per cent facility. The poorer teams would still go to proprietary tunnels such as Southampton University's, which was also 40 per cent, but the new Stewart Grand Prix stole a march in 1996 when technical director Alan Jenkins insisted on going to Swift's 50 per cent facility in Ste Clemente, California. All of them have moving ground tunnel floors. The test model is suspended atop a belt to simulate the interplay between vehicle and ground, and since it is, of course, impractical for the model to move, the belt or 'ground' does instead.

Opinions are divided as to the point of diminishing returns for larger and larger scale tunnels. Early in 1997 Benetton had two concurrent wind-tunnel pro-grammes running. One was for very advanced research and development conducted in Italy by former Tyrrell and Ferrari man Jean-Claude Migeot; the other involved the everyday grafting work down at Farnborough's facility in England. But Wirth also had his pet project, about which he admitted to being 'very excited.' This was an all-new tunnel at Benetton's Enstone factory, whose scale he was reluctant to divulge. 'Every day it's looking absolutely enormous. Flavio [Briatore] comes to my office, looks out the window, and says "Oh, my God!" The thing is growing like a monstrosity. It's a big, big wind-tunnel. I think it will be the biggest one there is. I know ours is bigger than Ferrari's.' It was due for completion in the late summer of 1997, so that it would be operating in time to make a significant contribution to the team's 1998 challenger. Informed sources suggested it was 65 or even 70 per cent.

Wirth agreed whole-heartedly that Williams's continued success had proved beyond any doubt that aerodynamic excellence was the overall key to success, given the necessary factors of power and reliability. 'If you are talking about a technical renaissance at Benetton,' he said, 'it's going to be centred around that. I know what it's like having your own tunnel. We had that at Simtek, though obviously nothing like the scale and complexity of our new one, and the advantage that you have in that is so large. The big gains at Benetton are going to come in 1998 and '99.'

'There's no doubt that aerodynamic testing is a remote task to the racing, in the sense that people do very little on-car aerodynamic testing these days,' said Ross Brawn. 'It's all done away from the track, in the wind-tunnels. So the better quality the wind-tunnel facility, the better quality results you'll get.

'But it is diminishing returns, for sure. But the thing about motor racing, and Formula 1, is that it chases diminishing returns. You know, it's half a million pounds for another five brake horse-power. It's a very expensive business, and it's at a very thin end, so somebody may look at it and feel that they could run a 60 per cent model and learn a bit more than they could from a 50 per cent model, and they are happy to pay the hundreds of thousands that would take.'

'If you had a full-scale wind-tunnel, you wouldn't worry about the scale effect,' Frank Dernie thought. 'And the data you got back would be better. Much better! It's just that nobody so far has put their hand deep enough into their pocket to build one. I believe you could do it. Definitely. The problem isn't the technology, it's the cash, I think.'

Gary Anderson agreed. 'I think if you are looking at more than 50 per cent scale then it's time to bite the bullet and look to whole scale, because then you've got the actual car and your costs are balanced and maybe even lowered because you haven't got the cost of making wind-tunnel models. And the car is really what's it's all about anyway, isn't it, not models. A full-scale tunnel is feasible, sure, but it's not easy. But then, at the end of the day, nothing in Formula 1 ever is.'

Caution is an essential part of wind-tunnel testing and data interpretation, as Adrian Newey revealed in a story about his days with Leyton House, designing the March 881 and 891 models:

'At that time we were testing at a rather small Southampton wind-tunnel and as we started to become more and more ambitious with the aerodynamics we started to fall foul of a few scaling factors which were incorrect. So we got into a position where we had things which looked very good in the tunnel and then didn't work on the circuit. The trouble is that once you get into that it's not a science any more, it becomes an art. You don't know what to trust and what not to. People started saying that the car was designed to run at only one ride height, which wasn't actually true. If we tried the car with what happened in the tunnel, it only tended to work on the track at a narrow band of ride heights, whereas in the tunnel our findings had made it look as if it worked over a wide band. That was certainly a large factor, and led us down the wrong route for a year or so. When we finally got the March wind-tunnel at Comtec sorted out, things got better. We had our own tunnel – Leyton House inherited it from March Engineering – and though it had several inherent faults we could chop it up to cure them.'

★ ★ ★

Wind tunnel models are beautiful works of art, very highly detailed replicas of their full-scale counterparts, and are therefore very expensive. They are usually made entirely in-house, by full-time model makers. Typically, they comprise a central aluminium spine, precise replica carbon fibre bodywork and (springless) suspension which can be articulated. Each model has at least 30 interchangeable pieces, plus sundry moving parts, all of them beautifully integrated. Consistency of manufacture ensures that accurate, repeatable tests can be made and, more importantly, that the findings can be relied upon. The research entails laborious tests and analysis of the effects of each small change, which is recorded on data sheets. Though it sounds exotic it isn't, unless you have a boffin mentality and like and understand figures, because it's primarily about attention to detail, sheer hard slog, and the elimination of anomalies.

It is also very, very expensive, whether a team owns its tunnel or hires time in one. The figures can make scary reading, and provide yet another indication why Formula 1 costs so much. In 1996 typical costs for an eight-hour wind-tunnel day would seldom be less than £2,000. Even a relatively small team such as Tyrrell had 15 six-day weeks booked annually at Southampton, and each of those days lasted a full 12 hours. And deputy technical director Mike Gascoyne, a trained aerodynamicist, would have liked far more tunnel time than that. Model costs could easily run into six figures, all of which translated into some £2.5 million – just for one aspect, albeit a crucial one, of the basic research. For the bigger teams those costs could treble, especially since ownership of a tunnel not only meant maximizing its use and, in some cases, paying for its cost in instalments, but also hiring a staff to run it and paying them wages suitable to the unsociable hours.

Aerodynamic development work is continuous, and no specification is ever settled for long. The wind-tunnel team will continuously be seeking out fresh advantages, which it can take the production department two or three months to create: a new front or rear wing, modified sidepods, or a new nose shape.

One unfortunate corollary of all this intensive effort is that there is a great temptation to believe that all Formula 1

The other problem of modern Formula 1 car aerodynamics is that following cars lose their downforce in the preceding car's dirty air. Here, at Imola in 1997, Irvine's Ferrari heads Giancarlo Fisichella's Jordan by inches as they exit the slow last corner and cross the finish line, but on the faster parts of the lap Fisichella had no option but to drop back to preserve front-end grip. (ICN UK Bureau)

cars would look almost identical were they to be lined up side-by-side in their naked carbon fibre state, but if you were to compare the lap times at the high downforce circuits such as Hungaroring, and then at Hockenheim where, for once, aerodynamics are less important than pure grunt, you could detect which cars had superior aerodynamics. But because the increments come from such small factors, what you will never be able to see is why. This invisibility of advantage is another reason why the expense is so high, yet so justified, because any easily identified technical 'tweak', such as Tyrrell's X wings that were introduced in Argentina in 1997, tends to be copied within days if other teams perceive them to offer a performance advantage. But advantages that embrace a subtle combination of aerodynamic nuances can be much, much harder to spot.

'I think the chassis has got as small as it can,' said Gascoyne. 'By the time you've observed all the FIA's fixed dimensions, plus the driver's, and then made it as small as you can for aerodynamic reasons, you end up with a pretty fixed pattern. That's really why cars have become more and more alike over the past five years. Having said that, though they look very similar they are quite different in aerodynamic form. It's very small things on each that add up to the aerodynamic efficiency.'

Gascoyne holds a PhD in fluid dynamics, but is a great believer in the old adage, 'the more you learn the less you know'. 'If somebody tells me they understand the aerodynamics of racing cars, then they don't understand the problem. The more you know about it, the more you realize it's a very difficult subject. And there might be many who disagree, but it's still a basically experimental subject.'

Most Formula 1 circuits require high downforce, but Hockenheim and Monza are quick enough to trade it for maximum straight-line speed. Here, to help in that quest, Heinz-Harald Frentzen's Sauber–Ford wears a rear 'speed' wing at Monza in 1995. Note, too, that in the wake of Wendlinger's accident the previous year, the Swiss team was in the vanguard of safety cockpit development. (ICN UK Bureau)

Whatever, the potential gains from aerodynamic development, in terms of reductions in lap times, are far greater, dollar for dollar, than those relating to engines.

* * *

Computational fluid dynamics has gained in popularity in recent years as teams come to appreciate more what it can offer in terms of modelling and prediction. When Ron Ayers was conducting his initial research during the conception of Richard Noble's supersonic land speed record-seeking Thrust SSC jetcar, he compared a cfd programme with empirical testing of a scale model strapped to an 800 mph rocket sled, and when the two sets of figures provided sufficiently encouraging correlation, he and Noble knew that they had a valid project. But Formula 1 teams have yet to embrace cfd to that extent, and those that use it tend to employ it as a model for future wind-tunnel test programmes. Ross Brawn said: 'At this stage it's all really for making comparisons, but we are a long way yet from designing a car via cfd. I would say that that's a long way ahead.'

Cfd also requires a lot of number crunching. Noble gained access to a Cray computer for the aero work, and Brawn said of Ferrari: 'We have some pretty powerful computers.' But when he was at Benetton they came up with a novel solution to the problem of finding a sufficiently powerful machine. 'What we did was to run a lot of the stuff overnight and just link all the work stations, so we'd use all the processing power. So come eight o'clock at night when people were beginning to drift home, as they turned their machines off we'd commandeer them and link them into the processing network. Of course we could have used a Cray, by buying time on it, but that's very expensive and there were other ways. All the Benetton equipment was effectively redundant

overnight, so we used to organize ourselves that way.'

There is no question that aerodynamic testing will become ever more intense in Formula 1, but that is only likely to make it even more esoteric and less likely to have any practical use in road car applications. Adrian Newey provided some last thoughts.

'Regarding specifics, I think it probably is too specialized. It's partly a function of the regulations, insofar as you're stuck with what is basically a very messy aerodynamic vehicle; you're not allowed to fair the wheels in, there are all sorts of regulation restrictions on front overhang, rear overhang, front wing endplates and so on, so I suppose a Group C type of car would be closer to having a direct spin-off.

'One of the things that was interesting with Group C was where they were pushing to get the frontal area down and comply with the windscreen regulation, and that was important in developing the windscreen technology. That spun off more and more into road cars. But I don't think there's any direct relevance of Formula 1 aerodynamics to road cars, though having said that, I think it's good if it makes people aware of how important aerodynamics are. The fact that aerodynamics are talked about more and more in motor racing has spun off as a buzzword to the man in the street, so he thinks that aerodynamics are important. That makes the road car people hype it more, and that's a good thing.

'In a road car, generally speaking, there's little point in having a lot of downforce. To generate enough downforce to make it significant to the driver, you'd start to make the fuel consumption worse, because of the drag that goes with downforce, and because the rolling resistance goes up. In road cars drag is the main thing, and neutral buoyancy. And, of course, speed limits naturally curb the potential for real efficiency which can only come with high speed.'

Chapter 4

Aerodynamics at work

'Now I think we have to recognize that with modern cars and aerodynamics, slip-streaming as we knew it in the 'sixties does not exist any more. The cars of the 'six-ties were not developed in rolling road wind-tunnels with endless resources and technical facilities . . .'

Max Mosley, President, FIA

THE AERODYNAMIC EFFICIENCY FOR the modern Formula 1 car has brought in its wake some seemingly insuperable problems, not the least of which concerns overtaking. In the 1960s and 1970s Formula 1 drivers could reg-ularly indulge in slipstreaming epics, particularly at really quick tracks such as the pre-chicane Monza. In 1969 Jackie Stewart just clinched his first World Championship by winning the Italian GP there by 0.08 sec from Jochen Rindt, with Jean-Pierre Beltoise and Bruce McLaren in their wheel-tracks, 0.09 sec and 0.02 sec further adrift respectively. Two years later Peter Gethin won his-tory's fastest GP at 242.61 kmh (150.76 mph), leading Ronnie Peterson, Francois Cevert, Mike Hailwood, and Howden Ganley across the finish line with only 0.61 sec covering the five of them. The first four were a mere 0.18 sec apart, and Gethin's margin over Peterson was officially one hundredth of a second!

In those days the slipstream effect behind a car could literally suck another along in its wake, saving the following driver horsepower and fuel and allowing him to slingshot by at the appropriate moment. But today this is no longer the case. The closer a following driver gets, the more trouble he is likely to run into. The Williams team's telemetry indicates that whenever one of its cars gets close to another at high speed, it loses 30 per cent of its frontal downforce. This is because the diffusors at the back of the cars, what is left of them, spew out such fast-moving, turbulent air.

In a laudable attempt to do something about this, the FIA came up with the idea of conducting wind-tunnel experi-ments with two cars running close together. It was an inspired piece of lat-eral thinking that sadly led nowhere. 'A lot of the ideas come from the FIA,' president Max Mosley said modestly, 'then Charlie Whiting and Peter Wright bring it in front of the Technical Working Group of Formula 1 engineers and out of this usually comes a pretty sensible view. There is a high degree of mutual respect. There is the odd eccentric, but fundamentally it works quite well.'

Unfortunately, the tests proved inconclusive. 'We spent a lot of money, in conjunction with taking advice from the various teams' engineers, to try to find an answer to cars losing their front-end grip,' Mosley lamented. 'But we came to the conclusion we would have had to eliminate the downforce factor altogether in order to resolve the problem.' Many observers wondered why the already truncated diffusor could not be deleted altogether, but this, it seemed, was not an acceptable option. However, from these tests sprang another idea that everyone liked very much, where cars would be permitted to run with active front wings, which could be used in close-running situations to generate sufficient extra downforce by adopting a new angle of attack, to make up for the amount lost in running in turbulent, or 'dirty', air. 'We felt that the only way to control the situation was to have an active, computer-controlled front wing to do whatever is necessary to maintain the balance of the car when it gets close up behind,' said Mosley.

Ron Dennis grinned in recollection, and said: 'I think we could have done that very well indeed at McLaren,' while Patrick Head at Williams had rubbed his hands at the prospect. The idea was simply to have an area of the front wing where the normal rules on movable bodywork wouldn't apply. But it never happened. The wing would have been an echo of the movable mid-mounted device that Ferrari introduced way back in 1968, the year in which a leak in its hydraulic system had prompted the massive but little publicized accident that Chris Amon suffered during that year's Italian GP at Monza when the fluid got on to his rear tyres and caused him to spin at very high speed. Sadly, the modern equivalent was never even tried in the wind-tunnel. Ferrari was rumoured

to have been the stick in the mud that said no, and the idea died.

'It was very radical and it made me nervous,' Mosley admitted. 'because I thought if there was a crash somebody might say it was mad to allow something we had prohibited for 30 years, but it was technically so interesting. I found it very attractive, as several others did. And it was very interesting in the Technical Working Group. The engineers for whom we always had a lot of respect were in favour of this fascinating new technical challenge. The lesser engineers were against.

'Now I think we have to recognize that with modern cars and aerodynamics, slipstreaming as we knew it in the 'sixties does not exist any more. The cars of the 'sixties were not developed in rolling road wind-tunnels with endless resources and technical facilities . . .'

Instead, another compromise sprang from that Technical Working Group discussion, and this was to reduce a car's track by 20 cm, from 200 cm to 180. McLaren is thought to have propounded the idea. 'On the face of it,' Mosley continued, 'that would have two or three effects. Number one, it would reduce the overall downforce by amounts for which the estimates varied considerably. Number two, it made the cars quicker on the straights. And number three, it made them slower in the corners. All of those things are beneficial in the sense that it increases the braking distance and decreases the grip and so on, so we immediately said okay. But one has to recognize that if you do that, the only part of a 1997 car that you may be able to fit to a 1998 car, talking of the chassis, is probably the steering wheel. Everything else must be new.

'The trouble is, if, for example, you change the underbody rules, you may end up forcing manufacturers to build a new engine, never mind a new gearbox. Any change to the car is catastrophically expensive. So if you can find some way of keeping the performance under control, without doing that, then that in a way is the best way.' And the manner in which the FIA finally opted to try and slay that dragon was not, as many had desperately hoped, aerodynamics, but by re-introducing grooved tyres in place of the familiar slicks (see Chapter 13).

Jordan technical director Gary Anderson provided an insight into the reasons why any technical changes tend to demand a complete rethink of a car's packaging, and why such a relatively minor change as narrowing the track actually means going back to first principles in the wind-tunnel and starting to optimize the package all over again.

'It's a lesson that we've learned because of getting a bit bigger. With aerodynamics we've been guilty in the past, because of time being short and only one bloke doing the work, of finalizing this bit before we finalized that bit and then finalized that bit. Really, that's wrong. You need to do it as a full package. Everything is so interrelated that you have to go all round the car. Even with something like narrowing the track, everything in the package has to be re-assessed and re-optimized. That's why we need to have five people working on aerodynamics now. It's just too much for one man to do the job as efficiently as it needs to be done.

'If you are going to do it better, then you have to do it that way, and I think Williams and people like that do it a bit better again than us. But we may have closed the gap a bit by realizing that we had to increase staff levels.' It is mainly aerodynamics that demands such human resources.

'If you can have a constant load on the tyre,' Anderson continued, 'that is the main thing that keeps the car on the road and going round the corner. Aerodynamics dictates all the sensitivity. Everything comes, basically, from aerodynamics. Yeah, the rest of it has all got to work as well, it goes without saying:

the engine, the gearbox, the mechanical side of the car. Of course they've all got to work and be understood, and if any of it is wrong it can lose you a lot of time, but the difference in working and finding a better solution to that side is pretty small reward, to be honest. You keep looking at it, to try and make it better, but the rewards are tiny compared to aerodynamic rewards.'

Tyrrell's Mike Gascoyne once summarized Formula 1 feelings when he said: 'One of our guys might come to us and say, "I can redesign our uprights to be half a kilo lighter. I'm really sure I can do a great job of it." But I would have to say to him, "what's the point?" We can't afford to spend a lot of time doing something like that, even if he were to save a kilo an upright, because at the end of the day it isn't going to give you any performance advantage whatsoever, so you tend to concentrate on those areas where there are serious gains to be made. And that means you concentrate on the aerodynamics.'

As an indication of the wisdom of this philosophy, John Barnard explained precisely how the sleek shape of his 1995 Ferrari 412T2 had evolved, and why it did not slavishly follow the trend of really high noses, such as the one Barnard himself had designed for the Benetton B191. 'It started off when we were looking at a brand new set of aerodynamic regulations. You start with something and you may have a deficiency. When we started with the T2 with a high nose we lacked front downforce, or front grunt as we call it. The way that we had it then, there was a slight element of lift with the high nose. And so one of the reactions was, "Let's try the other way." At that time we got an improvement with the low nose, which allowed us to generate what we wanted at the front.'

At the time he did not write off reversion to the underhanging front wing, which duly appeared on the 412T2's successor, the F310, half-way through

John Barnard's Ferrari 412T2 continued with the low nose configuration, though its designer admitted that it could probably have raced as successfully with a high nose had the basic aerodynamic research programme pushed hard enough in that direction initially. (ICN UK Bureau)

The car's rear winglets are just visible in this shot, together with the complex front wing design and the 'barge boards' or turning vanes located just behind the front wheels. (ICN UK Bureau)

the following season. 'Well, having gone through the development cycle of the 412T2 it was quite possible that we'd have gone back and done a high nose. The key element was that there wasn't a big difference. There might have been a small one, but it was not big. It was a case of: "If you develop enough in either direction . . ." We'd had a very seriously developed low-nose car by the middle of 1995. But at that point, if we'd put on a high nose we probably would have got what we wanted. But basic development just isn't enough. You've got to follow it

Barge boards had begun to appear in 1994. Christian Fittipaldi's Footwork Arrows FA16 shows its vestigial board, which is immediately behind the extension from its front wing endplate (above), while the boards on Jean Alesi's Ferrari are more significant (below). Also visible is the Ferrari's mini rear wing, mounted just ahead of the main plane. (Proaction)

through. It's like the stories of Honda building V12, V10 and V8 engines to test, and then choosing the best one to race; it's no good unless you develop them all thoroughly.'

The turning vanes, or 'barge boards' as they became popularly known, were also very important. 'They were very sensitive and also very individual. It's no good looking at somebody else's vanes unless your cars are identical packages. They tend to control the vortexes from the front wing, like the old wing end-plate gutters. The turning vanes now do that job.

'Dropping the rear wing cost quite a bit. The lower it gets, it becomes so interactive with the bodywork that it can be doing as much to improve the down-force from the body as it does working as a wing. So when you start changing things such as engine covers it becomes critical, because it's all so interactive. That's the problem.'

One of the 412T2's major characteristics was that the winglet and the sponson were united. And having pioneered the coke bottle shape in the past with his McLarens, Barnard revealed why he had chosen something less pronounced for the 412T2.

'It was because the winglet thing was a big step for us. That's why the car came out with them originally, whereas a lot of other people had no winglets and then we saw a lot of winglets coming along. Because we looked at them early on, we sort of built them into the package, so the actual coke was underneath that area. There was still a reasonable coke there, but we found that we didn't need it all the way up. Again, it was part of the raised floor, stepped floor concept.'

Early in 1997, Anderson quantified the manner in which the aerodynamicists had all but regained all of the downforce lost since 1994, using 1993 figures as the 100 per cent baseline:

'If you take the downforce levels that we had at the beginning of 1994, we are

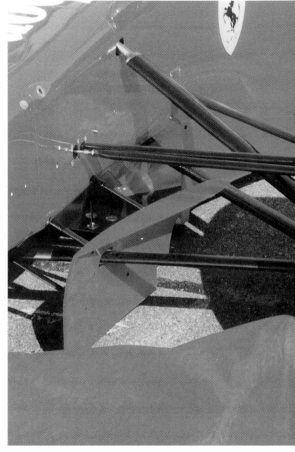

By 1997 Ferrari's boards had become more complex, the foremost incorporating a control lip on its upper surface. Sporting Director Jean Todt confirmed that they had exerted a significant influence in curing the car's original tendency to understeer during pre-season testing. (Author)

almost there now. But it dropped down quite dramatically initially, then it sort of crept back at the end of 1994. I'd say the initial loss was a good 35, 40 per cent of the level of downforce that we saw in 1993, mainly because of cutting back the diffusor. Generally it crept back by 25, 30 per cent by the end of the season. In our specific case it was reasonably similar in 1995, 1996 was a little bit better, and now we have gained a lot from

Besides the long strakes which channelled air towards the rear wing, Ferrari's F310B also incorporated winglets at the rear of the sidepods. (Author)

increasing our staff level.'

At the beginning of 1994 most of the downforce came from the diffusor and the front wing endplate area, but though diffusors were cut back dramatically in time for the Spanish GP in 1994, Anderson feels that these two areas continue to exert similar overall influence. 'The diffusor isn't as strong as it used to be, of course, but it's how the things relate to each other. To get it to still work to its maximum still takes the same progress, but it's even harder because there aren't the same rewards from it. It's quite a fine line between being good and bad.'

Asked his opinion of the most influential areas, Frank Dernie replied: 'I wish I knew! Certainly it isn't as much as 70 per cent from the diffusor, like perhaps it used to be in the early 'nineties, thanks to the 50 mm step and the tiny front wing endplates. But there isn't anything that's not important on the aerodynamic side: the brake ducts, the diffusor, the

aerodynamic wishbones, the engine cover, the airbox, the driver's helmet, the steering wheel, the windscreen, the rear-view mirrors. Literally everything makes a contribution.'

A team can build in a disadvantage by following the rules literally, where others interpret the spirit of them. Those that lose out in such situations tend to accuse their rivals of cutting corners, while those rivals bridle at the very thought of it.

'We were guilty for a while with our long sidepod thing,' Anderson continued. 'It was an area we were into because of the regulations. Because of the side impact safety thing we built the car to the intention of the regulations. A few other people didn't and at the end of the day it was acceptable, what they did. Making a car to pass the regulations as opposed to making a car better for an impact. Again, because of having only one aerodynamicist, it was one of those things where you evolve a solution to

Once the absolute heart of a car's aerodynamic downforce, the diffusors at the rear – which helped to exhaust fast-flowing air – were cut back to the axle centreline in May 1994. This had a dramatic effect on the amount of downforce generated, until designers found other ways to recover it. (Author)

various bits before you've finished off other bits. For our 1997 car we discovered the reasons why the longer sidepods weren't as good as the shorter pods. The longer ones were very good for cooling and for driver safety, but unfortunately performance becomes paramount.'

Anyone tempted to suggest that Jordan doesn't build very strong cars, however, has only to look at Rubens Barrichello's escape from his Imola accident in 1994, or Martin Brundle's from his barrel-roll at Melbourne in 1996. 'That's the problem with the regulations, in my opinion,' Anderson reflected. 'A lot of cars are built to pass the regulations, as opposed to complying with the intention of them. And you've got to join the club, haven't you?'

It should be recorded that others said much the same of the 1996 Jordan and Williams as they sited their drivers much lower than rivals did, by building low

monocoques and adding a small spike just ahead of the steering wheel which was nominally the front rollover bar datum through which the FIA would take its measurement which ensured that a line drawn between the front rollover hoop by the dashboard, and the rollover hoop behind the driver's head, would pass above his helmet with him seated in the cockpit. Neither team is remotely the sort to place driver safety after performance, and both Anderson and Patrick Head at Williams were stung by such suggestions, but that's the way things are in Formula 1. There were protests at the first race, in Melbourne, but the FIA turned them down. 'A lot of people didn't agree with what we'd done,' Anderson recalled. 'What irritated me is that others said they had taken a conscious decision not to do what we had done in order not to compromise safety, yet all of them have done it now.

We never looked at it and did it in any way thinking it would be less safe than a higher one. It annoys me when people do that, and then go back on their word. It's cheap.'

Both teams had come up with elegant solutions to the ugly compromise of safety cockpits, which ruined aerodynamics and made most cars look as if somebody had stuffed an old armchair

McLaren's mini wing appeared on the ill-starred MP4/10 on occasion in 1995, in an attempt to increase downforce by exploiting a loophole in the regulations. Jordan also tried a mini wing, but most other teams refused the bait. (McLaren)

into the cockpit, or else obliged the driver to wear a horse's collar, but regretfully, from the aesthetic viewpoint at least, the FIA introduced another new regulation for 1998 which outlawed such spikes. It also increased cockpit opening dimensions again, thus re-introducing the 1996 design conundrum.

★ ★ ★

Though the post-'gizmo' period did not see any major breakthroughs in aerodynamic design on the scale of ground effect or even the raised nose, there was no shortage of interesting novelties. On its ill-starred 1995 MP4/10 McLaren introduced an engine cover-mounted intermediate wing, to maximize downforce on tight circuits such as Monaco and the Hungaroring. Chief designer Neil Oatley's concept exploited a loophole in Article 3.8 of the technical regulations, which stated: 'No part of the bodywork between the rear roll structure and the front edge of the complete rear wheels, which is more than 60 cm above the reference plane, may be more than 25 cm from the centreline of the car.' By specifying the rear edge of the rollover hoop as the forward boundary of the exclusion zone for aerodynamic surfaces, the FIA had left open a 'grey area' into which such a wing could be inserted, and McLaren mounted it on an elongated airbox. The rules also allowed this wing to be sited higher than the rear wing, thus ensuring that the intermediate surface did not materially affect airflow to the main wing. 'To optimize such a relatively small aerodynamic device, you have to get it in the absolute perfect position,' said Ron Dennis, 'and that is where we believe it is worth having.'

McLaren ran with its intermediate wing on and off in 1995, and Jordan introduced something similar the following year. Asked what he thought of the McLaren wing, Barnard had laughed and said: 'Well. . . . No comment!'

Minardi tried a different type of mini

rear wing in 1995, actually mounting it on the forward edge of the main rear wing. Andy Tilley was Alessandro Zanardi's race engineer at Lotus before moving to a similar position with Luca Badoer at Minardi and thence, via a spell at Benetton, to engineer Martin Brundle and Giancarlo Fisichella at Jordan. When Aldo Costa and Rene Hilhorst left Minardi midway through 1995, the main mechanical design work had devolved to him.

Hilhorst had came up with some unusual ideas initially, and was responsible for the 'upside down' front wing, the panelled-in front wishbones, top-exit radiator ducting, and the small wing that was fitted on circuits where maximum downforce was required. 'If you need the maximum downforce,' said Tilley, 'that extra wing was about the only weapon we had, but the only time that we really ran maximum downforce was in Hungary when we ran that "swan" rear wing and some extra elements in the main wing too.

'I revised the initial front wing, which was low in the centre and high at the tips, with a very highly loaded centre section, and I also changed the wishbones, the canards, and the top exits for the radiators, which were sort of 10 year-old McLaren ideas. I didn't think that much of what we had to begin with seemed a good idea, to be honest. The last changes were introduced at Hockenheim, where we achieved our ultimate specification.'

To show that very little is new under the sun in Formula 1, faired-in top wishbones

The performance, if not the aesthetics, of Ferrari's 1996 F310 was improved marginally by its raised nose. Just visible behind the front wheel is the outlet at the bottom of the sidepod, for its unusual twin-floor air channels. (ICN UK Bureau)

This is how Tyrrell's 025 looked when it first appeared early in 1997. Its most notable feature, apart from its clean lines, was the single-post mounting for the front wing. The last time such a feature had been tried was on the ill-fated Footwork FA12 of 1991. (Tyrrell)

The front of Tyrrell's 025 also featured revisions, with these 'moustache' wings augmenting the main plane. (Author)

such as Minardi's had actually appeared on Jackie Stewart's Ken Tyrrell Matra MS10 at the Race of Champions at Brands Hatch – as long ago as 1968 . . .

Also interesting was the element of the 1992 F92A 'twin-floor' concept that had crept back into John Barnard's 1996 Ferrari F310. This took the form of a splitter sited not far back from the exit of air from the low nose, which then channelled air into a tunnel, between the high-set twin radiator intakes (which were immediately likened by the Italian media to those on a jet fighter) and the undertray, which expanded where the air exited half-way down the flanks.

1997 brought further novelty with Tyrrell's X wings, first seen in Argentina. Like the McLaren and Jordan mini wings, these were located – on the sides of the 025's cockpit – in an area that the rules had left open, and the idea was again to maximize downforce. At the same time Tyrrell, which had re-introduced the markedly more elegant single-post front wing mounting last tried back in 1991 by Footwork, also introduced further front wing area by incorporating stub wings either side at the top of the nose, above the main plane.

'We're not making any extravagant claims,' said Mike Gascoyne, 'but we've seen significant extra downforce in the wind-tunnel with these wings, after testing a lot of combinations, and generally we seem to get pretty good correlation between our tunnel tests and our track results.'

Tyrrell also tried aerofoil-section suspension (see Chapter 12).

* * *

What precise influence do the various parts of a Formula 1 car exert? Working from the front of the car backwards, Gary Anderson helped to provide a layman's guide to parts and terminology:

Front wing The front wing still plays an important role. At the end of Estoril's main straight, for example, downforce is around 560 kg, which means that at least eight full-grown men could step on to the wings without causing them to deflect. The front wing probably accounts for 25 per cent of overall downforce.

Front wing endplates The front wing endplates help to draw air over the wing to maximize its efficiency, 'but mostly they are good for airflow over the rear of the car. They help to send the best possible airflow back towards the undertray and then to the diffusor to make them work better. It's all about getting more out of the things. More front downforce costs you nothing in drag; it's the rear end that costs you big penalties. So you try to do everything you can to make the rear of the car work better, so that you can run with less rear wing and have a more efficient car. The old front wing endplates used to be very good for influencing the airflow around the front wheel, and the new smaller ones still are, though not to the same extent because of the regulation changes.'

Nose Upswept noses were virtually *de rigeur* in Formula 1 by 1997, since they helped to channel air round the front wing and direct it efficiently back towards the undertray and diffusor.

Suspension Aerofoil-section wishbones and steering arms do their modest bit to help minimize drag.

Barge boards The turning vanes, which are more commonly known as 'barge boards', are similar in function to the front wing endplates and first appeared when the latter were cut down for 1994. They may be horizontal or, more usually, vertical, and their job is to influence the wake of the air flowing over the front wing and to tidy it up before it gets to the back of the car. As an indication of their importance, the barge boards on Ferrari's 1997 F310B, with their distinctive curved top lip, were instrumental in

The Jordan 196 wing (above) shows its black Gurney strip on the trailing edge, a device named after legendary American racer Dan Gurney, who, along with his driver Bobby Unser, had added a small lip to their Eagle's wings during testing and discovered a massive jump in downforce. Now most wings feature some sort of Gurney. (Author)

Jordan's barge boards on its 196 were relatively simple. (Author)

cutting down the serious understeer which plagued the car's handling during its initial test sessions.

Sidepods These are usually nice looking, but they are not just a cosmetic means of housing the water radiators; they also play a safety role by providing deformable structure on the side of the car.

Undertray The undertray is extremely important, especially round the kinked area by the rear wheels, though not so important as it used to be when it directed airflow to the extended diffusors before the rule changes to limit downforce were introduced midway through 1994.

Safety cockpits These exerted a malign influence on aerodynamic efficiency when they were mandated for the 1996 season, because of the increase in drag brought about by their bulky shape. 'It hurts the rear downforce a little bit, because the flow-through round the back of the cockpit is not quite as good. But we're talking about only a very, very small amount.'

Airboxes Ferrari and Benetton in particular had big problems with airflow into the engines' airboxes sited above their drivers' heads – and thus lost out on the efficiency of ram air-boosting horsepower at high speeds. This was mainly because they did not achieve such low-line seating positions as Williams or Jordan achieved in 1996. As a result the Ferrari drivers in particular were obliged to cock their heads to one side to alleviate the problem on the straights. In 1997 Frank Dernie's first effort with the Arrows–Yamaha was too much of a compromise in Australia, for example, but by Brazil a new version was ready, with a smaller intake, and another revision for Argentina proved more efficient still.

Winglets These are usually mounted high on the sidepods, just ahead of the rear wheels, and, like Tyrrell's cockpit-located X wings, are designed to maximize downforce.

Rear wheel scallops These are the shaped sections ahead of the rear tyres, where the coke bottle effect begins as the

Detached from the car, an undertray with truncated diffusor appears a complex piece of composite moulding. (Author)

Moulded scallops ahead of the rear wheels, seen here on Jordan's 196, aim to smooth airflow before it reaches the rear wing, thus maximizing aerodynamic efficiency. (Author)

bodywork sweeps in. 'Again it's a matter of cleaning up the air and influencing the flow round the rear tyre to maximize the efficiency of the diffusor.'

Diffusor This is the section of the undertray that sweeps up to release the air that has been speeded up during its journey beneath the car. In the old days, when diffusors extended well beyond the rear axle centreline, they could account for up to 70 per cent of a car's downforce. Now the figure is probably closer to 42 per cent, and the diffusor affects the whole pressure distribution beneath the car.

Rear wing Now that diffusors have been cut back by regulation, the rear wing generates around 33 per cent of the

downforce. Again taking the example of Estoril's main straight, this would result in 1,000 kg of downforce, equivalent to a car carrying 16 unwanted passengers at the back, assuming they could all fit on . . .

Wheels 'These four things are pretty bad to the car. They create in excess of 30 per cent of the drag. The actual drag went down when the tyres were narrowed for 1993, because frontal area was reduced. It went down from 40 per cent to around 33 of the total drag. But the overall influence of drag on the performance of the car hasn't really changed.'

Downforce The pressure generated by the car's motion through the air, which tends either to push it (in the case of high-pressure flow over the body) or suck it (in the case of low-pressure flow beneath the car) on to the track.

Lift The pressure of air flowing over or under the car when it is in motion, that tends to try and lift it off the road.

Drag Air resistance to the car's forward motion. Something that all aerodynamic research aims to reduce to a minimum.

Lift over drag The ratio of downforce (negative lift) to drag. High figures are the best.

Pitch sensitivity This is a key to good handling. On a car that has low pitch sensitivity the aerodynamic balance doesn't shift around as the car pitches up and down over bumps, or tends to shift its centre of gravity under acceleration or deceleration. Pitch sensitivity tends to be more influential on a car's overall behaviour than either yaw or roll stability. Anderson observed: 'These cars with the steps shouldn't pitch much. I don't think I could make a pitch-sensitive car. The cars that we make today should be inherently fairly nice aerodynamically.'

Centre of pressure The point on the car through which all of the aerodynamic forces may be said to act.

★ ★ ★

One final thought: at 240 kmh (150 mph) a Formula 1 car generates around 1,600 kg, or 2,600 lb of downforce, and weighs just over 550 kg (1,212 lb) with fuel and driver aboard, so it could literally stick to the ceiling if the road could suddenly be inverted . . .

Chapter 5

The impact of safety: the cars

'There is no question that we can make the cars strong enough to withstand most sorts of impact that we encounter nowadays, but you can make things too strong. If we are not careful, you could have a situation where you find a driver dead within the cockpit of a car whose own structure has been able to withstand a very high impact.'

John Barnard, Technical Director, TWR Arrows

UNTIL 30 APRIL 1994, the Formula 1 world held the belief that cars had reached an acceptable ratio of performance to safety. This was not due to any inherent complacency, because by and large Formula 1 is not a complacent world on any level. And the designers in particular are men who never stop thinking of fresh ways not just of enhancing performance, but of safeguarding the drivers. It's what they do, and they do it well.

The previous day Rubens Barrichello had escaped from a massive wall-of-death accident which befell his Jordan when he made a mistake at the Variante Bassa corner at Imola, and Formula 1 sages nodded their heads and spoke wisely on what a safe sport it had become. And they were right. It was.

But then came the death of Roland Ratzenberger. An intensely likeable fellow who had just graduated to Formula 1 with Nick Wirth's equally fledgling Simtek team, Ratzenberger died at the Villeneuve curve as a result of massive impact with the outer wall, after his car had failed to make the very fast right-hand curve leading down to the Tosa hairpin. Analysis of the incident later pinpointed front wing damage as the cause, probably resulting from running over a kerb. There still seems to be doubt whether this was sustained on the previous lap, or earlier in the day. Whatever, when the wing failed approaching Villeneuve, Roland had no chance. The impact destroyed the Simtek chassis, ripping open one side, and Ratzenberger is thought to have died instantly. He was the first man to die in a Formula 1 car since Elio de Angelis perished at Paul Ricard during a post-Monaco test in May 1986, and the first to die in a Formula 1 race since Riccardo Paletti at Montreal in 1982.

Given its nature, Formula 1 is a sport that focuses on the famous. It is a hard fact that had the Imola weekend held but that one tragedy, the sport would

The death of Ayrton Senna, seen here in practice at Imola prior to the fateful San Marino GP of 1994, sparked off a new wave of safety investigation in Formula 1. (ICN UK Bureau)

have carried on regardless, putting the incident down to the Austrian's own misfortune, just as it chose largely to forget about Philippe Streiff's scandalous paralysis as a result of the testing accident he suffered in an AGS at the Jacarapagua circuit in Rio early in 1989.

But then came 1 May, and the accident which killed Ayrton Senna. It was every bit as shocking as the death of Jim Clark had been 26 years earlier, for the sport lost its yardstick, a man who had seemed superhuman. And it lost him live on television. This is not the place to pick over the bones of that accident, nor to try and pinpoint its causes since an Italian court is still doing that with relentless sloth. But the accident's effects would materially change the face of the sport.

Back in 1990 the last really big Formula 1 accident had befallen the unfortunate Martin Donnelly, when some sort of suspension failure had pitched his Lotus 102 into the barriers at Jerez, where it had literally exploded into fragments and left him lying on the track with just the remains of the seat back strapped to him like a haversack. He survived, and even drove a Jordan briefly in a test three years later, but his racing career was over.

'If you looked at Martin's chassis,' said his friend, Jordan technical director Gary Anderson, 'you could figure out that what happened was going to happen. That chassis was going to explode, because of its structure. Now the regulations have changed, and they're not far off what we proposed in the aftermath of that, via the Technical Working Group. I think the lay-up had a lot to do with it. I'm not saying they were wrong to do it like that; the regulations were like that, and they went as far as they could.'

There is a problem attached to significant changes in chassis regulations, however, as Anderson points out. 'Okay, if changes make a chassis stiffer and safer, that's good. But that's the bit that people complain about, because the smaller teams have got to build a new chassis. I'm sure that they would all be building a new chassis anyway, but they could simply sit down and say we wouldn't have had to do this if you hadn't changed the rules.'

Though Ratzenberger's chassis had been severely compromised by the impact, which was almost at maximum speed, the irony of Senna's death is that the Williams tub withstood its own impact extremely well. Had the right front wheel not remained attached by the steering arm and come back to hit him on the head – in a carbon copy of the tragedy that befell Mike Spence at Indianapolis in May 1968 – he would have survived. But, equally, Barrichello had been even luckier than it had seemed at the time.

'If the safety facilities hadn't been so good at Imola, with Professor Watkins getting to the scene so quickly, Rubens would have been dead as well,' Anderson revealed. 'He'd swallowed his tongue and was choking to death, but Sid got there and helped him.'

Prior to Imola, Formula 1 thought it had beaten back old spectres, but the accidents forced it to re-examine its safety philosophies. Car design came under the microscope in the most intensive soul-searching since 1968.

The carbon fibre composite monocoque chassis had been on the scene since 1981, when both John Barnard at McLaren and Colin Chapman at Lotus had pioneered it, and provided the FIA's increasingly stringent crash tests were applied equally to every team, there was less and less cause to doubt the inherent integrity of this kind of structure. But controlled deceleration was critical at Formula 1 speeds, and Barnard made a chilling point when he said: 'There is no question that we can make the cars strong enough to withstand most sorts of impact that we encounter nowadays, but you can make things too strong. If we are not careful, you could have a situation where you find a driver dead within the cockpit of a car whose own structure has been able to withstand a very high impact. We must retain a degree of deformability.'

Jean-Marie Balestre, Max Mosley's predecessor as president of the FISA, was a mercurial character, full of Gallic gesture and hyperbole which often tended to disguise his true contribution to a sport that he clearly loved with a passion. It is probably true to say that such characteristics militated against him being accorded the recognition and credit that he deserved for introducing the concept of mandatory crash testing.

'He tried very hard on safety,' Mosley conceded. 'And it has to be said that his was really the era and administration that began all that. Because up to the end of the 'seventies it was just the teams doing the best that they could. There were no rules, and the fact of the matter is that when there are rules, people try harder. With our crash tests now, people quite often fail, and I think that shows how effective they are.'

Besides truncating diffusors in the aftermath of Imola (see Chapters 3 and 4) the FIA also set in train means of ensuring that wheels sheared off in accidents rather than being retained by one link and thus swinging back dangerously into the cockpit. The actual opening of the cockpit was changed too, for 1995, and higher sides were mandated to offer better driver protection. And in the wake of Austrian Karl Wendlinger's accident at Monaco, further changes were put under development. Wendlinger had spun his Sauber–Mercedes at the chicane and had struck a protective water barrel sideways on at cockpit level, probably at little more than 50 kmh (30 mph). The impact left him comatose for 18 days, and though he recovered and briefly raced again in Formula 1, his

The most visually obvious change in the outward appearance of current Grand Prix cars is the high-sided cockpit, which now incorporates a deformable structure designed to minimize head injuries such as those sustained by Karl Wendlinger in his accident at Monaco in 1994. These are the solutions offered by Tyrrell and Jordan. (Author)

The superior protection afforded by the revised cockpit regulations is nicely illustrated in this shot of Jacques Villeneuve testing a Williams FW17 at Monza in 1995. (ICN UK Bureau)

promising career was over. Working with the FIA's chief medical delegate Professor Sid Watkins's Safety Group, designers came up with the protective padded cockpits that were ready for introduction in 1996.

By then, however, there had been two more serious accidents, one of which focused attention not just on the need for the safety cockpits, but for something more. For the first time serious consideration was given to the use of air bags in the cockpits of Formula 1 cars.

Both accidents involved McLarens, and the first came when Mark Blundell crashed heavily at the notorious 130R left-hander at Suzuka, a bend taken at as close to maximum speed as the car's behaviour and the drivers' courage and commitment will allow. The McLaren spun, and hit the barriers almost head-on. A resilient character, Blundell got himself out of the car, which had withstood the very heavy impact extremely well and performed its job of protecting

him perfectly, but he retched immediately afterwards. Blundell was later advised by the team not to participate in the final qualifying session. After a check-up at the medical centre he underwent physiotherapy, but was determined to compete in Sunday's race.

'I was sore and stiff, as you'd expect to be after a crash like that,' he said the following day. 'I was focused on getting into the apex as quick as possible but I went in a bit too late into the corner. I looked at the data later and I was doing 298 kmh [179 mph] on the grass. The car took off about 30 kmh [18 mph] of that when it spun, but from that point on it was airborne anyway. I went in at a slight angle, because I sustained 6g frontal impact and 6g lateral at the same point. There was quite a lot of force . . . They reckon I hit the barrier at around 250 kmh (155 mph). So considering, I think we did fairly well. I'm quite fortunate.

'I think I was probably knocked out

for a little bit, because I didn't move at first in the car. I was certainly winded and the reason I didn't run in qualifying was that my vision was slightly blurred, and I didn't feel 100 per cent fit, so there was no point in putting myself out there and putting the car at any risk. It was the best option to actually walk away. But I can assure you that walking away from qualifying was a harder thing than going out there and doing it.'

Even more serious was Mika Hakkinen's crash at Adelaide in the next race, when a tyre deflation sent the Finn crashing very hard into a concrete wall protected by two layers of old tyres. Such was the force of the impact that he struck his head on the steering wheel, and suffered a skull fracture. Only a track-side tracheotomy saved his life, performed by a medic with suitable experience who happened to be among the team at that part of the circuit. He returned to racing the following season, apparently none the worse for the experience.

Hakkinen's accident prompted serious research into air bag technology. 'Mika hit his head on the steering column, so you can appreciate just how far the safety belts stretched and how far his body elasticated,' said McLaren chief Ron Dennis. 'It's a long way from where his head started and where it struck. I'm told by Prof Watkins that the forces required to fracture a skull in that way are very, very high.'

The Italian driver Alessandro Zanardi had likewise had his spine temporarily 'elongated' in an incident during practice for the Belgian Grand Prix in 1993, when he spun his Lotus in the dauntingly fast Eau Rouge corner and struck the outer barriers very hard.

Now the FIA Technical Working Group, which had been set up after Imola, and had already been looking into means of restricting driver movement, pinpointed air bags as an avenue in which serious research needed to be

undertaken. Gerhard Berger, the GPDA representative on safety matters at that time, said in Adelaide: 'I have seen some of the work they have been doing, and it certainly impressed me.'

Dennis, however, was sceptical about air bags. They are relatively simple devices designed to expand rapidly in an accident so that the vehicle's occupants are effectively protected from the impact by a large balloon-like bag which has sufficient 'give' to prevent them striking a solid object. At the time they were already to be found fitted on many up-market road cars and the results had been impressive, though the explosive charge that detonated the bags could damage the interior of the car and there were problems relating to where they should be installed. In road cars neither problem was particularly significant, but when the situation was transferred to the tight confines of a race car cockpit, some serious considerations arose, not the least of which concerned precisely where to locate them, and the potential risk that the close-proximity detonation might harm the driver.

There were further problems in safe-guarding against premature or accidental deployment, such as when a car might be jolted over sharp bumps or collide with another vehicle. Choosing the g-loading at which the bag would be triggered would also be critical – the dangers of accidental deployment when the driver was travelling at maximum speed were self-evident.

'The speed of these accidents is so much higher than anything experienced on a production car that our engineers believe there is no system that could inflate fast enough to accommodate this sort of impact,' Dennis claimed. He believed that the sport should look to other areas, among them things such as more progressively deformable crash barriers.

Ross Brawn, then technical director of champion constructor Benetton, was more optimistic. 'What you are trying to do is decelerate the head, and there is a very arbitrary figure arrived at for the average human being which gives a critical impact figure for cranial deceleration. If you decelerate it too quickly, you will extrude a driver's brains through his ears, and we don't want to do that. So what we try to do is slow the head in a progressive way, but if you let it move too far laterally you then start to risk neck problems. It's a juggling act between deceleration rates, duration and size of impact. You can have a relatively low impact, but if it's sustained for a long time that can do a lot of damage. Or you can have a higher impact for a much shorter period.'

Brawn, like all designers, favoured increased deformable structures on the cars themselves, for in any impact getting rid of a car's kinetic energy is vitally important. By 1997 Formula 1 cars had better crushable nose structures and sidepods, and the newly introduced deformable structure at the rear, as well as the crushable head restraints on the side and back of the cockpits.

'We need to be able to get more information to verify that any trigger mechanism can react quickly enough,' he continued in 1995 when discussing the possibility of air bags, 'but the people who make the air bag believe they can come up with one that will be viable.'

Watkins harboured no doubts about the desirability of air bags, and believed then that they could be seen as soon as 1996: 'Naturally we want them to inflate as soon as possible but not to hinder a driver's escape or extrication from the cockpit. They also need to be small enough so that if they did go off accidentally they would not be a hazard.' He envisaged a small bag mounted in the steering wheel.

Though air bags were not, after all, deemed ready for 1996, nor even 1997, investigation went on, and at Monaco in that latter year Mosley said: 'Our research is continuing, in collaboration with Daimler–Benz, and we have learned some very interesting things. It would be premature to discuss details, but we will not impose any regulations until we can be sure that they are entirely safe.'

The structural integrity of the latest Formula 1 cars was soon put to the test when Martin Brundle's Jordan–Peugeot was launched over the top of other cars on the first lap of the Australian GP at Melbourne, which opened the 1996 season. The gold car barrel-rolled into a sand-trap, but though the engine was all but torn from the chassis, the driver's safety cell was completely intact. Just as Derek Warwick had done after rolling his Lotus at Monza in 1990, Brundle was able to run back to the pits to take the spare car for the restart.

Later still, the Dutch driver Jos Verstappen escaped from a very heavy accident during the Belgian GP, when his Arrows suffered a stub axle failure. Because the incident was not shown on television its severity went largely unnoticed, but Mosley brought the matter up at Monaco in 1997 when discussing safety matters: 'You may be interested to know what we have learned about the cockpit padding that we required on Formula 1 cars at the beginning of last season,' he said. 'After the accident which Jos Verstappen had we have studied both his helmet and the padding on his Arrows. We now have conclusive scientific evidence that without the cockpit padding, his accident would have been fatal.'

Verstappen himself was amused by this revelation, as only racing drivers can be. 'I hear Max is saying that my accident at Spa would have been fatal if I hadn't had a safety cockpit?' he inquired with a smile. And he thought for a moment or two, before adding: 'You know, I guess he's probably right!'

'I think that safety cockpits are one of the biggest areas of safety that we've

Rollover protection has always been good during the period of Formula 1 covered by this book. Luca Badoer had cause to be thankful for it after this inversion during the 1996 Argentinean GP. (ICN UK Bureau)

had,' Gary Anderson said. 'I felt that the sides could be narrower and closer to the driver's head, all that sort of stuff, like IndyCars, but . . . It's better if the guy is taking the load vertically, down through his head, through the spine rather than through the neck.'

After 1994 the FIA had toughened its crash testing and impact resistance requirements, and the rear impact test came in for 1997. While still planning Tyrrell's 025 in 1996, Mike Gascoyne said: 'The regulations are quite simple for the rear impact; it's almost the front impact test in reverse. I think basically the rear cover will incorporate some sort of crash structure, maybe tied into the rear wing pylon. But you'll have to put everything on for the test that's going to affect the impact, so it'll be tougher than the frontal impact, where you can put the nose-cone on the pendulum rig rather than using the entire chassis as well.'

The promising Italian driver Giancarlo Fisichella was the first to test the structure empirically, when he lost control of his Jordan–Peugeot at Silverstone during a test early in 1997, and went off backwards at Stowe corner in a similar accident to the one which had damaged J. J. Lehto's neck in 1994, or Jean Alesi's mirror repeat for Ferrari at Mugello around the same time. The Jordan was fitted with the new black box (see Chapter 9) which had been made mandatory that season, and this recorded that the car went from 141 mph (227 kmh) to zero in 0.72 sec, with an impact speed of 50g and a deceleration of 12g. But the new rear impact structure saved him from any serious injury, and the cockpit structure also did its bit.

'It helped Giancarlo enormously,' Anderson said, 'and he was able to get himself out. He did a couple of circles, found out he'd hurt his knee, then lay down. But it was a cut knee like a kid falling off a bicycle, nothing worse. For that to be the end result of that sort of accident was pretty impressive. We'd also have done in the gearbox there, no prob-

The FIA's continual tightening of its crash test regulations undoubtedly helped Johnny Herbert when he crashed his Sauber–Petronas head-on into the barriers at Ste Devote during the 1997 Monaco GP. The Englishman not only escaped unharmed despite the speed of the impact, but scarcely deemed the incident worth mentioning afterwards! (ICN UK Bureau)

lem, without the structure. We were actually able to use the same gearbox casing in Brazil the following weekend.'

It was further tribute to the far-reaching investigations instigated by the FIA in 1994, which had already seen solutions to the problems that arose from accidents such as Hakkinen's being sought before they actually occurred. But all along the designers and safety delegates never lost sight of the fact that motor racing was still a knife-edge sport. Mosley had several times professed his personal aim to ensure that it would no longer be a sport that might kill its participants, and while others might privately have thought that this was an impossible aspiration, given its very nature, none of them was going to draw back from trying to achieve it. But for every step forward that they took, they were only too aware that all progress brings in its wake a different set of problems. The trick was not to introduce more than you solved. And never to feel complacent.

Chapter 6

The impact of safety: the circuits

'In my capacity with the GPDA I visited most of the circuits to do a sort of safety inspection, and to be honest it was beginning to do my head in, walking round them looking at all the places we had previously taken for granted, where now if you had an accident you stood a good chance of dying.'

Martin Brundle

NOT SINCE JACKIE STEWART'S crusading days had such attention been paid to circuit safety as in the aftermath of Imola 1994. The immediate manifest-ation of this took some decidedly less than credible forms.

At Monaco the drivers banded together to reform the Grand Prix

Of all circuits, the Autodromo Enzo e Dino Ferrari at Imola received the greatest revamp in the aftermath of the deaths of Roland Ratzenberger and Ayrton Senna. All round the world gravel traps were extended, in the search for greater run-off areas. (ICN UK Bureau)

Drivers' Association, with Michael Schumacher, Gerhard Berger, and Martin Brundle taking leading roles. This was an understandable unification that, in its own way, echoed the drivers' private thinking after Senna's death and reflected the feeling that Chris Amon had summarized when Jim Clark was killed: 'We all felt that, if it could happen to Jimmy, what chance did the rest of us have?'

There had been aspects of concern over the manner in which drivers were treated at Imola, not the least of which was the official who told Senna that he had no business visiting the scene of Ratzenberger's accident and threatened to fine him. And even before the Brazilian's death moves were afoot to revive the GPDA. Now they attempted to speak with one voice, and it was indeed a vocal majority that faced down the governing body at the Circuit du Catalunya for the Spanish GP, where they insisted that they would not race until a chicane had been installed on the back straight where drivers faced hard braking just before an immovable wall. They stood firm and won that round, and then in Canada there was the ridiculous sight of the old sweeps down by the Olympic rowing basin being sullied by a chicane marked out by, of all things, orange and white rubber cones.

Other circuits suffered the same chicane malaise. Spa's glorious and very quick Eau Rouge corner was singled out after the accident that befell Alessandro

The organizers of the Belgian GP proved conclusively that good circuit management and a bit of imagination could create a challenging but acceptably safe corner when they revised Spa's famous Eau Rouge corner after the accident in 1993 that befell Alessandro Zanardi. Though a chicane was in place for the 1994 race, increased run-off areas allowed Eau Rouge to revert to its former glory from 1995 onwards. (LAT)

Zanardi there in 1993. The corner could not be modified in time, so another chicane went in, and the purists secretly felt that they had just witnessed the demise of the last Great Corner left in Formula 1. But true to their words the organizers and the FIA worked together brilliantly to recreate the corner for 1995 with sensible and acceptable run-off areas, while preserving its steely challenge. It was a tribute to what could be done, when people put the right mindset to it.

At Monza arguments raged with environmentalist parties about cutting down fewer trees than the authorities were actually prepared to plant in compensation, to ensure an adequate run-off area at the second Lesmo corner, and it took a threat by the FIA to cancel the race before a sensible compromise was achieved. At Estoril the dangerous second corner, with its two-tier Armco barrier which would barely contain errant cars from a steep drop, remained untouched, while the ridiculous Corkscrew chicane (where Eddie Irvine inadvertently tipped Damon Hill on his head during practice in 1995) was installed on the back stretch. Other circuits made changes, too.

And then there was Imola itself, which became a mere shadow of its former self with chicanes at Tamburello and Villeneuve, and only a more sensible Acque Minerali corner as compensation. Jacques Villeneuve, who had raced there in Formula 3, said in 1997: 'It's not a very nice track any more, with chicanes everywhere. It doesn't feel like there's a natural rhythm to it. It's a very modern track, basically. I guess Piratella is a nice corner, but . . .'

When he announced Tyrrell's 1996 contender, the 024, Harvey Postlethwaite, the team's managing director of engineering, had only part of his tongue in his cheek when he said: 'We have analysed the characteristics of all the circuits hosting Grands Prix and found the most common Formula 1 cor-

ner is second-gear at 75 mph. Accordingly, we have optimized our car for second-gear 75 mph corners.'

It was probably the saddest comment of the year, but Mosley flatly denied popular suggestions that an 'official' FIA circuit design handbook existed, whereby new organizers had to produce circuit designs that flattered advertising locations and opportunities rather than concentrating on providing an interesting configuration or any overtaking sites. 'That is definitely untrue. What we would like is some magician to find a way of building a circuit that was both safe and where you've got overtaking and thrilling racing. Do that, and circuit advertising looks after itself, because people watch it if it's exciting.'

Martin Brundle, however, who would narrowly escape serious injury or worse at Suzuka in the 1994 season when his McLaren spun on standing water and nearly ploughed into a tractor parked the wrong side of the barriers, offered another telling comment. 'In my capacity with the GPDA I visited most of the circuits to do a sort of safety inspection,' he said, 'and to be honest it was beginning to do my head in, walking round them looking at all the places we had previously taken for granted, where now if you had an accident you stood a good chance of dying.'

Mosley said at one stage in 1995 that the FIA had identified 16 unacceptably dangerous corners left in Formula 1, and had whittled them down to eight, but declined to be specific. 'I can only tell you some of them, and it would be invidious to do that! And it raises the question that eventually you are going to end up with a few – three or four – where you can't solve the problem because if you slow the cars down enough to make those corners safe, you'd definitely be interfering too much with the performances of the cars. You know there's a mountain or a cliff or a lake or something that stops you changing the cor-

Damon Hill and Shinji Nakano put the gravel trap at Imola's last corner to the test when they collided during the 1997 San Marino GP. On that occasion both cars were swiftly arrested, but at other times and venues gravel traps occasionally left something to be desired. (ICN UK Bureau)

ner. We are almost getting to that point, so that raises a very interesting question of principle which is going to get raised at the World Council. Is it acceptable that there is the odd dangerous corner?

'I've always felt that the governing body should push safety to the point where the drivers are saying, "We want to take more risks". It shouldn't be the other way round. It's completely wrong if the drivers should be put in a position where they are saying, "This is dangerous", and the governing body is saying, "It's all right". I want to discuss this basic philosophical point with the World Council; and also it's one of those things it's quite interesting to talk to the drivers about.'

By 1997 drivers were indeed moaning that their cars were not quick enough, and that the circuits had no decent fast

corners left, and Jacques Villeneuve was the most vocal complainant. But Mosley proffered a different response to the one his previous comments had led observers to expect. 'If the 1998 specification cars are not "fun" to drive, then I can only say sorry. When Jacques claimed that slower drivers would find it easier on grooved tyres to stay close to the most skilled drivers, all the evidence is to the contrary. Indeed, if you believe that you wipe out the history of motor sport. In effect, Jacques suggests that all racing drivers were mediocre until he came along . . .'

Villeneuve's response had been trenchant when he was asked if he had talked to Mosley. 'Talking is one thing,' he said, 'but listening is another.'

But, perhaps surprisingly, Villeneuve found a champion in Bernie Ecclestone, who early in 1997 said: 'I think there will always be accidents and we need to look after the drivers when the accidents happen. And that's what we've been doing for the last 20 years. Steadily improving every year. Villeneuve doesn't say that motor racing should be dangerous, he just says we want more challenging circuits. I agree with him 100 per cent. Since the accident at Imola, I think the FIA panicked a little under pressure from the media and went a bit over the top with chicanes all over the place. Which was proved at Barcelona, the next race, where we had chicanes everywhere, which was completely wrong and unnecessary.'

Ecclestone also said he was in favour of quicker corners. 'Sure. You don't want to tempt people to have accidents, but a lot of these drivers like big balls corners. They don't want the slow stuff. The fast stuff sorts the men out from the boys, and that's what it's all about, after all. Nothing says you have to go flat out. You can always go nine-tenths.

'In particular, when the new circuits are being built, we should be a bit more careful, rather than saying let's put a chicane in there. But you couldn't really keep corners like the old Boschkurve at the Osterreichring, could you? That would be a bit naughty.'

Mosley was aware that risk is a part of the attraction for drivers, having raced himself up to Formula 2 level. 'I remember asking Berger about something once at Monza, and he said to me, "Well, what do you think?" And I said to him, "I don't have to drive the car". And that really is the difference. Yet if you said to mountaineers, "We're going to let you climb that north face of the Eiger, but you've got to have safety ropes attached all the way up and you've got to take the following precautions so if you slip you can't hurt yourselves", they probably wouldn't like it.'

He spread his hands in helpless gesture at the problem of living in a society that likes to protect adventurers from themselves, and told another little story. 'A very, very well-known former Grand Prix driver, who shall remain nameless, phoned me up and said, "This is ridiculous, I'm not allowed to race in an old car race in the helmet I wore back in the Dark Ages, and now I've got to wear one of these new helmets". And I thought, "Well, he's got a point. He's the same sort of age as I am and if he wants to wear a funny helmet, really, who are we to tell him he can't?"'

The moral judgement can be difficult, especially when it comes to circuit safety and deciding what is and what isn't acceptable. 'If you go back to the 'sixties, the main objective was to make sure the spectators didn't get hurt, and really the drivers knew damn well they were doing something really dangerous and if they didn't like it, they didn't have to do it. And if you marked the part of the circuit where they could get killed or injured in red, then the circuit would be virtually red all round. Then in the 'seventies we started, fairly haphazardly, shrinking the red bits, and that process accelerated during the 'eighties and further during the 'nineties, and then really, after Senna, we set out to eliminate the red bits altogether. Now maybe we shouldn't be doing that. It's a question to discuss with the drivers, because in the end they've got to take the risk. And, to be honest, I think it is true that the wish to eliminate the red bits diminishes the further we get away from Imola.'

Behind the scenes, meanwhile, Professor Sid Watkins's Safety Group continued to undertake long-term investigation into subjects as far-reaching as barrier design and materials, and systems to arrest errant cars. At Monaco in 1997, for example, Johnny Herbert's Sauber–Petronas hit the barrier head-on at the Ste Devote corner, at very high speed. Three years earlier David Coulthard had struck metal barriers head-on at around 30 mph (48 kmh) at

Barriers formed by stacks of old tyres bonded together have become an increasingly important means of arresting errant cars progressively. Damon Hill crashed his Williams heavily enough during the 1995 GP of Europe at the Nürburgring to sustain a minor leg fracture, but had he struck a solid barrier his injuries might have been worse. (ICN UK Bureau)

the Hungaroring, and recalled: 'That hurt far more than the accident I had later that weekend when I ripped two wheels off the car.' Yet Herbert walked away and barely mentioned the incident later in the day, such was the improved barrier design which had allowed the barrier to 'give' without arresting the car instantly.

And the FIA is now very close to being able to apply standardized circuit safety criteria across the globe.

Time will tell whether fast corners do reappear in Formula 1, but Professor Watkins's comment in the foreword to this author's book *Echoes of Imola* tended to arrest flights of fancy while summarizing the feeling after the events of that black weekend. 'Given a retrospective choice,' he wrote, 'between a Tamburello or a Senna, I do not believe any sane person would now select the wall.'

Chapter 7

Power games

'Our aim is, in fact, to produce an engine which drivers can forget all about. It is often said that an engine on its own cannot win a race, but that it can lose one. An engine which puts out 10 or 20 extra horsepower will not change a car's overall competitiveness. However, an engine which fails does.'

Axel Plasse, Track Test Engineer, Renault Sport

ENZO FERRARI ALWAYS HELD dear to the belief that the engine was the heart of any racing car, and steadfastly refused to accept the view that a good chassis was more important than a good powerplant. This is interesting, because in the late-1980s and the early-1990s two disparate views were on offer. Though the coming of ground effect had tended to sway most observers to the chassis view, McLaren's tremendous run of success from 1988 to 1991 was generally put down by its rivals not to the capability of its chassis engineering – far from it in some cases – but to the immense power of Honda's engines, particularly when Ayrton Senna was sitting ahead of them. According to this school, McLaren won races not because it had a great car but because the Honda had so much horsepower to spare in comparison with its rivals that Senna could run with a massive amount of wing to create downforce, yet still get down the straights in this high drag mode with sufficient alacrity to outrun the opposition.

To some extent the performance of the McLarens after 1992, when, following Honda's withdrawal, they were fitted with customer Ford and then works Peugeot engines, tended to endorse this view, and the initial months of its alliance with Mercedes-Benz simply strengthened that endorsement.

The other view took it that Williams was the best simply because it had the best engine, Renault's Honda-matching V10. When Benetton also used the French engine and Michael Schumacher used it to beat Williams in 1995, the sages nodded wisely, but a year later they were scratching their heads as Williams raced away from Gerhard Berger and Jean Alesi, prompting the alternative view that the Williams was the best because it had competent drivers, a good engine, and a chassis with excellent aerodynamic performance.

This is not to suggest that engines are not important any more, because quite obviously they play a key role. But the indications are that it is far more feasible

The champion of them all, Renault's RS7 3-litre engine swept the board on its debut in 1995. (Renault)

to make up on the track for a deficiency of 10 to 15 bhp than it is to make up for a chassis that lacks aerodynamic grip. And indeed, apart from the downsizing from 3.5 to 3 litres for 1995 the engine manufacturers have been treated well by the rule-makers, leading to feelings in some circles that they are something of a protected species, and that the FIA is loathe to frighten them off by making any radical changes which might affect the engine. As a result the teams often feel put upon, since they have habitually borne the brunt of changes in the regulations. Jordan's technical director Gary Anderson put such feelings into words when he said: 'The regulations are there to make the formula more stable, but the FIA still don't want to hurt the engine manufacturers in changing the regulations every year. Most Formula 1 teams build a car, then the regulations change

and they're having to go along with them and build another one for the next year. Most engine manufacturers build a new engine as well, but they don't want to change their process because it's too big a loss for a major company to stand.

'You're committed to Formula 1 when you're in it, so as teams we have to accept that. The big manufacturers don't have to, because they can always pull out. It's a bit annoying that, because engine performance does make a difference to the cars, of course. But it's not that big a difference; a good engine is a good engine, obviously, and will be faster than one that's not so good. But to lose a couple of seconds a lap because of the engine is fairly dramatic; half a second, yes. A couple of seconds, no.'

* * *

When the 3.5 litre normally aspirated

Formula 1 replaced the 1.5 litre turbocharged formula for 1989, the ideal concept of engine was still open to debate. While Ferrari remained faithful to its ingrained belief in the advantages of the traditional V12, and Ford to its equally entrenched favour of the V8, Renault, Honda, and Ilmor (Mercedes) opted for the 'half-way house' approach of the V10.

By the time the formula had been downgraded to 3 litres for 1995, in the wake of the outcry for reductions in lap speed following the tragedies of Imola the previous May, the V10 had gained in favour, with Peugeot and Yamaha vaulting aboard the bandwagon. And though Ferrari and Ford both started out with V12 and V8 respectively, the latter had wanted to go V10 but had insufficient time in which to develop one, and Ferrari was being lobbied very hard by John Barnard to go a similar route, and

had earmarked 1 September as the date for completion of the prototype. This left only the indefatigable Brian Hart to row the V8 boat (and even he had produced a V10 in the 3.5 litre years), together with Ford and its customer engines.

Barnard explained why, as a vehicle designer, he had been driving Ferrari so hard for a 10-cylinder engine: 'I had been pushing ever since I came back to Ferrari, in 1992. To be honest, going right back to the first time I was with them, my position was slightly different. I was overall technical director, so the engine division came under me, although I was only inputting basics. But the 12 was an input. I felt in those days probably that was the right way to go.

'But when I went back the second time I pushed for a V10 because I felt that a 12 was wrong. At Ferrari we looked at Brian Hart's V10, but there were so many political problems in all

Peugeot's A14 was another power unit to follow the increasingly popular V10 configuration, and by 1996 was deemed to be one of the most powerful engines in the sport. (Peugeot)

areas that it didn't materialize. We then had a very good designer from Cosworth, who designed an eight, which I pushed hard to get built. But again it didn't get built because of the inherent 12 cylinder philosophy at Maranello.'

Eventually the walls came down at Ferrari, and the V10 was ready for the 1996 season. 'There was much less of a 12 cylinder band at Ferrari, which after all had done eights in the past,' Barnard continued. 'And eventually the 10 came along. In general terms it's the safest thing to do. Underneath, though, I still think we should have been looking at an eight. After all, if you go to an eight from a 10, you can say that pretty much everything else is a negative on a 10 than it is on an eight.'

Nick Hayes, who took over in 1997 as Formula 1 Programme Director at Cosworth Racing when previous incumbent Martyn Walters was promoted to Chief Engineer, explained the relative merits of the three configurations from the engine designer's viewpoint:

'In terms of more cylinders, 12 versus 10 versus eight, in general more cylinders mean more valve area, so you can in theory get more airflow in an engine per revolution. More cylinders also tend to have lighter pieces for a given capacity, so you are often able to run them to a higher rpm. And both of those things mean more airflow, to which you put more fuel, and that means you get more base power. But what you do is take off some things, too. More cylinders give you greater losses. Though you are producing more indicated horsepower, because there are more bits it takes more power to turn them all round, so in theory you get a situation where a 12 versus a 10, or a 10 versus an eight, will each respectively have more power but a lot more losses, so that the actual brake horsepower number will be different. But there is obviously a lot more to it, because of the losses. More cylinders are less efficient, so you have to use a lot more fuel.

'The big thing against more cylinders is that the engines get longer and heavier, and the teams don't like that as part of the car package, and also they tend to have greater heat rejection so the radiators tend to get bigger, the drag is worse . . . So you've got a lot of things going against more cylinders and a few things going for them.'

Barnard echoed the view. 'If you analyse a 12, what do you get, in theory? Theoretically you should get more top power. Revs mean top-end power, but let's look at the rest of it. In the mid-range and bottom end it's more difficult to match an eight or a 10. We still ran movable inlet trumpets at Ferrari, and I don't think anyone else did any more. We had to do all those tricks just to keep up with the 10s and eights.

'Then the 12 was longer, it was heavier, it used more fuel, it was fundamentally less torsionally stiff, you'd got more exhaust pipes to package – which was no small thing in itself – your radiators tended to be bigger because you were expending more heat because overall you'd probably got more friction, and that increased drag. Your driveability was more difficult to obtain. Everything else apart from the top power was a negative.'

Hayes continued: 'In 1993 we did an exercise with Rory Byrne at Benetton, looking at eights, 10s and 12s and we came up with the result that an eight would be best, so we did the Zetec R for 1994, based on an eight being better everywhere but Hockenheim and Monza according to our prediction. Unfortunately, that was for a race and it didn't include refuelling. That calculation was based on start-line weight with a full tank of fuel. Half-way through 1993 refuelling was introduced, and I think that swung the balance slightly towards a 10.

'We did a 10 at the first opportunity. With the rule changes after the Senna accident, nearly all the engine people had to do three litre versions of what they already had in the time available. So for us the first opportunity for a 10 was for 1996. Now we are pretty convinced that with the way the regulations are, a 10 is the best compromise. We know an eight would be smaller and lighter, won't rev as high, won't have quite as much power, but will have lower heat rejection. So there are plusses and minuses. A 12, similarly the other way. You'll have slightly more power but the engine will be longer and heavier, and there will be a lot more heat rejection so the radiators will be bigger. So at the end of the day, looking at the compromises, we were right in doing an eight for 1994, and we were right to do a 10 since refuelling came in.'

Barnard retains his forthright views on engines, and said: 'I think people make too much hype about making a new engine. Teams make new cars all the time. Look at an engine today and one 10 years ago, and what's new on it? What is new? Pneumatic valves? So what? We had them then! There's a certain amount of expense in tooling, but let's say it takes half a million pounds. In today's world that's not a huge amount. Brian Hart does it . . . The newest thing seems to be materials, or at least improvements in them.'

In a typical Formula 1 engine 63 per cent of the components are made of aluminium, things such as the cylinder heads, the crankcase, the sump, cam covers, pistons, and sundries such as water pump casings. Steel accounts for almost 30 per cent, for the long lead-time things such as the crankshaft, the camshafts, and the timing gears. Titanium, an expensive light-weight metal, amounts to five per cent of the mix and is used for parts such as the connecting rods, the valves, and sundry fasteners, while magnesium is used in very small proportions for sundry housings. Carbon fibre is also used to a small extent, for items such as the airbox

through which air is ducted into the intakes, and the inlet trumpets and their carrier.

Interestingly ceramics, once a buzz word in engineering circles along with oval pistons (which are proscribed by the regulations) appear less likely to play a significant role than is generally supposed in lay circles. 'I can't see them being used,' said Mario Illien, the co-founder and chief designer of Ilmor Engineering, which manufactures Formula 1 and IndyCar engines for Mercedes-Benz in its factory in Brixworth, near Northampton. He put down the improvements in engine power outputs and longevity to better basic materials. 'Today you get much better aluminiums, casting techniques are much better and the aluminium has better properties. You get titaniums with better properties, you get better finishing techniques and coatings. It's a lot of things in those areas, and you can make lighter components to do the same jobs as they used to.'

Ford has had plenty of experience with materials, too, though it hasn't necessarily had a great deal of success to show for it. In the course of developing several Formula 1 engines in a short space of time, its engine manufacturer Cosworth Racing has perfected its casting techniques to improve the products and cut down production times. First there was the HB, the final successor to derivatives of the legendary DFV, and the first pukka Ford for the 3.5 litre formula. Then came a stillborn 12, followed by the Zetec R V8, another stillborn 12, a stillborn 3.5 litre V10 which was killed by the sudden change in engine regulations for 1995, and then the pukka 3 litre Zetec R V10. As an indication of the developmental time that goes into a modern powerplant, the latter completed almost 330 hours of running on the dynamometer before it ran in a chassis for the first time.

Despite this, Ford did not have as easy

Among several engines that it has created in the past five years, Cosworth's 3.5-litre Ford V12 proved stillborn after the FIA changed the regulations to 3 litres for 1995 in the wake of the Imola accidents. (Ford)

a time with its first V10 as Ferrari seemed to, though both engines appeared for the 1996 season. While Ferrari survived a brief spate of piston failures caused by a faulty batch, and went on to win three races, Ford's drivers Heinz-Harald Frentzen and Johnny Herbert bemoaned the lack of horsepower, the latter being moved to suggest that it had no more than the Zetec R V8 Sauber had used the previous season. Hayes acknowledged that some of the criticism was justified, but qualified it. 'I think at the beginning of the year the engine was very difficult as far as driveability was concerned, and it was also a fair way behind on top-end power too. So, yes, that criticism was justified. But I think through the year it was far less so. We did a lot of work and moved on a lot. Drivers always say they lack horsepower, they always will, and I don't blame

them. But as I say, in the beginning it was behind, but I think we caught up a lot during the season, and we caught up further during the winter.'

Naturally, priority development resources at Cosworth were allocated to the V10, which was destined for Stewart Grand Prix's fledgling team. Hayes and his team modified it significantly during the winter of 1996. 'We concentrated nearly everything on performance,' he said, 'by which I mean peak power and shape and width of the power curve. We went for a lot of work on top-end power and the power curve. Quite a lot of the engine's mechanicals were new. It still revved to 16,500 rpm, and that's what we would qualify and race it at.'

He was optimistic that Cosworth would be in a better position to bring upgrades on line faster in 1997 than it could in the past, as a direct product of significantly greater – and long overdue – commitment from Ford to its Formula 1 effort. Other companies had been on the ball markedly longer, however, in particular Renault, Mercedes-Benz, and Peugeot, all of whom upheld Honda's expensive yet effective policy of continuous development.

When the first 3 litre Formula 1 was introduced in 1966 it was heralded as 'The Return To Power'. At that time a power output figure of 400 bhp was a big deal, though in fact it's unlikely that anybody truly produced this in a car until the Lotus 49 appeared in 1967 with its Ford–Cosworth DFV V8. 450 bhp was whispered of as the great goal – 150 bhp per litre – with 600 bhp as the ultimate target many years down the line.

Towards the end of the 3.5 litre formula in 1994, Ferrari was generally reckoned to have the most powerful engine in racing, with 800 bhp, but Renault was not far behind with 780, while Mercedes-Benz and Peugeot were thought to be pumping out 770. The Ford Zetec R in Michael Schumacher's World Championship-winning Benetton probably peaked at 735/740 bhp, proving that power was not everything. But like bore and stroke measurements, all of this was the sort of information that was harder to come by than Schumacher's home telephone number or the secret of eternal life. When Ford had first launched the HB at its Warley headquarters in mid-1989, Mike Kranefuss, then its head of motor sport, stood up and uttered the immortal words: 'This is our new engine. It's called a Ford and it's a 3.5 litre V8. Other than that, we're not going to tell you anything!' It set the tone for a generation.

★ ★ ★

By the beginning of the 1997 season, after two years of development, the 3 litre Formula 1 engines were beginning to hit their stride. By now Renault was

adjudged to have the powerhouse, with 740 bhp at 17,400 rpm, possibly matched by the Mugen–Honda, with Peugeot, Mercedes-Benz, and Ferrari next in line with around 720. Engine speeds were well in excess of 17,000 rpm on the better designs. That's over 280 revs per second, or an explosion of the fuel mixture in the combustion chamber around 1,400 times per second!

Electronics have undoubtedly helped to make an engine designer's life easier, but the main reason for the startling advance in performance is the increase in revs per minute, a corollary of better materials technology and general design progress. Mario Illien cited one further reason. 'For sure, the pneumatic valve control is the most important factor.'

This technology had its roots firmly in the 1980s and was but part of the legacy bequeathed to the sport by Renault Sport's genius designer Bernard Dudot, father not only of the highly successful V10, but its turbocharged V6 predecessor which had changed the path of racing. Instead of relying on old-fashioned coil springs to close the valves, or adopting the sort of desmodromic mechanical means that Mercedes-Benz had used to sound effect in the 1950s, Dudot developed a system whereby compressed air was used instead of the springs to close the valves. Without frail springs, which were prone to breaking with abuse, engines were able to rev far higher, and thus to develop greater horsepower.

Maximum power, however, was but part of the equation. 'Out of power, torque and driveability I would think the driveability is the most important thing,' Illien said. 'You've got to have the top-end performance as well, but there are only two really fast circuits, Hockenheim and Monza, where you really need it. The rest are high downforce tracks and wherever you go you need to have a very driveable torque band, as even as possible with no sharp changes. That is very important.'

Axel Plasse, track test engineer at Renault Sport, agreed. 'We place significant importance on the driveability of our engine, and driver comfort. We are not obsessed with engine power. We endeavour to produce an engine which is driveable in all conditions and which gives drivers no reason for complaint. Our aim is, in fact, to produce an engine which drivers can forget all about. It is often said that an engine on its own cannot win a race, but that it can lose one. An engine which puts out 10 or 20 extra horsepower will not change a car's overall competitiveness. However, an engine which fails does.'

Initially, drivers complained that the 3 litre engines lacked the torque of their 3.5 forebears. 'Obviously,' Illien agreed. 'The three litres are revving more, or are at least using a similar rpm band, and when we went to the three litres we had other changes too, and to make these engines more driveable at the lower end was a bit more difficult.'

'Of course there is less torque,' said Dudot, 'but to balance that there is less of a problem with traction.'

* * *

Hand in hand with the advent of the 3 litre engines came modifications to slow circuits down. 'So many of the circuits now are dependent on mid-range, low-end, accelerating power out of corners,' Barnard noted. 'Look at the modified Imola.' Renault's 1995 RS7A had revealed a change in power philosophy, too, prompting Barnard to comment: 'It definitely beat the V12 Ferrari when accelerating out of corners at Imola. So what was important was changing. So this engine thing was quite interesting, but like all these things, at the end of the day the guy building the engine wants to see the big numbers and the guy building the car wants to see something tiny to package.'

Barnard, of course, had been instrumental in packaging the TAG Porsche

turbo V6 into his McLaren MP4/2s in 1983, working very closely with Hans Metzger at Porsche to ensure that engine and car mated perfectly. Today the same process is ever more important, for nothing can be allowed to compromise optimal aerodynamics. Accordingly the new breed of engines were universally low, minimalist designs, aiming for the lowest centre of gravity, minimum weight and the smallest possible packaging. But it was possible to go too far, as John Judd at Engine Developments had discovered when Yamaha produced what was deemed to be the smallest engine of them all in 1996.

'We got good reliability early on,' Judd said, 'but then it became apparent that we had a problem with the casting quality of the blocks, which began cracking and leaking water with greater use.' This was deemed to be a by-product of the attempt to make the engine as light as possible, partly by minimizing the thickness of the cylinder walls. The problem was eventually solved once new casting techniques had been introduced.

'It's all really about integration, about designing an engine around a car rather than vice versa,' said Ross Brawn, technical director of Ferrari. 'One of the great examples was the TAG Porsche V6. And it's something that Renault seems to understand best.'

At Ferrari the engine people historically tend to have their own problems, but now there is a far greater understanding of the need not just for power but general usability, driveability, and fuel economy, the integration of the whole package. An engine that uses more fuel isn't going to be competitive. Even at Ferrari, traditionally the home of the most powerful engines of any Formula 1 era, there has come the general recognition that having an engine that looks good on the dyno doesn't mean much these days. It's how that engine performs in the car, how it can be

Yamaha's OX10C 3-litre broke new ground as the Japanese company, best known for its motor cycle racing successes, worked in conjunction with Engine Developments in England to create the lightest and most compact unit. The quest was not entirely successful. (Yamaha)

used by the driver, that really counts.

It's more difficult for Ferrari because it gets little feedback apart from via its own team. Brawn made an interesting point that reflected this. 'Renault really knows what's required because they talk to the teams. When I was at Benetton we spent a lot of time with Renault talking about what would happen if we did this or did that, moving away from just the power aspects. And of course they were getting the same from Williams. Now Paulo Martinelli and his people at Ferrari are doing the same with me. Engines are difficult, because they've got a longer lead time than the car. I mean, we'd be designing bits for the following year's engines as early as March the previous season. So it needs more time to steer an engine in a certain direction.'

Mario Illien might disagree with that view, however, for Ilmor and Mercedes-Benz were the only partnership to bite the bullet and opt to build an all-new 3 litre engine for 1995. On the face of it a reduction of a mere 500 cc might seem relatively easy, but it actually called for a complete redesign of the engine and Ilmor achieved the feat in record time. Its FO110 unit was conceived and built in a staggering three months. Illien explained why he did not see an alternative:

'I wouldn't actually say it was difficult. I would say it would have been more difficult to compromise by taking the three and a half litre and downsizing it. That would definitely have been a compromise. And there would have been a slight weight penalty by using the three and a half litre. So I felt we should go

Mario Illien's FO110 series of V10 engines for Mercedes–Benz echoed Renault's ceaseless development in the quest for better performance and reliability. When the 3-litre formula was announced, Illien was the first to opt for a completely new engine, rather than modifying his existing 3.5, and the project was completed in an astonishing three months. (Mercedes–Benz)

straight away to the three litre and make a proper job, though obviously it was a bigger risk, to start with at least. But it gave us something to build on. At that time we were still very much in the game of closing the gap, we still had to catch up, and I felt that would be another way of getting closer, but quicker closer, to the opposition.'

Formula 1 engines are oversquare; the bore is larger than the stroke. This is because short-stroke engines rev higher, and higher revs mean great power. If Ilmor had compromised by sleeving down the bore, the block would have been slightly longer than necessary. Likewise, reducing the stroke might have left the block too high. That in turn might have necessitated a longer than optimum con-rod and so the compro-

mises would have run full circle throughout the unit. In most applications it would not strictly have mattered, but in Formula 1 such things are critical.

* * *

For many seasons Formula 1 engines have simply been plugged in and out like light bulbs, and the sight of a unit stripped down for attention in the garage has long since faded. 'The days have long gone when you might try and make an engine work at the track,' said Brian Hart, the racer turned engine-builder who worked wonders with his private project on minimal funding. 'When an engine arrives at the circuit today it's like a set of tyres. You just put them in and take them out.'

All the engines are set up before they

arrive too, with the right details such as fuel mapping for specific circuits. Mercedes-Benz, for instance, uses its transient dynamometer not just for test work, but for setting up. 'We can simulate race distances and certain conditions, as well as how well the engine picks up out of corners, its driveability,' said Illien. 'Mainly we are using it for endurance running, for reliability.' Mercedes can programme in the characteristics of different circuits, to provide empirical evaluation of various configurations, based on data acquired in previous races at a given venue, and the transient dyno time is shared between Ilmor's Formula 1 and CART IndyCar projects.

The majority of engine development is thus done on the test benches, but some aspects can only be conducted at the track. 'Generally speaking, testing is a means of validating a new development or a new component,' explained Axel Plasse. 'It is an indispensable phase of the development process and rare indeed are the fields of technology in which engineers can allow themselves not to test. Despite the importance of calculation work both within teams and at Renault Sport, nothing can replace testing. To be able to predict on paper what is likely to work and what isn't has effectively become increasingly important, but testing is still essential.

'Although bench testing attempts to reproduce real conditions as closely as possible, it has its limits. A Formula 1 car moves, turns, and accelerates whereas an engine on the bench is fixed, which means that a whole host of situations cannot be simulated.

'Having said that, the test bench remains a rigorous tool which is capable of determining, for example, whether a particular engine is developing, say, three brake horsepower more than another. This is something which a driver is incapable of doing. However, a bench test is a bit like a computer inasmuch as it can only quantify parameters that are quantifiable. Some parameters – such as the characteristics of a new type of fuel – are difficult to put into figures in order to evaluate performance gains. On the other hand, there are many subjective considerations – such as driveability and response – which can only be judged by a driver. Track testing is an intermediate phase between bench testing and race use. It's the final link in the chain before a part or a new development can be raced.'

★ ★ ★

Besides the switch from 3.5 to 3 litre engines, the most significant regulation change affecting engines was the ban on fly-by-wire throttles which accompanied the ban on other electronic driver aids. FIA President Max Mosley was concerned that traction control would be very difficult to police, just as in the past it had proved almost impossible to police ground clearance once a car was in motion. And early in 1994 he cited three primary reasons why he wanted fly-by-wire throttles outlawed.

'The first is that it is impossible for the scrutineers at any reasonable time to check the integrity of the hardware and the software, so they can't be sure that the throttle wouldn't behave in a wholly unpredictable way. Whereas with a classic throttle you can be reasonably sure of that.

'Secondly, it is extremely difficult for a team that has such a system to demonstrate that it doesn't have traction control. Which, after all, they have to. It is up to them to demonstrate that they don't have it.

'Thirdly, it enables an engine to be set at a more critical level, so as to give more power than if a driver drove it. All racing engines are difficult to drive; that's the main difference between a racing and a road engine as far as using it is concerned. An engine that is extremely difficult to drive may give more power but you need an electronic throttle to help anyone except the most competent driver to extract the power from the engine. And we see that as a driver aid. So those are the three reasons.'

Mosley added: 'All of the teams know what the rules are, and on all the grey areas or difficult areas they know what our view is, and although our view is not necessarily the view of the stewards – they can make their own minds up – it will probably be quite persuasive. So I think that anybody who wants to go to the first race in Brazil with an uncontentious car, can.'

The teams eventually produced persuasive arguments in favour of keeping fly-by-wire throttles, and once he had ascertained the effectiveness of his engineers' own ability to police software systems, Mosley relented and they were reinstated.

'Originally people just used them for traction control,' explained Gary Anderson. 'The engine didn't have to do what the driver was telling it, it could do what the rear wheels were telling it. It's not so much a system of transmitting faster signals than a driver's foot; what you can have is a non-linear throttle, so originally you could map the engine throttle opening differently from the pedal. But since 1994 the rules have been that you have to have a fixed map. You could do that with a mechanical linkage as well, if you really got carried away, but not very easily. Also, with the blippers for down-changes, that's all built into the one system, whereas with the old cable you had to have two systems. It's just made it a bit easier. It's all legal, so long as there are no inputs to it other than the driver moving his foot, and the computer can take control momentarily for a gear change. But you have to have that fixed map, not a variable map, or a different map for each gear. They can check all that now, so everybody has to comply with it. It's all fads, to be honest; if you had mechanical throttles, you wouldn't see any difference, either. It's just probably a little bit easier, and at tracks such as Monaco you can alter the map slightly so you have lower throttle openings and the guy's got a little bit more control. That can improve pick-up, and you can do things to it that can help the amount of power you've got at the rear wheels for a given throttle opening, or you can give the driver a bigger window to play with. If he has good control over the throttle, say with three-quarters of the pedal movement rather than a quarter, he can cope with a lot of power, and that can be very useful at a track like Monaco.'

'We have made great progress with power throttles,' said Bernard Dudot. 'Fly-by-wire is a very good thing, and now the FIA is happy it can check systems for traction control so we can use them again. This is very sensible.'

In mid 1997 the FIA sanctioned three-dimensional engine mapping, which Ferrari had developed with beneficial result and which others regarded as a form of traction control. Such mapping allows power or torque outputs to be plotted simultaneously against throttle position and revs, but some worried that clever programmers could turn the throttle into a 'torque command control' which, working in conjunction with the right engine management system, could vary engine parameters to produce a desired overall level of performance rather than just leaving the driver to cope with unrestricted power or torque. In other words, to limit wheelspin like a traction control device.

The FIA ruled this was not illegal provided it remained purely within the driver's physical control.

Mario Illien firmly believed that it was a legal means to an end, suggesting that Mercedes-Benz had already been working along such lines, while Patrick Head also felt it to be acceptable, though he was less impressed with the way in which it was ratified. "I don't think it is a very good idea to ratify a rule in such a way, effectively making a 180 degree turn, halfway through a season," he said. "But I'm sure Renault will catch up." It did.

★ ★ ★

Giving the lie somewhat to those who felt that the FIA did little to contain the excesses of engine manufacturers, or to persuade them to change their programmes, the FIA sought in 1993, at the height of the arguments over the ban on electronic 'gizmos', to initiate a limit on the number of engines teams could use during a season. The idea was that the same engine must remain in a car throughout an entire event subject to a maximum of 12 engines per team per season. Use of the spare car was to count as an engine change, as would removal of the sump or the cylinder heads. The smaller teams had proposed a limit of six to eight engines per team per race meeting, to try and counter the 'grenade' qualifying engines that were prevalent at the time.

The plan was ridiculous and completely unworkable, and predictably it fell into abeyance and was never mentioned again . . .

Around this time Dudot gave some typical figures for race engine life, which make interesting reading. 'Our engines can go to 500 miles, no problem, but we usually rebuild them after 325 just to be safe. As a general rule we rebuild them after every race, after they have done an official qualifying session, or after a lengthy private test.'

In fact 'grenade' qualifying engines largely disappeared anyway, on economic grounds, and it was on the same grounds – once Formula 1's final V12 had wailed its glorious last – that Ford's trusty V8s kept rumbling along. In any formula a supply of customer engines is an essential backstop if a situation is to be avoided where there are insufficient power units to go round, especially as the majority of major manufacturers avoid the cost and logistical problems of supplying more than one team if they possibly can. Into this breach, commendably, stepped Ford. Naturally, the V10 development programme was much more intensive than that for the V8, since the works Stewart alliance received precedence. But under Motorsport Manager Mark Parrish the ED3 V8 (which dated back to the 3.5 litre HB introduced for 1989) was given a new lease of life as it was massaged first into the ED4, and then into the ED5. He explained the confused situation where Ford started the 1997 season by supplying not one but two V8s (a logistical problem that Lola soon solved for Cosworth by going out of business).

'We were not allowed to supply customer V10s, and we knew that the ED3 wasn't going to do the job that year, so we needed to do something about it. The EC, or the Zetec R V8, which Sauber used in 1995, was a heavier engine. It probably made the ultimate V8 as a 3.5 litre engine, but as a 3 litre it had been compromised. We thought that with the development we had done, the old HB would form the basis of a better 3 litre V8 engine.

'Our development programme on the ED4 hadn't been as intense as that on the Zetec R V10 because our resources were more limited. It's difficult to say what the proportion was, but ours was definitely a more low-key programme.'

Parrish's team concentrated primarily on getting the engine to rev higher and on increasing horsepower. 'With the ED3 upgrade that we did for Minardi in 1996 we concentrated on the bottom end, which was new and allowed the engine to run faster, to 14,500 rpm. What we did with ED4 in 1997 was to revise the cylinder heads and camshafts, and the inlet system, and that's where the majority of benefit came from. There were some other minor modifications to the auxiliaries. It didn't rev any higher, but the peak power came in higher than it did with ED3, which had been one of Minardi's complaints.' The ED5 appeared later that season, again for Tyrrell.

Chapter 8

Fuellish things

'If refuelling makes the racing more exciting, then fine. If it flambéd 10 mechanics, then I'd think it was a bad decision. I think you are playing with fire, simply, no pun intended.'

Damon Hill, World Champion

IN THE ANGST THAT accompanied the FIA's ban on electronic 'gizmos' for the 1994 season, and the sudden 'discovery' at the Canadian GP that virtually all of the cars were illegal, one very salient point went almost unnoticed – the plan to reintroduce refuelling for the forthcoming season.

The manner in which the FISA suggested that the Formula 1 teams would have to wait until October for the FIA World Council to rule one way or another on the legality issue kept everyone on tenterhooks, with the veiled threat that they really ought to comply with the governing body's wishes. The teams thus had many things on their minds when Bernie Ecclestone put refuelling on the agenda at a crucial seven-hour meeting, which centred mainly on the vexed subject of electronics, at the German GP at Hockenheim in 1993. With consummate acumen Ecclestone left the controversial subject of refuelling until the point at which most of the team owners had argued themselves to the brink of emotional exhaustion and were prepared to

agree in principle to anything just to bring the meeting to a close.

By the Portuguese GP in September some of them had already started wondering just what they had been thinking of, and as the dust of Hockenheim began to settle had been able to determine with greater clarity the direction in which they had so adroitly been led. It is said that even Ecclestone himself was entertaining second thoughts at this stage, but while everyone else appeared to be in favour of dropping the idea, Ferrari and Minardi were not. These were the days when the Concorde Agreement called for unanimity, and Ferrari resolutely blocked the new proposal. Minardi, a past user of Ferrari engines, politically followed suit. Refuelling had been given the okay, so it would be going ahead. After all, with a thirsty V12 which often began races with the in-built disadvantage of carrying more fuel, Ferrari stood to gain a great deal, since refuelling would alleviate that shortcoming to an extent, while also allowing its designers to package the long V12 engine around a smaller tank. Moreover, it was believed that the red cars had gone to the line in some of the 1993 races with their 240-litre tanks full to the brim, and that the drivers had been obliged to back off at key stages to make sure of getting to the finish line. Refuelling would suit Ferrari very nicely, thank you.

Thus it gradually became apparent that it was going to be a reality, and also that it was going to be around for some time, for the FIA had written into the 1995 stepped bottom regulations that cars need no longer have a minimum fuel capacity of 200 litres. Effectively, everyone would thus build smaller cars, and once that had happened there was no way they would want to go back to cars with larger tanks. The FIA shrewdly knew that, ultimately, this might prove another compelling reason to retain refuelling.

Ecclestone and Mosley wanted refuelling because it would liven up races, and Patrick Head of Williams was open-minded enough to agree. 'I think it will brighten them up,' he said. 'Races will be sprints from beginning to end, and they'll be more exciting from the entertainment point of view.' Frank Williams, meanwhile, did not share his partner's enthusiasm, but said: 'Despite our misgivings we're going to give it a shot. Obviously we're going to try very hard not to have an accident.'

This was Formula-1-speak for 'Bernie and Max have us over a barrel, so there is nothing we can do but go along with their wishes.'

Ron Dennis of McLaren was particularly vocal in the early part of 1994, by which time the matter had long been a *fait accompli* and everybody had been obliged, in order to remain competitive, to produce new cars with smaller tanks because there was no longer a necessity to carry enough fuel to do a full race distance.

'The chances are there will be a con-flagration,' he said, and, indeed, events would more than once prove him right. 'We haven't seen the hardware yet, though; we have only had access so far to drawings. From what we have seen it looks well designed, and the process should be safer than those previously used in motor racing. But we will be handling a flammable liquid in an area

During the first major test session of 1994, at the Imola circuit, Ayrton Senna's Williams FW16 betrays the move back to refuelling by the presence of the hose coupling just behind the Brazilian's left shoulder. (ICN UK Bureau)

of stress, and therefore there will be risks.'

This was a time when any team manager would grimace at the very mention of refuelling, and when the majority of them harboured serious fears of a pit lane holocaust. Those with longer memories recalled the fire in the Porsche pit during the World Sportscar Championship race at Hockenheim in 1985, when high ambient temperatures had led fuel tanks to expand and then caused a huge blowback of fuel over the Ickx/Mass Porsche 956. Porsche's team manager Norbert Singer had been badly burned in the incident, along with engineer Helmut Schmidt. Williams, in particular, recalled Keke Rosberg's car catching fire briefly during a refuelling stop in Rio 12 years earlier. 'When the accident happens,' Dennis continued, 'we have to ask, "Will it be controllable? Will people be hurt?"'

Dennis could not be accused of scaremongering; he was simply having the courage to voice the concerns that his

This is the bulky, aircraft-standard refuelling equipment designed specifically for Formula 1 use by the French company, Intertechnique. Teams use one rig per car, and while one refueller supports the hose, the other grasps the axial handle at the end as he connects its to the valve on the side of the car's fuel tank. (Author)

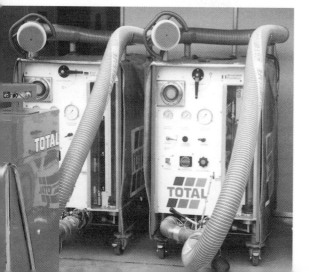

fellow team owners felt. But Jackie Oliver of Footwork sounded a note of optimism when he described a visit to the factory of the company that would manufacture the equipment under exclusive licence, Intertechnique. 'We tried it out, and it's super equipment. It's very well made, to an excellent standard of workmanship. It works just fine and I believe that it's foolproof. It's safer than the systems we used before. If we are going to have any problems this year, they will be because of people failure or because of a freak circumstance.'

'If you could guarantee that there wouldn't be a fire with refuelling, then fine,' said Adrian Newey. 'If Bernie then thinks that it would make a better spectacle, then that's his prerogative. I'd have no engineering objection to it. But the Imola race in 1993 was a classic example. Some marshals nearly got run over as Senna left the pits because a load of camera people were pushing them forward. Okay, Bernie can make sure there are no camera crews in the pit lane, although I'd find that hard to believe with the television thing. But there isn't enough room. And on a boiling hot day like that, even if we were to go back to ordinary four star fuel, it's pretty volatile in that sort of heat. In those very cramped conditions I think it would be very, very dangerous.'

Damon Hill spoke for most of the drivers when he said: 'If refuelling makes the racing more exciting, then fine. If it flambéd 10 mechanics then I'd think it was a bad decision. I think you are playing with fire, simply, no pun intended. For me, I don't know if it's any more dangerous, because I sit in the car when they are refuelling it anyway. I sit in the car at the start with 200 litres behind me. There is precious little difference with a fire with 200 litres and one with 50. But if there is a spillage there are two things that can happen. The fuel can go into the cockpit and not catch fire, in which case I drive the rest of the race sit-

The smiles didn't last long for Damon Hill in 1997 after the launch of the Arrows A18, which followed the broad outlines of the Williams FW18. Though it handled well, the design required continual upgrading throughout the season. (ICN UK Bureau)

Nestling in rural Oxfordshire, TWR's Leafield facility is an impressive and dramatic indication of the sort of headquarters that serious F1 teams required as the Millennium approached. (TWR)

The classical shape of the Formula 1 car of the mid-1990s is nicely illustrated in this view of the Williams FW17 driven by David Coulthard and Damon Hill. Though they look different in some ways to the FW15s (see Prologue), they were essentially an evolution of that basic concept. (ICN UK Bureau)

Computer-controlled machinery cuts the basic shape of a car's rear bodywork from solid material, dramatically reducing manufacturing time and enhancing accuracy. (Fondmetal)

The prototype stage entails trial fitting the components together in their intended orientations. Here a McLaren chassis mock-up is united with a Mercedes engine, plus gearbox and radiators, to check the installation. (Sutton Motorsport)

Alan Jenkins's Stewart SF-1 design was the new Stewart Grand Prix team's first offspring for the 1997 season, but that didn't stop Jenkins stealing a march by conducting all of its aerodynamic testing in a 50 per cent wind-tunnel, the same size as used by the omnipotent Williams team. (ICN UK Bureau)

Above *The Ferrari 310 of 1996 echoes the F92A's unsuccessful twin-floor aerodynamics, and the influence of the safety cockpit can clearly be seen, together with the manner in which Eddie Irvine's helmet interferes with airflow into the engine's airbox. The car typified the new breed of 'aero' cars which, in marked contrast to the preceding 412T2, had a dislike of being driven sideways. (ICN UK Bureau)*

Right *At Monaco in 1997 Mika Salo splashes to fifth place, his Tyrrell 025 sporting the distinctive X wings for maximum downforce on a circuit where grip is everything. (ICN UK Bureau)*

Below *Though barge boards look like tacked on afterthoughts they play a crucial role in smoothing airflow through the front suspension arms and back towards the rear wing. This is Ferrari's 1997 F310B. (Author)*

Seen from head-on (see page 58) McLaren's mini-wing on the unloved MP4/10 looked integrated, but from the side the design was less harmonious. Opinion was sharply divided as to whether it conferred any aerodynamic advantage. (McLaren)

In Argentina the Tyrrell appeared for the first time with its cockpit-mounted wings, which were quickly christened X wings in the Formula 1 pit lane. Like McLaren's mini wing, they exploited a loophole in the regulations to increase downforce. (Author)

Front wing endplates are shadows of their former selves, thanks to regulation changes. The Minardi M197 wing features a small outer winglet. (Author)

Another close-up of Tyrrell's 'moustache' wings on the 025, which embraced the theme of the high nose that Tyrrell designer Harvey Postlethwaite had pioneered on the 019 back in 1990. (Author)

The improved protection provided by the revised cockpit regulations is well shown in this view of Jacques Villeneuve in a Williams FW18 during the 1996 season. (ICN UK Bureau)

Jordan 197 winglets, designed to maximize downforce. (Author)

Hill again sampled the gravel at Estoril in 1995, when Eddie Irvine inadvertently tipped the Williams over after a minor collision in the tight Corkscrew chicane. It was the first time in his career that Hill had been on his head, and, though he emerged unharmed, he and several other drivers were openly critical of this very slow new addition to the Portuguese circuit. (ICN UK Bureau)

In a pose that television has made familiar the world over, a driver carefully monitors the progress of rivals on the movable television screen resting on his car's scuttle. Here, Jacques Villeneuve awaits the right moment to make his qualifying attempt, watched by his race engineer Jock Clear and girlfriend Sandrine. (ICN UK Bureau)

ting in a pool of fuel. Or it can catch fire, in which case I have got to get out of the car, among other things. The prospect of that happening, and the fact that you put it into the middle of a Grand Prix, when everyone is trying to work as hard as they can to try to avoid making mistakes, means that the potential is there. On those basic terms I am dubious about it.'

It was apparent from the start, however, that the FIA had made a serious effort to select the safest possible equipment, even though some other teams did not share Oliver's benign view after a few initial testing glitches. The Jordan team had a problem with the hose-to-tank connection during a test in Barcelona, while veteran mechanic Bob Dance was doused with fuel – which mercifully did not ignite – when the Lotus team experienced a similar thing. Intertechnique overcame the problem by fitting stronger hose connecting springs.

When Gordon Murray had brought the spectacle of refuelling back to Formula 1 at the 1982 British GP, the equipment used required two men. One presented the fuel hose to one side of the car, the other simultaneously offered up a ventilating bottle to a similar coupling on the other side. As the fuel hose went home, the fuel tank vented displaced air

Previous spread *When things go awry, refuelling is much less acceptable. This is the fire that engulfed the Benetton pit during Jos Verstappen's dramatic stop in the 1994 German GP at Hockenheim. Only a small amount of fuel actually spilled over, but the fire could have had serious consequences. Fortunately, nobody sustained lasting injuries.* (LAT)

Left *It's not often that you see a car's dampers left open for inspection, since secrecy is all part of the game and most are covered up even while adjustments are being made. This is the Arrows A18's triple-damper system.* (Author)

into the big plastic bottle. The problems arose if either of them got themselves out of synchronisation. In the pressure of the moment this was eminently possible, especially as both men were on their mettle not to be the one who let the team down.

Intertechnique's background was in the aviation business, and its refuelling rigs were pressurised to 1.1 bar, with a flow rate between nine and 12 litres per second. Fuel flowed from a reservoir in the garage down a thick co-axial hose – which comprised one hose inside another. The inner supplied the fuel, the outer acted as the vital vent for the air in the fuel tank. The nozzle on the end of the hose had to be locked on to a similar mechanism on the side of the car and as it connected it opened the vent valve first. Only when that was open did the inlet pipe open to allow the fuel to flow. When the nozzle was disconnected the inlet valves closed first, then the tank vent.

The teams were obliged to have two tanks in the garage, one low pressure, the other high. When the team decided how much fuel it wanted to put into a car the amount was transferred in advance of the fuel stop to the high pressure tank. That was then locked off and pressurised. A large piston in the top of the tank was driven downwards when the system was activated, to expel the fuel.

The fuel hose was very heavy, and thus required two men, one to locate the nozzle, the other to support the weight of the hose itself. It was at its most difficult before attachment to the car because it was full of fuel and was rigid because of the pressure in it. The fuellers wore flame-proof clothing, and each man had a light in his helmet which let him know when the pressure had dropped, which in turn indicated when the fuel had been transferred. Backing this up there was also a tactile message as the hose went limp when empty.

Despite the misgivings, the introduction of refuelling went well, adding a new spectacle to Formula 1 not only in terms of the dramatic pit stops, but also because of the new race strategies that the teams had to adopt, though in terms of public entertainment the one tended to cancel out the other because trying to predict or perceive strategy could be a complex business. Overall, however, the sight of cars wobbling on their jacks as four wheels and tyres were changed and 60 litres of fuel were thrown aboard in little over eight seconds, became a source of enduring fascination in living rooms across the globe.

It was at the German GP at Hockenheim – ironically enough – that the disaster everybody had predicted came close to realization.

It came on the 15th lap, and it involved the young Dutch driver Jos Verstappen, driving the second Benetton alongside pace-setter Michael Schumacher. As Verstappen pulled up in the Benetton pit, which was situated just below the Paddock Club in which the wealthiest visitors to the race were entertained by the teams who had invited them, some fuel was spilt. For moments nothing happened, then the back of the car, and the mechanics surrounding it, were engulfed in an orange ball of flame. It took just four seconds for the fire to be extinguished, itself an admirable feat, but the damage had been done. Mechanics Paul Seaby, Dave Redding and Wayne Bennett were all released from hospital that evening with minor burns, but Michael Jakeman and Kenny Handkammer were kept in overnight for observation. They were lucky too, but Simon Morley, who had been in charge of the refuelling hose, was detained longer.

In cool analysis it was an horrific incident that mercifully did no enduring damage, except to the credibility of refuelling and Intertechnique's equipment, and doubtless to the sleeping ability of

When everything goes right, refuelling is an exciting and welcome addition to the Formula 1 spectacle. Here McLaren services Martin Brundle during the 1994 Hungarian GP. (ICN UK Bureau)

those involved at its epicentre. But one of the more worrying aspects was that the sizeable conflagration had been caused by a spillage estimated at little over two litres of fuel.

Verstappen himself was commendably cool about the whole thing. 'I saw the liquid and thought at first that it was water,' he said. 'The next second . . . Boom! All I could see were the flames licking round the cockpit. I was really panicking, because those few seconds seemed like half an hour. I hit the safety belt and managed to scramble clear just as the flames were being put out.'

For Benetton, worse was to come, for in a season in which the legality of its cars' transmission had already been called into question, subsequent investigation of the refuelling equipment revealed that a fuel filter had been removed from the system. This would have improved the flow rate, and by the Hungarian GP had sparked off fresh allegations that the team was cheating. The FIA alleged that removal of the filter had allowed debris to clog the docking mechanism of the refuelling equipment.

Use of such filters was made a legal requirement the previous February after the Jordan and Lotus teams' problems, and Article 6.5.1 of the Technical Regulations expressly forbade them to be removed. It also expressly forbade teams to modify the refuelling equipment in any way. Removal of the filter was estimated to offer a potential improvement in flow rate of 10 to 12 per cent, enough to make a highly significant difference to a pit stop.

Benetton claimed initially that it had received verbal permission from FIA Technical Delegate Charlie Whiting to remove the filter. Later it suggested that a 'junior employee' (thought to be team manager Joan Villadelprat) had received verbal permission to do so from Intertechnique and had received verbal approval from Whiting when it was men-

tioned to him in conversation. Intertechnique stressed, perhaps belatedly, that any proposal to modify its equipment had to be made in writing to the FIA, and that any permission, equally, had to be in writing. And it added that, after the problems in the Barcelona test, any such proposal to remove the filter would not have been granted. The gist of it all was that the systems could run without the filters but that it was not desirable that they should, and that Benetton had been in the wrong for doing so without written permission. Benetton insisted that an independent investigation by Accident and Failure Technical Analysis Ltd had not found any evidence to support the view that debris had been responsible for the malfunction, and issued a statement accusing Intertechnique of supplying faulty equipment. It also alleged that Intertechnique had, without telling any of the teams, begun changing refuelling valves in all of its systems along the pit lane, and that parts removed from other teams' rigs had 'five times the operating clearance' of the same part removed from the Verstappen rig.

The reality was that seven Benetton team members, not to mention other teams' personnel close by in the pit lane, or the hundreds of guests in the Paddock Club, could have suffered serious injury.

Explaining why the FIA had not penalised Benetton more heavily than it did, Mosley explained: 'The thing is that as far as the "junior employee" is concerned, and his removing the part, once you accept that he thought – at whatever level – that he could do that, then, immediately, the level of guilt changes. Now it was said by the team that Charlie said they could remove the filter. What Charlie actually said was, "It's okay by me if it's okay by Intertechnique". In other words, go and ask Intertechnique, because it's not within my competence. I think the junior employee thought that, because the Larrousse team had done something similar, that Intertechnique had said it was all right. Or at least, that was what was presented to us in Paris.'

In a way, the FIA didn't have to do more, for the way in which it handled matters blackened Benetton's name further in any case. Patrick Head of Williams clearly felt that was the case when he said: 'It is quite possible that the lack of a filter did not cause the fire, but I have no direct knowledge. However, I do know that a central and critical component in the fuel system has been changed here by Intertechnique with no explanation to any of the teams. Everyone has had the valve in the centre of the fuel hose replaced with a different one. I can understand Benetton being annoyed that it was changed without explanation. It's also a bit off that the FIA put out the Intertechnique report.' But he added, as an afterthought: 'I would also have to say that in my view the man who decided to remove the filter was . . . unwise.'

Shortly afterwards, at the Italian GP at Monza that September, the Williams team was also reprimanded by the FIA on race day morning, for running a modified part in its refuelling system. The governing body had not given permission for the change, but accepted that Intertechnique had sanctioned it and had supplied the revised component that was fitted to the Williams cars.

Early in 1995 McLaren suffered a fuel spill during a practice refuelling run using a chassis with no electronics and thus a cold engine. 'We lost around 10 kilos of fuel,' said Ron Dennis, 'when a fuel valve stuck.'

Dennis took the valve to the Defence Research Agency at RAE Farnborough for investigation, and explained: 'We found that there was a retaining spring which had not been correctly fitted in the valve, but also that that area had not been designed to be idiot proof. Therefore it was possible for that to be incorrectly fitted on all other valves. One of the other five valves had shown traces of the problem we had, and a design change has been effected.

'These things are quite normal – of course it's a little more nerve-wracking when you have a design fault on something like a refuelling rig – but I'm quite comfortable now that the problem has been eliminated and that the systems will operate safely.'

Then, at Spa, Eddie Irvine's Jordan suffered a similar problem to Verstappen, albeit with a smaller fire, while a sticking fuel tank valve caused Pedro Diniz to bail out of his Ligier in Argentina in 1996 when fuel that had slopped from the open vent ignited while he was travelling at speed following his pit stop. Fortunately the Brazilian, whose picture made the front pages of newspapers around the globe, escaped without injury, but it was too close for comfort.

Since then there have been no further incidents, and refuelling has become accepted as just another part of the Formula 1 routine. 'I think it's a reasonable system,' said Jordan's Gary Anderson, 'when you think how many couplings have been made each season by each team.'

Out of context it all seemed very easy, but add the tension and pressure of a Grand Prix, and the knowledge that a mistake could, at best, lose your driver a Grand Prix victory, or at worst risk igniting your team-mates, and refuelling was indeed a whole new dimension. From 1994 onwards it was no longer just the drivers who took risks in Formula 1, but the foot-soldiers, too.

* * *

Refuelling was not the sole controversy surrounding the subject of fuel in Formula 1 as the 1994 season drew near, for Max Mosley had made it clear that he intended to eradicate some of the more exotic fuel blends, with their high toluene contents, and substitute something closer to ordinary pump fuel – 'commercially available fuel' – at the earliest convenience. This process began in 1993 and was completed by 1994. And as it would with software, the FIA came up with the idea of establishing a basic 'fingerprint' to determine what comprised an acceptable fuel, and to monitor what the teams were using by matching race batches against it.

As the Formula 1 circus headed to the scrutineering bay in Interlagos for the first race of 1994, Mosley was optimistic that the legality of the leading cars wouldn't be the contentious factor that sceptics expected it to be. Few Formula 1 seasons had been quite so eagerly awaited, after the banning of the infamous 'gizmos', and fans hoped for closer racing. But there was concern whether the changes in the regulations actually would make any difference. And, even more, that there might be attempts to 'circumvent' them. But the FIA had made some none-too-veiled threats to persuade teams that the best policy was to play with a straight bat, and threatened 'Draconian' penalties for any transgressors.

In mid-March, all of the fuel companies finally acquiesced to the FIA dictate that they had to supply samples for analysis before the Brazilian GP, and once they had been vetted samples were certificated for use by the appropriate teams. It was a simple enough scheme: no certificate, no pass through scrutineering. Better still, Mosley had turned the regulations round on the teams; they had always had to comply with the rules, but he now made it expressly clear that wherever doubt over legality existed the onus was on them to prove that their cars complied.

Behind the scenes he was still stinging from Elf's threats to take legal action in 1992 over the expressed intention to outlaw exotic fuel brews in favour of 'pump' fuel, and the revisions in policy were designed to avoid leaving the FIA in an exposed position.

'We've checked all the fuel before the start of the season,' he said, 'so there won't be any of that hanging around afterwards, unless there's something that nobody's thought of. So I think the chances of problems, either in Brazil or after Brazil, are small. And if there are problems, I have to say it won't be our fault. We've done everything one possibly can so that everybody knows exactly where they are. We analyse the sample batches carefully and then we compare, as it were, the two fingerprints, like a DNA test.'

The sole problem arose after Michael Schumacher had won the 1995 Brazilian GP from David Coulthard's Williams, and a chromatography check revealed that the Elf fuel in both cars failed to match its sample batch. Fines of $30,000 had already been inflicted when samples taken in qualifying were found to have distinct differences from the fuel submitted for approval. For a while both cars were excluded, temporarily handing the win to Gerhard Berger, but subsequent appeals were upheld when Elf proved that it had mixed an almost identical batch after the original had been ratified.

'When we first found a non-conforming fuel in Brazil in 1995 the then Elf PR person was saying that we were using outdated machinery,' Mosley said. 'Then, of course, when our results were confirmed to the letter by the German, Swiss, and French national testing laboratories, the PR person was instructed by the scientists as to what machines were used and realised that we *were* using the very latest and best equipment. So again there is no problem there. They weren't cheating in any way; but what had happened was that they submitted one lot of fuel and then they made up a different batch which was almost the same but not quite. And we picked up the difference and said sorry, it's not the same. Now everybody knows that you send the sample from the batch that you're actually going to use, and you make enough fuel before you send the sample.'

It was a minor embarrassment for Elf, and for Formula 1 in general, but since then there have been no problems. In the 16 races of the 1996 World Championship, 116 fuel samples were analysed, from the cars, from the re-fuelling rigs, and from containers in team garages, and all were found to conform to the regulations.

★ ★ ★

One positive note concerning refuelling was the way in which pit stop strategy would play a key role in the outcome of a race, and Ron Dennis was more optimistic about that aspect. 'The strategy you adopt will be very interesting,' he said, 'and teams will contribute a great deal more.'

This was certainly true, but for those not intimately in the know – spectators and journalists alike – team strategies often proved harder to figure out than much of the advanced technology. Frequently this meant that the early stages of an event were not necessarily an accurate reflection of the true underlying form. In the 1996 San Marino GP, for example, David Coulthard and Michael Schumacher appeared to outrun Damon Hill initially during the early stages. But Hill was carrying a greater fuel load and was biding his time, looking after his tyres because of the greater fuel weight, though he was not devoid of misgivings in so doing.

'Before the start I sat down with Adrian Newey and asked him if he was really sure that starting with a lot of fuel and then making two quick top-up stops really was the right way to go,' Hill admitted. 'And he said it would be okay.' History records that it was a perfect strategy thanks to Newey's mental acuity. Hill won easily.

Benetton, too, had an enviable reputation for getting it right, especially in its Schumacher era when time and again it benefited more than any other from pit stop work. Yet even Benetton could get it wrong, as Jean Alesi confirmed in the wet 1996 Spanish GP 'The team made a terrible choice to stop only once,' he said. 'It was a big mistake.' Almost as big a mistake, team members were prompted to suggest, as his own in Melbourne a year later when he ignored pit signals and kept running until his otherwise healthy Benetton rolled to a silent halt . . . having run out of fuel.

There was, then, a fine line to be drawn in this game of tactical juggling between success and failure, praise and embarrassment.

McLaren appeared to have fluffed its chance to win the Monaco Grand Prix in 1996 because it brought Mika Hakkinen in first, when it might have been better off calling in higher-placed David Coulthard, who at that time lay third. When the Scot finally did stop he rejoined fifth, behind eventual race winner Olivier Panis. But just to show how difficult it can be to judge strategies without access to the full facts, there were underlying reasons. The initial plan had been to let Coulthard run non-stop, but indications from the telemetry warned that as the track dried he was using more fuel than Hakkinen. Having decided that Coulthard would need a top-up, McLaren thus had to bring Mika in first and leave David out as long as it dared, so it could be sure of getting sufficient extra fuel into the tank to see him through at the higher consumption. By such vagaries can Formula 1 races be decided.

In the Schumacher days Benetton's pit stop strategy assumed almost mystical status, but then it seemed in 1996 as if somebody had dropped the crystal ball. But who was the guru? Had it been Schumacher? Tom Walkinshaw? Ross Brawn? Nick Wirth, who took over from Rory Byrne as chief designer in 1997, chuckled at the suggestions but conceded the subject was no laughing matter.

'I think it was a joint effort, with the discipline coming from Tom. And for sure, strategy is ever more important with the tyre war situation. Not only must you decide what to do about fuel and strategy, you've got to decide what tyres to use. And the way that we work technically, that can only be done in a scientific way. Pat Symonds will be in charge of that, and having a race engineer of his calibre, taking that oversight in the background, is fantastic.'

Frank Dernie explained some of the mystique: 'It's pretty calculable what might happen, so long as you get good practice. If practice goes well and you manage to get all the information about tyres going off; the difference between old tyres and new ones; how they degrade; what the difference is between full and empty tanks; then you can calculate pretty accurately what the result would be of various strategies. So you can start looking at previous data, and when you are likely to catch up with the first of the slow people you won't be able to overtake, and planning your pit stop for then. It's actually quite easy.

'The thing which is difficult is when you're not on the first two rows of the grid. Then all those calculations come unstuck, because the performance of various people in midfield becomes less predictable. If you've assumed you are going to catch somebody by lap 18 and you get stuck behind a slow car for six laps and don't catch them until lap 25, that throws the whole thing into the air.'

Where a team can also spin off strategically is when conditions are variable, for example if a race starts wet, dries out, then perhaps is wet again close to half distance. 'Then you just need to be a bit of a racer, really, and having done it before you just think it through and keep an eye on what's going on. At Monte Carlo in 1996, for example, I was surprised that people didn't stop for dry tyres sooner. Normally they stop for them about the time when they are as quick as wets, and yet when people did stop in Monaco that year they were 10 seconds quicker straight away on dries. But obviously some people were trying to drag it out, so that when they did stop they could put enough fuel in to finish the race. But all that just varies according to how experienced people are, and how clever, I guess. And whether they've got good systems to make sure they can call the driver in at the shortest notice.'

Thinking under the massive pressure of the heat of battle is undoubtedly a taxing mental exercise. 'It's not easy,' Dernie agreed. 'But the television link that we get from the FIA is really, really useful. I only look at the screen which provides section times, and you can tell within a third of a lap from that whether somebody is quick or not. Which means you are not waiting each time for a whole lap of information. At Monaco you could see 30 seconds after Frentzen went out on slicks that it was the way to go, and you could actually stop your own car that lap if you hadn't already decided to do so. So it's a question of using the information you are given well. And you have to remain calm.'

Besides all this, changing tyres is relatively easy, unless you happen to be the unfortunate fellow on the outer rear wheel with everyone else whizzing by. Benetton, for example, has some 150 dry runs during the winter to bring its men up to scratch, then at least seven on a Thursday at a race meeting. Small wonder they are reckoned to be the best in the game.

The drivers can do their bit too, by making up time coming into the pits, even with the mandatory speed limits, though there have been occasions when some who tried to build a Schumacher-style advantage this way came to grief – such as David Coulthard, who crashed into the pit wall and out of the lead in the 1995 Australian GP.

Chapter 9

Spy in the cab

'All this bloody telemetry makes everything too transparent, and takes away all the
. . . secrets, if you like. I think it would make racing much more interesting if we
didn't have telemetry any more.'

Gerhard Berger

IN THE PAST, IF A driver insisted to his team that he had taken a corner flat without lifting from the throttle, they simply had to take his word for it. But when Jacques Villeneuve set pole position for the 1996 Japanese Grand Prix, and informed Williams technical director Patrick Head afterwards that he had taken the demanding 130R left-hand bend at Suzuka without lifting his foot, Head was so disbelieving that he looked it all up on the telemetry that over the years has become a curious mixture of nemesis and salvation to the men in the cockpits.

Villeneuve's traces did bear out his claim. It wasn't that he was disposed to mendacity or exaggeration, nor even that Head was a natural sceptic. But such a feat was so unusual that it took a bit of digesting. So much so that Head even went back to see if Villeneuve, while keeping his right foot buried on the throttle, hadn't at least dabbed the brakes with his left. He hadn't done that, either . . .

The development of electronics has brought about a revolution in the way in which Formula 1 teams conduct their business. They have made massive differences where they have been applied to the management of suspension, throttle, traction control, transmission, and engine management systems, and they have entirely changed the relationship between the man in the cockpit and the men in the pits. Besides proving beyond question the sort of point that Villeneuve was making, onboard telemetry has also exposed drivers when they have been moved to make extravagant claims, or provided advance warning of imminent mechanical catastrophe so that the team has been able to slow a driver down sufficiently to preserve his machinery.

It is probably the broadest double-edged sword in racing history.

To celebrate the occasion of his 200th Grand Prix, at Imola in 1997, Gerhard Berger had an unusual suggestion regarding telemetry. 'I'm always careful when I'm asked about this, because I'm a driver and it's not my job to make regulations,' he began. 'But, leaving aside wings and tyres for a moment, I really think that if you took away the telemetry, it would transform the whole sport.'

He paused for his audience to let such apparent heresy sink in, before offering an explanation.

'To me, it's very important that a driver should make a personal contribution to the set-up, by communicating to the engineers what he feels in the car. These days it doesn't count like it did, because a driver who doesn't feel as much as his team-mate just has to sit with the engineer, and look at the traces. All this bloody telemetry makes everything too transparent, and takes away all the . . .

secrets, if you like. I think it would make racing much more interesting if we didn't have telemetry any more.

'Okay,' he went on, 'it's very interesting the way it's changed – for the engineers, for drivers who love to work on the technical side – but I doubt that many spectators understand the complexities of Formula 1, and that hurts me. The sport gets more and more technical all the time, but that doesn't give the fans anything. What they want to see, I'm sure, is a nice slide, power oversteer, overtaking. If we spend five hours reading telemetry, moving the aero balance by point two to the front or point one to

Festooned with onboard television cameras atop the airbox and to the left of the nose, Damon Hill's World Championship-winning Williams FW18 also reveals the black stub of its communications aerial just ahead of his helmet. This was as vital a part of his successful package as Renault's V10 engine. (ICN UK Bureau)

the back, or whatever, what does that do for the people who pay to watch us? Nothing. So from that point of view, I'm not sure Formula 1 has gone in the right direction at all.

'It's not that I hate the technology,' he summarized. 'A lot of it fascinates me. But you have to keep the racing human, too, with passion and drama and intuition all involved. For me, Formula 1 is still a sport, not a show.'

But Berger was one of few voices speaking out in the technological wilderness. Many years ago, when he was attacking the land speed record with Thrust 2 on the desolate wastes of Bonneville's salt flats, the British driver Richard Noble had run into the trouble that would eventually close him down for the season. Asked what was happening, he had snapped: 'We're not telling the press anything!' And when an organization says that it isn't telling the press anything, what it really means is that it is not telling anyone anything.

Noble always regarded testing and running Thrust 2 as being akin to a fighter pilot developing a new aircraft (an analogy that grew even more apposite in his subsequent supersonic project with Thrust SSC, since it was piloted by RAF Squadron Leader Andy Green). And as such he believed that, like fighter plane development, it should take place in private. There are times when spectators may be forgiven for feeling that Formula 1's power-brokers are thinking along similar lines, that there-on-the-day viewers are to be discouraged, and that they are to be given 'negative incentive' instead to watch on television, once removed. It is as if the cold science is elevating the sport to a much more remote, depersonalized level, where what the driver feels matters less now that his every move in the car is open to empirical rather than subjective analysis. At times one can believe that the engineering side of Formula 1 forgets that it is also supposed to be a form of entertainment.

Telemetry can undoubtedly be of immense help to a driver, but it also means that there is no hiding place. Everything he does is there, on the telemetry traces, for all his engineers to see. It is as if his very personality and soul as a driver can be laid bare for analysis.

The 1993 season was Damon Hill's first as a full-time Formula 1 driver, and driving as Alain Prost's team-mate in the Williams–Renault camp was at once the plum job but at the same time no sinecure. The man who would go on to win the World Championship three years later had good cause, on a number of occasions, to be grateful to the facilities that telemetry opened up to a newcomer trying to make it in a highly competitive and pressured environment.

'It certainly helped him that we had the sort of telemetry where he could overlay his performance against Alain's, to see where he was losing out and to rectify his shortcomings,' Patrick Head recalled. 'The telemetry helped, although one should not overlook that Damon also had a fierce determination. He would sit down with the data and go through with the Renault engineer the speeds and engine rpms round the track, look at his data and then have a look at Alain's, overlay the two and work it all out, and then go out the next day and be right on the pace.'

Head cited one example that he felt was particularly outstanding, early in Hill's Williams career, at Adelaide in 1993 during practice for the Australian GP. 'All of this certainly impressed us, and it happened all through the year. But Australia was a pretty notable occasion. He was at least a second behind Ayrton Senna's McLaren on the first day, and a second behind Alain, and he just sat down and worked it out and the next day he didn't quite beat Alain's time but he was the fastest car on the track and one of the few drivers who improved significantly that second day.

When he isn't out on the track a driver is more often than not to be found deep in reflection with his race engineer. Damon Hill was no exception throughout 1995, and with David Brown (who has since moved to McLaren) here peruses the telemetry in the quest for more speed. (ICN UK Bureau)

He worked out what he needed to do, and he just did it.'

Adrian Newey, who at that time was chief designer at Williams, and a close ally of Hill's, agreed: 'Damon would sometimes turn up the first day and be a reasonable amount off Alain's pace. Then he'd go back and think about it, and go through an overlay of their fastest laps, and work out what he'd got to do with his driving technique and what he'd have to do with the set-up of the car, to try and overcome those deficiencies. He really responded very well in those circumstances.' Without telemetry, Newey conceded, 'it would take longer for a driver to learn his way as to where he's losing out, that's for sure.'

Telemetry was not always a positive influence for Hill. At Suzuka in 1994 it revealed quite clearly that he was up to 20 kmh (12 mph) slower through the fastest sections of the track than teammate Nigel Mansell, and again at Spa-Francorchamps in 1996 the 'spy in the cab' told the tale that his new partner, Jacques Villeneuve, was taking the infamous Eau Rouge and other very quick sections appreciably faster.

It was such revelations that created the belief in some quarters that Hill was not an absolutely top-line driver – comparable, say, with Michael Schumacher – because he left such safety margins where more aggressive rivals were prepared to go right to the edge lap after lap. And, it must be said, they sowed the doubts in the minds of Frank Williams and Patrick Head, that led them to drop Hill in favour of Heinz-Harald Frentzen for the 1997 season. The fact that Hill was still generally recording competitive lap times – and that in 1996 he won half of the races en route to the world title – tended to go unnoticed at times in a team which was brought up on a diet of out-and-out racers such as Alan Jones and Keke Rosberg, champions in 1980 and 1982 respectively.

That said, telemetry also played a crucial role in that 1996 World Championship, on more than one occasion. On his remarkable Formula 1 debut in the Australian GP at Melbourne, Villeneuve took pole position for the Williams–Renault team, and regained the lead from Hill after their pit stops. He then seemed set to match the record of the Italian Giancarlo Baghetti back in 1961, of winning first time out. But then the team instructed him to slow his pace.

What had happened was that Villeneuve had made a small mistake under pressure from Hill and had slid over a kerb in the first corner. As the

The battery of screens in front of Frank Williams show not just the action out on the track, but the current list of practice or qualifying times, breakdowns of each driver's individual laps, and their times for each sector of the circuit. (ICN UK Bureau)

Williams's carbon fibre undertray struck the kerb it deflected sufficiently to crimp an oil line on the Renault V10 engine. This initiated a slow leak of lubricant which Villeneuve could not initially be aware of, but which Hill could appreciate only too well since much of the Elf was smearing his helmet visor like dark treacle. Hill had three options: he could try to overtake, jeopardizing the chance of both cars scoring valuable World Championship points for the team since Villeneuve would almost certainly resist; he could wait until Villeneuve's engine suffered the almost inevitable fate of failure if the French-Canadian maintained his pace; or he could wait for the team to advise Villeneuve to back off.

Meanwhile, in the pit garage, the drop in oil pressure and associated rise in engine temperatures had already communicated itself to the Renault Sport engineers, who told the Williams management, who in turn finally did advise Villeneuve to back off. Hill thus took the lead and went on to kick-start his World Championship campaign with a win (which, incidentally, matched his father's record of 14). And, because he eased back to preserve his engine, Villeneuve was able to scoop six points despite his problem, giving Williams–Renault the maximum score of 16 points for its afternoon's work and setting it well on the way to the Constructors' Championship which would bring the team on to an equal footing with Ferrari's record of eight.

Without telemetry, Villeneuve would probably have continued until it was too late, and broken his engine. And, who knows, Hill might have gone off on his oil, handing victory instead to Eddie Irvine's Ferrari . . .

Later in the year, at Estoril for the Portuguese GP, there was another instance of rescue by telemetry. At that time Williams had been having some problems with its clutch release bearings, which were relatively conventional ballraces. The underlying reason was that clutches had got smaller and smaller with development, and the only aperture that remained open at the centre of the plates tended to be filled up with the clutch release bearing. It was a hostile environment, with virtually no cooling airflow, and carbon clutch plates which, at various times, might heat up to 600 or 700°C. Meanwhile the carbon steels in the ballrace could start softening and tempering down at little over 150°C, and plastic seals on the bearing also disliked intense heat. Keeping all of this alive for a Grand Prix distance was a demanding engineering conundrum, and Williams had been experiencing a little difficulty in solving it from time to time. It had suffered a batch of failures in testing, and had effected a means of monitoring both the environment in which the clutch release bearing was working, and the actual bearing itself, by including a thermo-couple in the clutch housing which would then relay the vital information back to the pits and keep the engineers fully *au fait* with the operating temperatures.

At this stage of the season Hill and Villeneuve were locked in their *mano a mano* battle for the World Championship. Hill led the race initially by a significant margin after Villeneuve made a poor start, but in a storming recovery that saw Villeneuve pass Schumacher on the outside of the last corner, the French-Canadian overtook Hill for the lead. Shortly after this the telemetry began to indicate that the temperature in Hill's gearbox bellhousing had risen unacceptably, and that the position and displacement of the clutch on his car was incorrect.

Williams's semi-automatic transmission was deliberately set up to use the clutch during downshifts, though it changed up without it, but now there might be a problem if Hill continued to use the clutch for the remainder of the race. And at this crucial point retirement for Hill could have had a devastating impact, both psychologically and physically, on his championship challenge. However, the team had done a lot of testing with the transmission set up to downshift without the clutch, should the necessity arise, and all it had to do was tell Hill to change the position of a switch in the cockpit to enable this mode to become operative. He continued at slightly reduced pace and duly finished in second place, thus securing another six points in the penultimate race.

Both incidents highlight another advantage of telemetry to the driver; because he has a phalanx of engineers monitoring every second of his car's performance during its power running, he has to worry far less about watching his instruments and can thus devote more of his concentration to driving.

* * *

So how does the telemetry actually work?

Every Formula 1 car is festooned with telemetry sensors at strategic points, though usually it carries more in testing than during an actual race meeting. 'We can run hundreds if we wanted to,' said Patrick Head. 'In a race, Renault typically has 20 or so, and we probably have 20 different ones, maybe a few more than that.'

These sensors monitor vital functions such as engine revs, water and oil temperatures, oil pressure, and the pressure of the pneumatic valve actuation system, throttle opening, fuel flow, fuel consumption, ground speed, and the point at which the driver selects his gear. Equally, however, it may encompass more esoteric areas such as that Williams clutch housing temperature, brake temperature, brake wear and retardation, suspension movement and loading, g-force, etc.

All this data is stored in an onboard recording system and then transmitted in three ways by the telemetric sensors.

When Ayrton Senna's Williams crashed at the Tamburello corner during the 1994 San Marino Grand Prix, the majority of his car's data was being downloaded to the pits in semi-real time, every time he completed a lap. Therefore the crucial data from his uncompleted final lap was compromised. To obviate this the first method of transmission is for all cars to transmit data to the pits in real time, so that there is a continuous flow of information the whole time that the car is in action on the track.

The second method stores the information and downloads it directly to the computers on each lap. The car passes a radar unit about 300 m ahead of the pits, which in turn activates an onboard transmitter whose signal is picked up by an antenna located at the relevant pit garage. This antenna is linked directly to the engineers' computers.

The third method is activated when the car stops at the pits. An engineer connects his own portable lap-top computer to the car's onboard system and can download 12 million bits of data in moments. This third method provides a valuable safety net, since the two other methods rely on radio transmission from the car, and at times this may be compromised by fluctuations in radio reception due to buildings, changes in the elevation of the track, or interference from external electronic systems. This is particularly problematic at circuits such as Monaco.

'It's all very quick,' Gary Anderson said. 'I don't know just how much data there is, but it's huge! Good stuff, but too much of it. It should be banned! The problem is finding the time and staff to go through it all. We have one guy on each car just going through it all the time, looking at a certain set of parameters. At night you can spend hours and hours and hours, just dicking about, really. Sometimes it's important, but also sometimes it's just important to engineer the car from a gut feeling, because that's what is real and there. It's the driver driving it still. The bloke who is driving the car is still human, and if he can't transmit to you what he's feeling, you won't find the theoretical thing on a squiggly line. We can look at the squiggly lines which tells us the parameters of the car, and that it's working reasonably well within them, centre of pressure, roll stiffness, ride height, etc, but after that it's still down to driver feeling, how much porridge he's had in the morning, or something . . .'

As part of its electronic crackdown of 1994, the FIA has specifically proscribed two-way telemetric traffic. In 1993 teams were developing systems whereby they could effect changes to a car's set-up – in particular to its computer-controlled active suspension – while the car was racing on the track, thus alleviating any set-up shortcomings and removing the final 'guesswork' from one of the most highly demanding aspects of racing. Teams are now only allowed to relay information from the cars to the pits.

Most use a VHF radio link to provide 'ship-to-shore' communications between the driver and the pits. The driver's helmet carries a microphone which is controlled by a push button on the steering wheel. The driver can only speak while activating this button but can receive at any time without recourse to separate movement. Communication is on a specific frequency, and usually only the team manager will speak to the driver during the course of a race. All transmissions are encrypted to prevent rivals eavesdropping. And in case that might seem a breach of gentlemanly trust, one team had an independent base set up at the 1992 British GP whose specific task was to try and jam other teams' radio frequencies . . .

The telemetric sensors provide around 100 impulses per second. Real time information flow is around 1Mb of data per lap, while the semi-real time download each lap provides the engineers with around 0.5Mb.

Since the arguments of 1994 the FIA has initiated stringent checks on computer software, and all systems on board a car, or which can be connected to it, must be validated by the scrutineers before a race meeting. At the beginning of each season teams are given the choice of having their systems inspected on two different levels.

'Option 1' entails a full check of computer source code, to ensure that the system complies with the Technical Regulations. The FIA then copies the programmes and holds them as a template, so that when programmes are uploaded at race meetings they can be compared with the initial 'fingerprint' to ensure that no changes have been made to the approved software. Any updates must be re-inspected as an 'Option 1 re-check'.

'Option 2' involves a less detailed pre-season check on the control software but a detailed check of upload software. When programmes are uploaded at a race meeting the FIA will take copies which it keeps indefinitely. These may be inspected in detail at any time, even after the season has finished. Under 'Option 2' teams can make regular updates to their software without the need for continual reapproval. If a team chooses 'Option 2' it may be subjected to a full source code inspection at any time, and in either case all hardware must be inspected and documented to facilitate monitoring of changes during the season.

Liverpool Data Research Associates Ltd (LDRA), the independent company that the FIA employed to investigate teams' computer software, explained source codes thus: 'Computer instructions are usually called machine code and are represented internally as a series of noughts and ones, known as binary numbers. This form of instruction is very difficult for humans to understand, so computer languages have been devised that enable us to express instructions in a form that is more natural to us. Programmes written in these languages are known as source codes. A computer cannot use them directly but they can be translated into machine code that it can understand by using another programme called a compiler. When the machine code is loaded into the computer's memory, the processor can then execute the instructions that are described in the source code.'

More than any other aspect of Formula 1 technology, electronics held the most scope for potential cheating, and this was a source of extreme concern to Max Mosley. During that troubled 1994 season he spelled out to the teams in uncompromising terms the precise reasons why the FIA was not prepared to waive its demand of access to a company's source code. And he fined Benetton and McLaren $100,000 each for their failure to supply their source codes after the San Marino GP. Both teams had fallen back on reluctance to disclose information of a highly confidential nature, but Mosley was having none of that.

'Source codes are regarded by some people as confidential because there are big car manufacturers, for example, which use similar source codes on their road cars,' he said. 'Our position is simple. There are some things that we don't have to check: for example, suspension geometries. But in any area that we need to check, because it is an area that might conceal a breach of the rules, then our position is very simple: if you bring it to a race meeting, we are entitled the check it.

'So, if your source codes are so secret that you don't want us, or anybody, to look at them, don't bring those codes to a Formula 1 race, because we have to look at them. We have to be sure that there is no traction control, no automatic gearbox – or the thousand and one things that could be there. Each team must understand that it is our duty to be able to look them in the eye and to be able to say we know that the other teams are not cheating.

'Unless everybody gives us all the information that we require, we cannot do that. Under Article 2.6 of the regulations, it is the duty of the competitor to satisfy the stewards that his car complies. Thus they have an absolute duty to do it: they cannot refuse.

'Our attitude in the future – and arguably we should have done this immediately after Imola – is to simply say: "We have not received your source codes. Practice starts on Friday: if we have not got them by Friday we will report to the stewards that we are not satisfied that your car complies and it will not leave the pit lane until we have received the codes."

'If any team is using a state secret the solution is simple. Don't put it on the car. But if it is on the car, we must be allowed to look at it, in fairness to all the other competitors.'

It took a while for some teams, notably McLaren, to see the sense in all this. But as an indication of the zeal with which the FIA has policed computer systems, it carried out 89 random checks during the course of the 16 races counting towards the 1996 World Championship. And as an indication of the common sense of all the teams, there were no transgressions. Mosley had won a very important battle.

* * *

Racing drivers and their design engineers dedicate their lives to shaving split seconds from lap times, and today's telemetric technology ensures that every thousandth that they save is faithfully and accurately recorded. Lap timing, both in qualifying for Grands Prix and during the races themselves, is done so smoothly and efficiently that it is tempting to take it all for granted. It is one of the areas in which Formula 1 has made the greatest progress in the past decades.

At Monte Carlo for the Monaco Grand Prix in 1997, Heinz-Harald Frentzen secured the first pole position of his career, driving for Williams, and the intensity of his struggle with Michael Schumacher was borne out by the closeness of their times. Frentzen managed 1 min 18.216 sec, compared to Schumacher's 1 min 18.235 sec – a hair's breadth that the TAG-Heuer time-keeping equipment was able to separate into its minutest fractions.

Closer still had been the gap between Schumacher's Benetton and Gerhard Berger's Ferrari in qualifying at Imola for the San Marino Grand Prix in 1995. The timing system separated them by a mere eight thousandths of a second, and their respective lap times were 1 min 27.274 sec and 1 min 27.282 sec. On that occasion the distance between the cars was measured by calculating it as a function of their speed and the time gap between them. At the start/finish line the margin of difference amounted to nothing more than 57.2 cm (22.5 in), a minuscule difference at speeds such as Berger's recorded maximum of 257.4 kmh (159.9 mph).

Such unimpeachable accuracy is made possible by the small transmitter mounted in the nose of each car, which sends an individual radio signal to trackside receivers each time it crosses the start/finish line, and to intermediate measurement points elsewhere around the track. Each transponder corresponds to a specific vehicle, which is why teams change the nose of the spare car if the driver who was not due to have priority use of it during the weekend suddenly finds that he needs it. If the original nose was left in place, the times he recorded would be credited to his team-mate!

Fifty years ago, when the World Championship was inaugurated, the timing was often done simply to the nearest second, via hand-held stop-watches activated by fallible human fingers, and it was not uncommon for several cars to share the same lap time when qualifying had finished. At the British Grand Prix in 1956, for instance, Mike Hawthorn and Peter Collins were each credited with 1 min 43 sec, while Harry Schell, Froilan Gonzalez, Roy Salvadori, and Eugenio Castellotti were given 1 min 44 sec. Further back still, another four cars were bracketed together on 1 min 49 sec.

Had the old system still been in use at Monaco in 1997 it would have given both Frentzen and Schumacher a similar lap time, and would probably not even have been able to distinguish which of them set their time first. Frentzen thus might not have been given his rightful place at the head of the field.

Timing improved marginally in the late-1950s and early-1960s, so that lap times could be measured electronically to the nearest tenth of a second, but there still remained the problem that at certain events around the globe partisan organizers would suddenly 'find' a lap time for a local hero or marque, once qualifying had finished. This was often a good means of making sure that spectators came flooding through the gates on race day. Progress continued through the 1960s, when times were measured to the nearest hundredth of a second, and eventually the 1980s and 1990s brought times split to the nearest thousandth. Such is the sophisticated system that TAG-Heuer operates today that drivers receive a full printout of all of their laps, and can pinpoint precisely when they set their best. In the media centre all times are flashed on to television screens the moment they are recorded in each session, so that despite the pace in this fast-moving world, everyone knows exactly what is happening, as it happens. During races, electronic lap charts appear on-screen, and are automatically updated every lap. Teams also receive printouts of the fastest speeds at specific points, and even the optimal lap time by combining a driver's three best sector speeds.

Telemetry plays another key role in ensuring the fairness of Grand Prix racing. During the 1994 season the young French driver Olivier Panis, though not the only perpetrator, displayed an alarming tendency for premature getaways at the start of races. This reached crisis level in the Hungarian GP when, from ninth on the grid, he vaulted forwards before the green lights came on. He backed off slightly, but was nevertheless up into fifth place at the end of the first lap on a circuit on which overtaking is notably difficult. Mosley was among many who had seen the transgression, and at the Italian GP he voiced his strong disapproval of the Frenchman's escape without penalty.

'I was furious about Panis myself, just as everyone was,' he told journalists. 'And this is something that we have put right now. What happened was that judges of fact are employed on the start-line, with each judge looking at four cars. It is his job to say whether or not one of the four has jumped the start. This is a throwback to the days when the most sophisticated recording device would have been an 8 mm cine camera.

'There were six judges of fact at the Hungaroring: five to cover the first 20 cars, and one to watch the final six. The judge responsible for Panis's car was absolutely certain that he had not jumped the start. He was invited – as a judge of fact can be invited – to revise his opinion. And as the video made plain, it was completely obvious. But to the astonishment of everyone concerned, the judge refused to revise his opinion.

'When the Sporting Code was examined, it was discovered that the opinion of a judge cannot in fact be disputed. Again, this dates back to the old days, and is something that should have been corrected years ago. From now on, first of all the stewards will have access to the video, and will be able to overrule the judges of fact. And in addition to that, we hope that from Estoril onwards there will be a light beam at the start for each car. If anybody moves early, there will be an indicator in the control tower and the competitor will be penalized accordingly.

'But Hungary was a most unfortunate event, a combination of somebody's stubbornness and regulations which did not allow us to change anything. But that has now been put right.' The nationality of the judge of fact was never divulged.

Mosley was as good as his word, for by the Portuguese GP the FIA had indeed introduced an electronic judge of fact for each car on the grid, and the system remains in use. It comprises an infrared photocell mounted just ahead of each allocated grid position, which is tripped by an individual transponder on each car. If it is tripped too soon an automatic signal is sent to the timing room, and this is backed by video evidence. Within a few laps of the start transgressors are informed of their crime, and are required to suffer a 10 second stop-and-go penalty in the pits within a certain number of laps. To begin with there were several perpetrators, but it didn't take long before the message sank in, and the jump starts have largely become a thing of the past.

Likewise, telemetry is also used to monitor speed in the pit lane during refuelling and tyre stops. Again, this was another legacy of the 1994 San Marino GP at Imola, where Michele Alboreto's Minardi lost a wheel after a pit stop and injured Ferrari and Lotus mechanics as the car slewed to a halt. The timing centre at race meetings measures the speed of cars in the pit lane by detecting their arrival and departure, and 10 second stop-and-go penalties are awarded for those exceeding the limit. Probably the most costly penalty was levied on David Coulthard at the 1995 British GP at

Silverstone, for he had just wrested the lead from eventual winner Johnny Herbert when he was called in for his stop-and-go penalty. Most of the teams used onboard speed-limiting systems, and Williams's operated via sensors in the wheels which limited the revs to prevent the car exceeding a certain speed. But during Coulthard's previous refuelling stop a front wheel sensor had malfunctioned, allowing him to exceed the pit lane limit. 'That was doubly expensive,' Coulthard recalled in 1997. 'I lost the bonus money I'd have got from Williams for taking what would have been my first Grand Prix victory, and going to McLaren at the end of that season as a winner of two, not one, races would have allowed me to raise my price . . .'

For 1997 the FIA mandated the use of electronic black boxes, similar to those used on aircraft, to be fitted to all cars so that, in the event of an accident, empirical data would be available for analysis to understand what went wrong and to help take the necessary steps to prevent a repeat in the future. Gary Anderson, however, provided an insight into the gulf between the teams and the FIA when he said: 'Well, if I told you I don't actually know what they record because the FIA keeps that to itself, you'd get the idea. As far as I know what they are interested in is the things that could happen during an accident. It's mainly the accelerations in the car. There's no reason why the boxes should-

n't be there, but I don't know what they actually do with them. One of Max's things is that they were very surprised to learn that gravel traps don't work. When they'd looked at the data from cars that had gone off in Melbourne, at the start of 1997, they found that they had actually accelerated from when they went from the track to the gravel. As I said to him, if he'd watched television for the last six years he'd have known that . . . But the boxes are there, and they provide whatever data it is that the FIA wants.'

For the FIA, however, the boxes were seen as a valuable means of gathering data that would, among other things, be useful in putting empirical figures into calculations when it came to designing restraint systems for cars going off the track.

One final, if unlikely, use for electronics in Formula 1 came to light in 1996, at the Belgian GP at Spa-Francorchamps. Jacques Villeneuve had not raced at the ultra-fast venue before, but after qualifying he disclosed that he had gone a long way towards learning the track by using a proprietary Formula 1 computer game to familiarize himself with it. So realistic was the game, and so effective his use of it, that this inveterate computer game fan was immediately competitive, and after qualifying in pole position he went on to take second place behind Michael Schumacher. In Formula 1 every little bit helps.

Chapter 10

Putting
a stop to it

'There was not a lot of difference between carbon brakes and cast-iron when we tested the latter. But the problem was that I don't think they'd last as well during a race. But they were pretty good.'

Damon Hill, World Champion

O N TWO OCCASIONS DURING qualifying for the San Marino GP at Imola in April 1997, Williams–Renault driver Heinz-Harald Frentzen recorded readings of 5.99g under braking.

That bears some thinking about. It meant that, momentarily, his body weighed 5.99 times its normal figure.

This author once experienced 6g when driving a rocket-powered dragster from rest to almost 250 mph (400 kmh) in less than two seconds, and that indeed was a memorable experience. But that was on acceleration, not deceleration. Frentzen's figures were 'spikes', peak readings, and of course you are bound to generate greater gravity loading under deceleration because of the effect of drag working with you rather than having to be encountered and challenged, as it would be under acceleration, but 5g retardation was commonplace in Formula 1 at that time, and an indication of just how stunningly efficient braking systems had become.

'I'd say that we would normally pull high fours,' said Gary Anderson. 'Say 4.8,

something like that. We could make it 5.9 if you wanted, just take the peaks, but they're not real because the wheels would have to be locked up to keep it there. So you'll get little spikes, but we filter them out. High fours are a good figure. If you were pulling 4.5g on a big stop, that'd be pretty good. Not bad at all.'

All the more interesting, when you consider that, despite a good power-to-weight ratio, the modern Formula 1 car accelerates at no more than 2g, while producing lateral force of around 3.5g in fast corners.

Along with downforce, brakes had become something of a bogeyman among enthusiasts who bemoaned the lack of overtaking, and many held the firm belief that the introduction in the 1970s of carbon as a brake disc material, in place of the previous cast iron, had been a prime mover in the dramatic reduction of braking distances. Carbon discs, it was argued, were directly responsible for the growing lack of overtaking which had characterized Formula 1 in the 1990s. Every enthusiast had watched brake discs glowing cherry red hot whenever a driver would stand on the middle pedal braking from very high speed, but they had also cursed the use of carbon as its very efficiency had decimated braking distances. Since cars now braked so late, there was precious little opportunity for another driver to outbrake a rival before a corner. Naturally, it followed that there were several calls for carbon brake discs to be banned, even though they could be counted as one of the better sights of the sport.

'The problem with banning them is that it would be very hard to police what materials might be used,' said Max Mosley. 'There are so many additives that one might then put into a cast-iron brake disc that, really, it would probably make little difference, both to cost and to efficiency.'

This is something of a specious argument, for the FIA could quite simply specify materials if it so wished, and then test at random to ensure that no proscribed materials were being used. And,

indeed, for 1998 it intended to outlaw the use of exotic additives in brake calipers, thus indicating quite clearly that it did have faith in its policing ability. And it also planned to limit the number of pistons allowed per brake caliper.

In 1995 Williams carried out some interesting testing, at a time when the FIA was still pondering whether it should get rid of the carbon stoppers. Patrick Head and Adrian Newey came up with cast-iron discs that were very similar to those used in the pre-carbon brake days, but mated them to a different pad material. 'There was very little difference between them and carbon brakes,' Head confirmed. 'Very little. Carbon brakes are more powerful, it's just that what we were running in the old days was a cast-iron disc with a fibrous pad, and what we ran during those tests at Silverstone was a cast-iron disc with what's called a carbon metallic pad, which is sintered.' This means it was turned from powder state into solid state by the application of heat. 'It was a com-

One of the great sights of modern Formula 1 has been the bright red glow of carbon brake discs under very heavy retardation. (LAT)

Though they look innocuous enough, carbon discs have been vilified by enthusiasts who say they have decimated braking distances and thus taken away a primary source of overtaking moves. Sadly, cast-iron discs have proved as effective, albeit less durable. These carbon discs on Damon Hill's 1997 Arrows feature Brembo calipers. (Author)

pletely different pad, but the same sort of brakes that are on the touring cars. Very powerful, but a different deal. And no, I don't think they would last a race as well as a carbon disc, but as far as retardational power was concerned, they were pretty much the same.' Damon Hill, who conducted the tests, agreed. 'There was not a lot of difference. But the problem was that I don't think they'd last as well during a race. But they were pretty good.'

Newey threw in his own observations on the idea of banning carbon brakes on grounds of cost. 'The cost of them is nothing like people make it out to be. In the overall budget of Formula 1 the bit you spend on your brakes is not very much. So I think when people started using that old argument, that there was a lot of knee-jerk reaction going on.'

Brakes had suddenly became a major priority again in 1997, because the softer compound tyres spawned by the new war between Goodyear and Bridgestone suddenly hacked as much as six seconds off the lap times drivers had been recording the previous year.

Adelaide, once the home of the Australian GP at the end of each season, had traditionally been tough on brakes, and both Niki Lauda and Keke Rosberg had encountered problems with brake discs shattering in past races, when driving for McLaren. Melbourne's Albert Park, the new venue for the race when it switched to open the GP season, did not boast a straight long enough to rival Adelaide's Dequetteville Terrace, but in the 1997 race such brake problems raised their head again. Frentzen, in his first race for Williams, was chasing eventual winner David Coulthard in the closing stages, nursing a problem with deteriorating brake efficiency, when his left front carbon brake disc suddenly puffed into black shards and dust as he approached the first corner. He spun into retirement, fortunately without hitting anything solid, leaving Williams to do a good deal of head scratching.

By Imola, where the German was able to record those phenomenal retardation figures, Head had a far closer grasp of the problem as the brakes had now been fitted with sensors which enabled the team to monitor their performance. 'We didn't actually have sensors fitted to the brakes in Australia,' Head admitted reflectively in Italy. 'We do here, and with them we could have detected in Melbourne that there was a problem about to happen, but we didn't. We are slightly further down the road now. The amount of work being done by the brakes this year is significantly greater because of the tyre situation, so we are having to spend quite a bit of time on it.'

It was noticeable during Michael Schumacher's and Eddie Irvine's pit stops during the San Marino GP that Ferrari engineers could be seen measuring front brake disc width with calipers to check their thickness. This suggested either that their telemetry was not as sophisticated as Williams's, or that they had only partial faith in it. But it was the level of concern that was telling.

Jacques Villeneuve provided an insight into the drivers' concerns when he said: 'When you look at the computer graphics you realize that you are having to put 150 kilos [330 lb] on the pedal every time you brake. That's okay for qualifying, but for 62 laps of racing it's going to be a battle. Unfortunately, power brakes are not allowed!'

Frentzen agreed. 'The 5.99g that we saw on the telemetry in qualifying, at Rivazza and Tosa, was the highest recorded deceleration figure that Williams had ever seen! And that means pedal pressures of 150 kilos, and some 1,200 psi in the brake lines . . .'

By 1993 the FIA was getting very concerned about braking systems, and as well as banning any sort of anti-lock assistance, it also outlawed any system of power generation. In neither case was it actively seeking to place drivers at greater risk; but by curtailing some of the answers to designers' problems (such as power-assisted braking to enable really high pedal pressures to be generated and then controlled by the anti-lock mechanism) it was hoping to impose a limit on braking performance and thereby to open up braking distances and, possibly, regenerate some overtaking opportunities. Its primary concern, and rightly so, was that technically advantageous things such as anti-lock mechanisms removed yet another of the arts of the racing driver, that of being able to brake with greater sensitivity than the next man. Damon Hill was perplexed during his early days as Alain Prost's team-mate at Williams by the fact that he would brake later than the Frenchman, but Prost would be quicker overall through the corner. This was because Alain braked sooner but lighter and came off the brake pedal and back on to the power quicker, and his ability to extract the most under braking was part of the aura that surrounded him.

By 1997 brakes were again taxing FIA minds as well as the teams', though the fact that the development had been spurred by the tyre war, and had been increased to keep pace with its continual demands, appeared to have gone unnoticed. Lap times were down, therefore brakes must be modified to alter that trend, was the inference. Yet for all that, the FIA gave the nod to electronic brake balance mechanisms, which surely amount to a driver aid. The idea is that the driver can operate the system to move the brake balance fore or aft according to circumstance, thus optimizing braking efficiency.

'In the past we'd had cable-operated devices which, under load, had been hard to adjust,' Jordan's Gary Anderson explained. 'And now it's a device where the driver can change the brake balance easier. Brakes are becoming more and more critical, as you could see in Melbourne, for example. The wear rate on them is much higher. Mainly because of the tyre war and the lack of aerodynamic stability in the cars, people have been using more front brakes than they used to in the old days, so really the front brakes have been wearing out. Now we are trying to create a means of balance change, so that the driver can be more in control of that situation. When he has a problem, he can move the balance.'

The systems have buttons on the steering wheel and the driver can press the relevant button before, or going into, a corner, in order to shift the balance to the front or rear wheels. But it's not an active system. There is nothing automatic about it, but operating the buttons activates the system electronically so it is still within the driver's control.

Ferrari's system was said also to apportion load laterally as well as longitudinally, but there were development problems and Eddie Irvine's troubles in Australia and Brazil were traced to the electronic system on his car malfunc-

tioning. 'It was moving the balance backwards and forwards at random, almost like a rogue active system,' he explained at Imola. 'And it's happening here, too. That's three out of four races.'

If it didn't mind electronic balance systems, the FIA took a dim view of the exotic metals that were creeping into brake caliper design, and focused on this for 1998, partly as a means of reducing costs but also to lessen braking effectiveness. From 1998 all calipers would have to be manufactured just from aluminium, without any fancy additives.

By 1997 calipers were mostly manufactured in MMC – metal matrix composite – which in this application was strengthened and stiffened by the presence of a silicon carbide particulate in the aluminium. Some calipers were stiffer still, and these were manufactured in material called Albemet, a trade name which stood for aluminium beryllium metal, an alloy which has a remarkable performance. It enabled the companies concerned to create calipers that were some 20 per cent stiffer and 30 per cent lighter than standard units – a considerable saving in unsprung weight overall.

'It makes a very stiff caliper and that also means that you can use smaller master cylinders and get a lot of mechanical advantage so that you can put a lot of hydraulic pressure through the brakes,' Head said. 'The 1998 aluminium calipers are more flexible so it is difficult to put as much power on without having long pedal travel to regain the mechanical advantage. But we can still do that.'

So would the move really make that much difference to braking efficiency and effectiveness? Like so many things that ruffle the surface of the water in Formula 1 from time to time, it seemed unlikely to make the slightest difference in the long run.

Chapter 11

Getting the power down

'In the circumstances, I am not satisfied in accordance with Article 2.6 of the Formula One Technical Regulations that car number 5 (M. Schumacher) complied with the Regulations at all times during the San Marino Grand Prix and I therefore submit this matter to the World Council for their consideration.'

Charlie Whiting, technical delegate, FIA

THE SEMI-AUTOMATIC TRANSMISSION, with its fingertip-operated paddles behind the steering wheel, has made missed gearshifts virtually a thing of the past. Such systems were very well developed by 1993, and the saving they facilitated on engine bills persuaded the FISA that they should not be proscribed along with active suspension and anti-lock brakes. However, drivers once again had to be in control of the actual shifting, and automatic up and downshifts were banned from 1994.

It was not difficult to see why semi-automatic transmissions were so popular. Anything that makes a car more efficient can also make it quicker. Conventional manual transmissions, with gear lever and clutch operated entirely by the driver, can cost 150 milliseconds for every gear change. The new breed of semi-autos, ushered in by John Barnard's Ferrari 640 in 1989, allowed the driver to keep both hands on the wheel and change gear in a mere 20 milliseconds by using electronics to operate

hydraulic actuators which changed the gears and operated the clutch. In such ways is time saved in racing, and you can imagine the potential advantage on courses such as Monaco . . . There was also the further advantage that cockpits could be slimmed down slightly if two-pedal control were to be adopted, thereby conferring a small aerodynamic advantage due to reduced cross-sectional area.

When the 1994 season began, the FIA's greatest concern was that nobody should be foolhardy enough to try and use the banned traction control, the system which used sensors on the rear wheels to assess whenever wheelspin was imminent, and cut the power fractionally to avoid it. The worry was that the FIA would not be able to detect such systems, especially if they were installed in a car's RAM memory, so that all a driver need do if inspection was imminent would be to turn off the engine and thus kill anything held in RAM.

FIA president Max Mosley was sufficiently perturbed to outline just what might lay in wait for any miscreants, suspending the threat of Draconian penalties like a Sword of Damocles over the heads of the teams. 'I think if somebody was found to be cheating, if you could demonstrate that they deliberately cheated, not that they interpreted the rule differently to you or there was some debatable point which they may be wrong about, then I think Draconian penalties would be completely correct,' he warned.

What he proposed was a ban from the championship, and cancellation of any points scored up to the discovery of the infringement. This was indeed strong government, and as the season progressed it would be put to the test.

The Benetton team sprang a major surprise on everyone – not least the championship favourite, Ayrton Senna, who had switched from McLaren to Williams – when Michael Schumacher won the opening two races, the Brazilian GP at Interlagos and the Pacific GP at Aida in Japan. It was at the latter that the first controversy raised its head when Ferrari was found to be running a system that some believed constituted a traction control device.

When the 412T1 had been launched at Fiorano in February, sporting director Jean Todt had stressed: 'The car is perfectly in line with the 1994 rules and the spirit of the 1994 rules. Ferrari always works within the rules. The team has clarified everything that it proposes to run, not just with itself but with the FIA.' And designer John Barnard had added: 'We have certainly gone along with everything that is intended by the regulations, not just what is exactly written down. Therefore I would say that this car is at the moment 100 per cent legal, according to the interpretation of the regulations.'

An incident arose on Sunday morning in Aida, when it transpired that FIA technical delegate Charlie Whiting had observed something unusual about the behaviour of Gerhard Berger's Ferrari while watching it out on the track during practice the previous day. That was compounded when team-mate Nicola Larini, standing in for Jean Alesi who had injured his neck in an accident at Mugello days earlier, naively admitted that his car felt better with the system switched on. This started tongues wagging and a cloak-and-dagger farce of accusations and counter-accusations, allegations and denials. Todt indicated to third parties that Whiting had okayed the system, Whiting emphatically denied doing so and said off the record that he felt that Ferrari's system was beyond the spirit of the regulations.

It seemed that the Italian team had come up with a system that, while not traction control, acted as a variable rev limiter in each gear to avoid wheelspin. It was described officially by the team as an 'engine modulation system'.

There was talk of Williams, Benetton, and McLaren considering a protest if the Ferrari raced and finished in that form, but Benetton's Flavio Briatore scotched his team's involvement in such action by saying: 'It is too fantastic to believe that Ferrari would run with traction control, and in any case I never protest about anybody in Formula 1. The problem is that the FISA introduced this rule which cannot be policed, and it is up to the FISA to deal with these matters, not the teams. How can you prove it one way or another?'

It was an interesting question, and one for which the FISA would provide a stunning answer later in the season. An answer that, as events had it, would be addressed directly at Briatore.

The arguments raged all day. Berger raced home second in a Ferrari that was not using the system after the FIA had issued a statement advising the team not to do so until it had issued a ruling on the matter, and the suggestions did the rounds that with software these days it was possible to introduce a password that would act as a virus to destroy specific parts of a programme if somebody wished to eliminate it. Eventually the whole thing blew over. Ferrari was correctly cleared of cheating but was advised that its system was outside the spirit of the rules, and everyone went off to prepare for the fateful meeting at Imola. But even before that there was another problem brewing, for Senna was privately convinced that Schumacher's car was using some sort of traction control after the manner in which it had run rings round him in Brazil. His death at Imola removed the one man who had the clout to make the accusation public, and to have cleared the air before things dragged on through the season amidst grumbling and behind-hand accusations against Benetton. A series of demon starts by Schumacher, particularly in France where he simply blasted between the two Williams–Renaults on the front row of the grid and then left them for dead, would do nothing subsequently to dispel the dark thoughts, and nor did the superior attitude of the team, which only served to convince some of its 'guilt'.

After Imola the FIA had confiscated computer software from McLaren and Benetton (see Chapter 9), but in the aftermath of the Senna and Ratzenberger tragedies – and the teams' reluctance to reveal their source codes – it was to be some time before the FIA could properly examine it.

By the time the teams arrived at Hockenheim for the Hungarian GP, the ninth race of the season, Schumacher and Benetton were already in trouble. The German had breached the rules by passing pole position man Damon Hill on the grid formation lap for the British GP, and had then exacerbated that offence by ignoring the resultant black flag. This was also to be the weekend of the pit lane fire that had engulfed Jos Verstappen's Benetton (see Chapter 8). But even before that, the team was

rocked when the FIA revealed the findings of its detailed trawl through its Imola software. Formula 1 was about to be invited to unravel The Mystery of Option 13.

★ ★ ★

'An investigation into the software used in the computer systems of the cars finishing in the top three in the San Marino GP was undertaken by Liverpool Data Research Associates Ltd (LDRA),' an FIA statement from Whiting began. It then outlined the argument by which Benetton had stalled supplying its source code, before dropping its bombshell.

'Analysis of this [Benetton's] software, which had been used in the San Marino GP, revealed that it included a facility called "launch control". This is a system which, when armed, allows the driver to initiate a start with a single action. The system will control the clutch, gear shift and engine speed fully automatically to a predetermined pattern.

'Benetton stated that this system is used only in testing. Benetton further stated that "it (the system) can only be switched on by recompilation of the code." This means recompilation of the source code. Detailed analysis by LDRA experts of this complex code revealed that this statement was untrue. "Launch control" could in fact be switched on using a lap-top personal computer (PC) connected to the gearbox control unit (GCU).

'When confronted with this information, the Benetton representatives conceded that it was possible to switch on the "launch control" using a lap-top PC, but indicated that the availability of this feature came as a surprise to them.

'In order to enable "launch control", a particular menu with 10 options has to be selected on the PC screen. "Launch control" is not visibly listed as an option. The menu was so arranged that, after 10 items, nothing further appeared. If, however, the operator scrolled down the menu beyond the 10th listed option, to option 13, "launch control" can be enabled, even though this is not visible on the screen. No satisfactory explanation was offered for this apparent attempt to conceal the feature.

'Two conditions had to be satisfied before the computer would apply "launch control". First, the software had to be enabled either by recompiling the code, which would take some minutes, or by connecting the lap-top PC as outlined above, which could be done in a matter of a few seconds.

'Secondly, the driver had to work through a particular sequence of gear shift paddle positions, as well as clutch and throttle pedal positions. We are told by Benetton that to initiate "launch control" (assuming the software has been enabled) the vehicle must be stationary, in neutral and with no pressure in the clutch circuit. To arm the system, the driver must hold the downchange paddle and then flick the upchange paddle once. The downchange paddle must then be released. The driver then applies full throttle when appropriate and a flick of the upchange paddle will set the car in motion.

'Having thus initiated "launch control", the driver would be able to make a fully automatic start. Such a start is clearly a driver aid as it operates the clutch, changes gear and uses traction control by modulating engine power (by changing ignition or fuel settings), in response to wheel speed.

'When asked why, if this system was only used in testing, such an elaborate procedure was necessary in order to switch it on, we were told it was to prevent it being switched on accidentally.

'In the circumstances, I am not satisfied in accordance with Article 2.6 of the Formula One Technical Regulations that car number 5 (M. Schumacher) complied with the Regulations at all times

during the San Marino Grand Prix and I therefore submit this matter to the World Council for their consideration.'

So there it was, in FIA black and white. What appeared to be the clearest possible accusation that Benetton had been cheating. The Hockenheim paddock was as aflame with gossip as the pit lane would be with spilt fuel days later. And Benetton technical director Ross Brawn was left to face the fire of the media as he sought to offer an explanation.

He revealed that the launch control system was one that Benetton had used in the winter of 1993 during dynamometer testing of Ford's Zetec R engine, and had never actually been used in a car, and he said that it had never been deleted from the team's software because of the amount of work that would have been necessary to reconstruct the software. He said that deletion would have taken weeks and months and that other priorities had intervened. But Mike Hennell, a director of LDRA, dismissed the idea of the technology being a left-over, when he said: 'Benetton's 1993 traction control system worked on throttling back the engine. On its launch control there is no means of throttling. It is very different technology, so it doesn't look as if it is left-over.'

Brawn was then asked what evidence Benetton could demonstrate that launch control had not been used at Imola.

'LDRA produced a report of the second investigation and they stated: "We were shown a replay of the alleged start of the San Marino GP which we agree, within reasonable doubt, were true figures. The recorded wheel speed, throttle position and engine rpm figures appear to show a normal, not a launch, start. The readings show a large amount of rear wheelspin after initial depression of the throttle (on the green light). After a short pause, approximately a third of a second, the driver response can be seen as he lifts off the throttle pedal, wheelspin is reduced, and the driver follows this by depressing the throttle pedal. In our opinion these figures are characteristic of either a normal driver-controlled start, or possibly a poor automatic start."

'That latter statement we then challenged,' Brawn continued, 'and considered unsubstantiated . . . They were unable to substantiate this statement . . . Benetton was fined $100,000 because it was not possible to supply the required information within the timescale requested. And that was the only offence. Benetton was totally cleared by the FIA of using any illegal facility or function.'

Yet still his grilling continued. Why had launch control not been listed as a visible feature on the computer menu?

'On the subject of the engine calibration menu, the title "launch control" has been removed from that because our software is used by many engineers, not only the person who had written the software. Once we understood that these features would be illegal, that was removed from that menu so that other engineers using the software for tests and similar wouldn't initiate it accidentally. It was never removed with the intent of trying to deceive anyone that it wasn't there, because all the software showed that it was present . . .

'There was some distinction made between the fact that you could go to a menu to initiate this, or you could recompile the software. I think most experts in our field would show that if you wanted to, you could change the machine code relevant to these particular features on the grid. So the fact that it was available via a menu or was present in software which couldn't be changed, wasn't relevant . . . We had already let LDRA know that the feature was present in the software, so why should we try to conceal it?

'There was a genuine belief by the engineer who wrote the software that he had deleted references to it in that menu. So when he was asked the question, "Can you access launch control by that menu?" he said, "No, I have removed that from the menu." But by approaching the software from a different direction, LDRA was able to achieve that.'

He said Benetton had told the FIA that the launch control procedure was exactly as it had been in 1993, and that its apparent complexity was a safety measure. 'It was merely there to ensure that the driver didn't initiate launch control at the wrong time.'

And he denied that Benetton was guilty by insinuation. 'We haven't been found guilty by insinuation. That is very, very clear. Benetton has been very successful this year and in common with any team in this situation in Formula 1, people will talk. Our success has been gained by hard work and the talents of Michael Schumacher. Unfortunately it is a cross we have to bear that people will want easy reasons why we are successful. There never are any, and never will be.'

Hennell provided some further insight when he said: 'Once we had finally got the source code from Benetton, after a lot of arguing and cajoling, it was a very easy process to investigate the system. We have yet to receive a source code from McLaren, while Ferrari were absolute magic. They made everything available to us, drawings, cars, test rigs . . . they went to great lengths. Mind you, perhaps that was partly because they had been accused of cheating at the previous race, at TI Circuit Aida.'

In Formula 1 circles it was suggested that, unable to prove anything against Benetton, the FIA had sought other ways of balancing what it deemed to be a score, or that it had been setting careful traps that were one by one snapping shut – even that Schumacher's subsequent exclusion from two races for his black flag indiscretion at Silverstone was payback of a different kind. But Hennell again put things into perspective when

he put down the more fanciful suggestions of special self-consuming software
programmes that would remain unde-
tectable.

'People talk about this sort of technology and dream up all sorts of models,
but it's a lot harder to do than they
think. It is also very dangerous to have a
rogue code wandering about a system on
something that travels at 200 mph.
It could work against the system very
easily.'

Underlying all the controversy was a
sense of complete incredulity at the
detail in which LDRA had examined the
Benetton software, and how it had managed to uphold with such devastating
effectiveness Mosley's claim that the
FIA would get to the bottom of such
matters. Right there and then, he had
struck a body blow for the governing
body which staggered Formula 1's
habitually secretive fraternity.

Speaking some years later, Mosley
outlined his views on the whole affair. 'I
don't believe that Benetton were using
traction control, but it was entirely our
fault. In the heat of all the problems after
the Senna accident, we handed the stuff
we'd taken from the cars back to the
team. If we hadn't handed it back and
had checked it out at greater length we
would have known for sure whether they
were or they were not. But I believe
them when they say they weren't, and I
know the Benetton people a lot better
now than I knew them then and I don't
believe they were using it. I think that
they just left it in there because it was
more trouble to delete it all than it was
to leave it. And when you start deleting
things in your programme it might inter-
fere with other things; one can quite see
how that might happen under the pressure of racing.' And so, finally, expired
one of Formula 1's Great Technical
Controversies.

* * *

With all the pressure and acrimony of

the rampant politics that season, other
technological aspects rather tended to
be eclipsed, but there were some interesting developments for those who cared
to look beyond the dramas.

John Barnard's elegant 1994 Ferrari
412T1 registered the sort of departure
from conventional thinking that had
become his trademark, and came complete with a fabricated and welded gearbox casing for its six-speed sequential
shift transmission. This was a clever
idea, because the gearbox is one of the
most time-sensitive parts of the Formula
1 car since it usually has around a three-
month lead time due to the need to
make patterns and then have the casing
cast. By opting for fabrication Barnard
had alleviated this problem, while creating a lighter, stiffer structure that also
took up less space (thereby allowing a
very clean back end) and was more
adaptable.

'We aim to improve all areas of the
gearbox,' he said at the car's launch,
adding: 'What you are seeing today is
only a starting point for new gearbox
materials and construction techniques.
It might be several years, but eventually
when other designers see what we've
ended up with, they will start to copy it.'

That had yet to happen as this book
went to press, but he had kept his word
by introducing a carbon fibre bellhousing betwixt engine and gearbox in 1995,
and then adding a carbon rear end to the
unit on the 1996 F310, which retained
the otherwise similar six-speed transverse transmission. This time, however,
the part-fabricated, part-machined,
part-cast unit made even more use of
titanium, too. Both carbon epoxy and
titanium have reasonably low thermal
expansion coefficients, but titanium,
though a castable material, is not particularly easy to work with. The logistics of
running a fabricated, handmade gearbox
proved troublesome for Ferrari at times.
Other teams could put a dozen magnesium gearbox castings through their

Packaging is a vital part of Formula 1 design. To provide the optimum weight distribution engines tend to be located as far forward as possible, and this photograph of a customer Ford ED4 engine in Tyrrell's 1997 025 chassis illustrates the basic package, with the radiators fanning out ahead of the engine itself, and the longitudinal transmission occupying the space between the engine and the rear axle. With this design, as on most in Formula 1 today, the gears are carried ahead of the axle line, to reduce the polar moment of inertia and prevent the car behaving like a dumbbell being swung around. (Author)

machine shops in three weeks, whereas at times in 1996 Ferrari was struggling at races to put together one fully efficient box, as oil leaks were prevalent. It achieved the aim, however, and the F310 won three races, but most other teams took the view that it was an unnecessary and expensive complication with a performance contribution that was difficult to define.

Ferrari, like Williams, stuck with a transverse transmission when it carried the same transmission over into 1997 with the F310B. With the transverse unit the gear shafts run across the car, mak-

ing a shorter but wider unit, and by this time other teams had opted for the longitudinal system where the shafts ran lengthways. These had come back into fashion in consequence of aerodynamic considerations, but whereas in the past they had tended to locate the gear pack behind the rear axle line, now, in the interests of weight distribution, it was ahead of it. 'It was really because of the stepped floor, and the cut-off diffusor,' Gary Anderson explained. 'It gave us the opportunity to make the most out of what diffusor was left, by making a narrow gearbox, and the longitudinal was

Ferrari, like Williams, is unusual in retaining the transverse gearbox, but John Barnard's unit features some exciting uses of carbon fibre and titanium, and breaks fresh ground by fabricating rather than casting the casing. (Author)

Williams's transverse gearbox is so compact that some rivals were astonished to discover that it is as easy to package as their own longitudinal designs. (LAT)

the easier way to go. Putting the gears ahead of the rear axle line kept the weight within the wheelbase, which helped the weight distribution.'

Another difference of opinion surrounded the use of two- or three-pedal control in the cockpit, and nowhere was the dichotomy more apparent than at Williams, where Jacques Villeneuve ran the former and Damon Hill stuck with the latter. There was something to recommend the two-pedal layout from the point of view of helping to stabilize the car under full power with just a left-foot dab on the brakes, and this, in conjunction with a hand-operated clutch, suited Villeneuve's IndyCar mentality. Hill, however, who didn't have a karting background where he might have learned the art of left-foot braking, had an intense dislike of the system and at times in his 1996 campaign this may have cost him races after he made several poor starts with the three-pedal layout. It got so bad that at one stage they began to threaten his World Championship aspirations, the more so since the man making the good getaways was his main rival: Villeneuve.

Williams–Renault had used the same AP clutch for the past couple of seasons. When operated, it activated a potentiometer that determined how close the clutch was to its bite point, then informed the car's electronic system when to deploy the conventional hydraulic actuation system.

'AP was continuously making small modifications and improvements to the clutch, sometimes to help it stay alive. It rotated up to 16,000 and something rpm, so it was quite a critical item,' said Head while providing some interesting insights into Hill's apparent tardiness. 'If you can imagine having a hand clutch and only two pedals, you have the possibility of putting your right foot on the throttle and the left hard on the brake while simultaneously letting the clutch out by hand until you feel the car straining against the brakes as the clutch bites. And then taking your foot off the brakes when the lights change. You have found the bite point, the point at which the clutch starts gripping, in advance of the start, so all you have got to do is take your foot straight off the brake pedal and *boompf!* You're going.

'The thing you've obviously got to be careful of is that you don't pump too much heat into the clutch while you're doing that, and overheat it. Slipping clutches these days are not really a problem because the actual material of the plates is carbon, which is capable of taking enormous temperatures. The problem is the housings which hold the plates, which tend to be aluminium, and the diaphragm spring which is steel, so what tends to happen is that you destroy not the plates but the rest of the clutch. The steel diaphragm gets so hot that it tempers down and loses its spring strength, that sort of thing. It's a question of not getting the clutch itself too hot.

'The problem for Damon was that he'd got three pedals and only two feet. And if he'd got one foot on the accelerator and one foot on the clutch, he hadn't got one for the brake.' Head admitted that Williams could have provided him with an electronic handbrake, although Benetton's had left both Jean Alesi and Gerhard Berger stranded embarrassingly on the grid at the European GP at Nürburgring earlier in the season when they stuck on, and the problem with them was that they didn't provide a great deal of feel. 'You couldn't feel through the brake pedal when the car was beginning to creep as the clutch bites,' Head disclosed.

'In the existing situation, Damon had to keep one foot on the accelerator, and one on the clutch. He'd be off the brake pedal, and thus had nothing to stop the car moving, so he couldn't come back and find the bite point on the clutch. So when the lights changed he'd got to take his foot back on the clutch and find just the right point at which it was gripping to produce drive, but not get so much grip at low speed that it bogged the engine down. He'd got to find that point, whereas Jacques had already found it before the off.'

Starting had been Hill's strong suit, and at this point it seemed his championship might depend upon it. Ironically, however, it was Villeneuve who fluffed his start in the crucial deciding race at Suzuka, Hill getting away perfectly to win from the front and clinch his world title in style.

By late-1996 Benetton had started running an electronic differential, and by 1997 such devices were popular with other top teams, notably Ferrari and Williams. Predictably much fuss was made initially about their legality, but they were pronounced kosher by the FIA, so everyone started to investigate them. Effectively an hydraulic cylinder applied load to a clutch pack within the differential, and the pressure in the cylinder was controlled electronically by a software management system according to various strategies that the teams were permitted to use by the FIA. They could not use a closed loop strategy and sense and respond to wheelspin, for example, because that would be too much like the dreaded traction control. But they were allowed to mimic the behaviour of fairly conventional mechanical limited slip differentials such as the Salisbury – which provide progressively less slip as power is increased and have been in use for decades – or viscous couplings.

The big thing was that, while the driver had buttons on the steering wheel which enabled him to select a higher or lower degree of differential lock, depending upon prevailing conditions, the change could only be effected when he pressed the buttons. Like electronic brake balance, it was not automatic, and thus did not count as a driver aid as such.

The driver remained in control of it.

This was another vital part of race set-up, where the driver's relationship with his race engineer became even more critical, for the race engineer's empirical knowledge of what a car would do within a certain set-up, based on his past experience, could help to guide the driver to the right compromises. Heinz-Harald Frentzen, for example, struggled badly in the first three races of 1997, when he had joined the Williams team alongside Jacques Villeneuve, and was unable to find a chassis set-up that he liked with the car in qualifying trim. In Brazil, where he finished a demoralized eighth while Villeneuve won, he himself admitted: 'I'm the new guy at Williams and my way of setting up the car at Sauber was different. The team is giving me advice and at the moment I'm still working out my point of view of setting up the car, and also Williams' point of view. At the moment I'm using a mixed set-up based on Damon Hill's and my own ideas.

'Technically the Williams is a very advanced car, so from a driver's point of view, and mine especially, there is much more information which I have to sort out before I make the car 100 per cent. The more information, the more things you can make wrong!'

Patrick Head said curtly: 'If I knew what the problem is, we would fix it . . . Maybe the bumpiness of the track here threw him, but it's something we've got to work out. I'm not certain. He seems to like it better when we've got fuel in the car. It's pretty disappointing . . . I wouldn't say either of his performances so far have been very exciting, but the season's got a lot of races in it and he's going to have to come to grips with it. I think it's going to take him half the season to get into it. Obviously from our point of view we'd like him to step into the car and be on the pace straight away, but he's not and it's something he's got to work out.'

But by the fourth race, the San Marino GP at Imola, Frentzen had begun to do just that and to experiment more with differential settings. And finally he made the FW19 behave in a manner with which he felt comfortable. He won that race, his first Grand Prix victory, and his first for Williams, and went on to take his first pole position, two weeks later, in Monaco.

Despite the tightening of the regulations, transmissions have undergone continual development in the post-'gizmo' era, though one major potential breakthrough was nipped very firmly in the bud just as it had reached the testing stage. This was Patrick Head's development of the long-established continuously variable transmission (cvt) concept, which relies on maintaining an engine at peak power.

Head explained what it was that attracted him to the idea. 'It was purely that with a conventional gearbox, as road speed increases the engine speed increases, until the engine passes through peak power and then goes into the falling side of the curve after peak power, and then you change up to the next gear which puts you well below peak power, and then you've got to build up again. And there are lots of times, not just going down straights, when the car can take peak power but you aren't delivering it because you haven't got the engine at that speed.

'People get very confused by the difference between torque and power, but basically in order to get the maximum acceleration from a car you want to keep the engine at peak power. The transmission looks after providing the best tractive effort then at the wheels. So if you use a cvt you can keep the engine at constant speed and vary the speed of the car while the engine speed remains constant, sitting on peak power. And the cvt varies the ratio in order to keep that balance between the two.

'Now the downside of that is that your average power around the lap will be higher, and inevitably your average fuel consumption will be higher, so though your theoretical lap time is better the amount of fuel you need to achieve that lap time is more on the basis that you get very little for nothing.'

The engine is running more efficiently because it does not drop below peak power and have to build back up again. Head continued: 'You could say that you keep the engine running at peak power, but talking out of my natural knowledge I wouldn't necessarily say that peak power and peak efficiency are the same thing. Peak efficiency is much nearer to peak torque than peak power. The thing is that on the road a cvt can cause a car to be more efficient, because there are many times when you are actually needing only 30 hp to drive a car along at 110 kmh [70 mph]. And if you've got the right sort of management system on the cvt it will put you in a low gear and open the throttle wide, and put the engine at the most efficient speed to achieve that level of power. And then you can achieve remarkable overall efficiencies.

'The problem with a cvt is that none of the systems that exist can achieve the efficiency of a pair of spur gears such as you have in a conventional transmission, and although it's not as far away as might commonly be expected, the actual transmission itself is not as efficient in terms of managing the vehicle. On a road car it can be more efficient, but on a racing car it was just one way to see how we could use the power that's available from the engine better to do quicker lap times.'

Williams collaborated with Van Doorn in Holland, the company whose DAF car had, in the 1960s, introduced the simple 'Forward to go Forward, Back to go Back' philosophy that was so much a part of its marketing programme. Later the transmission found its way into Volvo's 343 series, and also had a competition application in Chequered Flag's

F3 Tecnos – raced with success in the mid-1960s by Mike Beckwith and Gijs van Lennep – and also in a series of rallycross cars. The F3 cars in particular were good on tight or wet circuits, but suffered horsepower losses on the straights.

The Formula 1 version did away with the DAF's rubber belts in place of complex steel belts, and ran for the first time in a car at Silverstone in 1993, with David Coulthard at the wheel. The test produced some interesting results. 'We've got video film of it!' Head beamed with reminiscent pride. 'The acceleration was better, but we never really got an accurate comparison of lap times, mainly because we never completely debugged the control system for it. But had we gone out for a proper test we'd probably have sorted that. From a purely technical view I don't think we saw anything from it that caused us to think that we were on a wrong route, but we didn't run it long enough to prove whether the theoretical advantage was actually practically achievable at that time.'

The machine made a constant engine noise, and Head chuckled at the recollection. 'It just went around going *naaaaaaa!* That's one of the reasons that Bernie arranged to ban it. He thought it would sound dull, and he was probably right!'

The project may be dead in Formula 1 terms, thanks to specific outlawing by the FIA, but it is alive for other uses. 'I'm sure Van Doorn can use some of the bits that were made,' Head said. 'The belt was a special one developed for that purpose and designed to be able to transmit 800 bhp, and the pulleys were normal by their standards, but certainly they spent a lot of time looking into stiffness of the mountings and rigidity of the pulleys themselves. I know they said they learned an awful lot from the programme themselves, and I'm sure some of that, if not the actual bits themselves, are applicable to other areas.

'Those old rallycross cars were very successful. They were very quick on twiddly circuits with a lot of ups and downs, not so much on faster tracks because they had more losses, and also this bloody heavy weight hung out the back because that system used one rather like the DAF with great big pulleys. The interesting thing for us on the development we did in 1993 was the packaging of it, because basically we weren't prepared to put a cvt into a vehicle which we felt, by virtue of its inclusion, had been rendered slower. And therefore it was very much on the basis of saying that we must package it so that there were no installation disadvantages, and I think we achieved that.

'It was within eight to 10 kilos [18 to 22 lb] of a conventional transmission, no more than that, and that's the sort of amount that we could have saved with a winter's work . . .'

Coulthard looked back fondly on the cvt experience. 'The actual acceleration was better, but it was bizarre at first because you had to get used to the constant rpm. You'd get to a corner and the initial feeling when you braked and all these millions of cogs kept the engine at the same revs, was that the throttle had stuck open because the note didn't change!

'We did a lot of running on airfields, where the acceleration was quicker than a standard car, but we only really did one test at Silverstone before it was banned, and we never took any comparative times. I think the engine note might have been a bit much for spectators, all the time, but I think it could have been competitive.'

Chapter 12

Suspended animation

'The people who had perhaps been the best dicking around with passive suspension had gone off and done active suspension, and their engineers hadn't looked at a passive system for two or three years; so they had to go back and drag out their old files and try and remember what the hell they used to do.'

Frank Dernie, former technical director, TWR Arrows

ONE OF THE BIGGEST areas of change in Formula 1 design was brought about when the FIA outlawed electronic computer-controlled active suspension after the 1993 season, obliging teams once again to come back within the province of the laws of physics, and revert to tried and tested springs and rollbars in place of the highly sophisticated systems which had allowed them to create cars whose handling could actually be altered once the vehicle was under power.

The fundamental purpose of active suspension had been to optimize a car's aerodynamic behaviour by allowing it to run at a controlled ride height (the distance of the chassis underside from the track surface). Normally, cars would try to pitch their noses under heavy braking, and lift them on hard acceleration, and over the years various means had been tried to control these two undesirable traits. Back in 1970 Colin Chapman introduced his innovative wedge-shaped Lotus 72 with anti-dive and anti-squat geometry in its front and rear suspensions. Though it transpired that the 72 ultimately ran markedly better without them, Chapman's fertile mind never stopped turning over the conundrum and in 1982 he introduced the first active system, wherein computer-controlled electronics took over from the laws of physics in deciding what rake the car would adopt during power running. By this time Chapman had also introduced ground effect, which threw the focus of attention on to the aerodynamic behaviour of the car, and the active system was intended to ensure that the Lotuses ran at just the right ride heights front and rear to create maximum undercar downforce. While the car might want to roll during cornering, or dip its nose under braking, electronically-controlled hydraulic actuators physically prevented this, and if necessary jacked up the part of the car that wanted to react to the force of gravity.

Both Lotus and Williams, which had introduced its own system in 1987, experienced a number of alarming failures, the latter in particular struggling in 1988 as its system let Nigel Mansell down so many times that the British driver finally refused to drive the car in such a configuration after receiving one fright too many. Williams thus took the active system off its cars overnight at the British GP that year, improvised with the sort of panache that only the British teams seem capable of, and produced a 'passive' car for him to drive the following day. In the wet race, Mansell drove his heart out to take second place.

Thereafter, active ride fell into abeyance until technical director Patrick Head and chief designer Adrian Newey began penning the FW14 that would dominate the 1991 season. This car was passive, too, but it was always intended that it would use a significantly upgraded active system with fail safe back-ups, and this came in on the FW14B with which Mansell, ironically enough, blitzed the 1992 World Championship. In the hands of Alain Prost and Damon Hill its successor, the FW15, was so superior in 1993 that the FIA finally decided that something needed to be done, and banned many of the electronic driver aids. Active suspension was the first to bow to the governing body's guillotine. By then it was clear that active was the only way to go for every other team, and McLaren, Benetton, Ferrari, Footwork (with a McLaren TAG system), and Jordan were all experimenting with varying levels of success. McLaren, for example, had created a very efficient system, whereas Ferrari's was so disastrous that Gerhard Berger's car turned the wrong way as he exited the pits during the 1993 Portuguese GP at Estoril and came close to wiping out Derek Warwick and J. J. Lehto as they steamed down the main straight at 290 kmh (180 mph). There was a massive outcry against the ban, especially since many hundreds of thousands of dollars had been invested in development, but for 1994 everybody was obliged to revert to passive suspension.

That season saw Benetton–Ford take on, and beat, Williams–Renault, amid tragedy and acrimony, and different people had different memories of the change. Ross Brawn, at that time technical director at Benetton, recalled it happily.

'We were very fortunate during 1994, if you remember, because we actually had a very good car. It's a comment I have made before, but World Championships are the result of your own efforts – and other peoples'. And that year a lot of people found the transition from active to passive quite difficult. I mean, Williams didn't have a very good car that year, Ferrari weren't competitive, and we managed to create a very good car in 1994, so for us it was a good experience from active to passive. But there are some different criteria. With an active car you can afford to be much more cavalier with some of the aerodynamic characteristics, because the car is a very stable platform. So you can afford to widen the allowable pitch change, for instance, with ride height, because there is very little pitch change and very little ride height change. You can compensate for the tyre deflection via the suspension. Whereas with a passive car you can't do that so you have to go back much further into the correct ratio between aerodynamic efficiency and pitch change. So those are the sort of parameters that changed. That was one of the fundamentals.

'For sure, that was where McLaren had a big advantage in their purple patch in the mid to late 'eighties. Undoubtedly John Barnard and subsequent people had a better understanding of that element than other teams. But everyone caught up again. It took a year or two to realize what was happening, but people caught up and now it's a really key element of the design of a Formula 1 car.'

Part of this is also due to the way in

which teams have grown, so that they have a larger staff capable of conducting the necessary research.

Frank Dernie, who was also with Benetton, took a different view. 'The most difficult aspect of reverting from active to passive, I should think, was the driver getting used to the feel of going over bumps again!' he remarked, alluding to the manner in which active systems also gave the drivers much smoother rides. 'Nothing fundamentally changed between the pre-'93 and post-'93 passive suspension designs. There was a bit of a lag, obviously. The people who had perhaps been the best dicking around with passive suspension had gone off and done active suspension and their engineers hadn't looked at a passive system for two or three years, so they had to go back and drag out their old files and try and remember what the hell they used to do. Two years is a hell of a long time in Formula 1. So for some there was a hiccup in the development curve.'

Teams still use the tried and trusted wishbone suspension systems established in the 1960s, with the pushrods on the lower wishbones that operate spring/damper units which are now universally mounted atop the monocoque chassis. They are located there because this provides the safest and most logical site, and usually obviates the need for integrity-compromising holes within the side of the chassis. Few designers can have failed to bear in mind Martin Donnelly's accident in a Lotus 102 at Jerez in 1990, when the car crashed into a barrier and literally disintegrated in the impact. Donnelly's survival owed more to fortune than anything else, and one theory suggested that damage sustained earlier to a suspension unit, by running hard over a chicane kerb, had led to the pullrod failing prior to the corner in which the accident occurred. Lotus sited its spring/damper units at the base of the monocoque, where they were in a much more vulnerable position, and if, indeed,

Though it looks like a plumbing nightmare, the typical three-damper system (seen here on the 1997 Arrows A18) has proved a successful means of maintaining a car's ride height while allowing it to cope with roll during cornering. (Author)

a pullrod broke it would have the effect of removing any suspension action from that side of the car, leading the driver to lose control while trying to guide it round the corner.

Back in 1990 Tyrrell's Harvey Postlethwaite had introduced a single front damper – the monoshock – on his 019 model in order to minimize the effect of the rise of one wheel, over a kerb, being transmitted to the other via the anti-roll bar. Effectively, Postlethwaite's system tended to create the opposite reaction, the rising wheel tending to push its fellow further into contact with the track. However, in the wake of the active ban teams found it more effective to start using three dampers at the front. Dernie explained the thinking behind them:

'The main idea is that one of the problems you always have with racing cars is that you've got to run them with downforce on the bodywork instead of on the suspension, so you've always got the problem of holding the thing up down the straight bits, and if you put bump rubbers on which are stiff enough to stop it grinding itself to death down the straights, it's sitting on them or rolling on to them going round fast corners and causing big upsets in the handling, particularly if you hit a bump. Now if you have a third damper in the middle, between those for each individual wheel, you can stick a bump rubber on that one to stop it hitting the ground, but in roll there are no bump rubbers in the side dampers so you don't encounter those handling problems.'

Gary Anderson took up the theme: 'Basically you've got two rockers on either side of the car, which are activated by each of the front suspension pushrods. When they move they compress the spring either side, then there's a linkage to an anti-roll bar. As the car rolls, the bar, which is a torsion spring, resists the rolling motion. Meanwhile, the central damper only sees vertical motion, so it holds the car's nose up at the end of a straight without changing the roll stiffness [the rate of resistance to roll], which any change in either of the other two dampers would influence. It's merely a means of, on that one damper, separating vertical movement from rolling movement. It's effectively like a bump stop, but acting as a damper too.'

A bump stop is basically a spring, made in most cases of metal (though it could be a carbon fibre leaf spring), that takes the form either of a torsion bar or a torsion bar wound up in a coil. It is made of a material which will take a very high degree of load before it goes what is called 'beyond yield', which means that it will take a permanent set. Designers are most concerned not to allow any spring on the car to go beyond its yield point because, basically, it will then have lost some load and the car won't sit straight. Classically, in the old days, bump stops were used to limit spring travel so that the spring would not go beyond its yield point. Today's designers tend to use them more to give themselves a sort of rising rate suspension characteristic, which means that the resistance of the spring rises with the forces applied to it.

This is desirable because at low speed designers want to have a reasonably compliant suspension system, and also want to run the car fairly low for aerodynamic reasons. But they also want to be able to take a very high level of downforce at high speed, so usually they will run a given spring at low speed and let the suspension move, and then, when the car gets above the speed of the fastest corner, when it is travelling down the fastest straight, they will let a bump stop start carrying some of the load. Generally, most people who are running a third damper at the front will probably take most of the very high-speed load on the central one, which means that at high speed they are carrying the load at the axle on the central one, and keeping the bottom of the car above the ground. This is particularly important to avoid wear on the undercar plank which might lead later to exclusion (see Chapter 3), but still effectively allows one wheel to go over a bump or debris without affecting displacement of its opposite number and without the whole front end of the car jumping about.

Formula 1 dampers are works of art, and while companies such as Penske or Ohlins supply units, several teams manufacture their own or else manufacture part of the system in conjunction with proprietary components. Compared to road car dampers, Formula 1 units are very small, and generally use remote reservoirs for the hydraulic fluid that is carried within the damper body itself in road car applications where space is not such a critical factor.

Electronic dampers are also commonplace. There are several different kinds, but mostly they use small motors to turn the knob that would normally be turned manually to alter the settings on an adjustable road car damper.

Damper tuning is now one of the fine arts of Formula 1 set-up, and the larger teams do a lot of development work using their four or seven poster rigs. 'The suspension development work we do on there makes the car go quicker,' Dernie said. 'We don't dick around any more with damper settings at race tracks. We have that figured out from test rig running before we get there. We do a certain amount of testing on the rig, come up with a few settings that look interesting from the point of view of grip or what have you, and then usually run those round the race track and see which ones the driver likes the feel of best. So we tend not to move very far from that once we get to a race track. We might change damping inasmuch as we change from one damper that we've tested on the rig and looks good, to another one that we've tested on the rig which also looks good. We wouldn't take the first

John Barnard broke more new ground in 1994 when his Ferrari 412T1 did away with conventional uniball suspension mountings and opted instead for straightforward hinges, the Englishman arguing that they provided sufficient compliance at a time when suspension movement was minimal due to stiff chassis set-ups. (ICN UK Bureau)

damper that we've got and say "Let's try two clicks more rebound damping on that one". It's a long time since we did that.'

John Barnard's 1994 Ferrari 412T1 broke new ground – in controversial style – when the innovative Englishman did away with conventional uniball joints for mounting its wishbones and instead opted for knife-edged hinged mounts and then effectively relied on the flexure of the suspension arms themselves to augment the springing medium. It was a nice bit of lateral thinking that was within the rules and the car ran in that form during the year, but Barnard reluctantly reverted to uniball pivots for the 412T2

the following year, admitting that he had bowed to 'political pressure' from within Ferrari. He felt strongly that it was the way to go, and planned to incorporate the flexures again later in the season, citing enhanced stiffness as their prime advantage. However, Jean Alesi was believed to be particularly ill-disposed to them, and as other developments took priority, they did not reappear.

In 1994 the Williams FW16 shrouded its rear suspension and driveshafts in a neat aerofoil section which was integrated with the rear wing mount in an elegant piece of packaging, and the Didcot cars raced successfully in this form right through until the rear suspension was

For 1995 Tyrrell's Harvey Postlethwaite (seen here, left, with Ken Tyrrell) introduced the Hydrolink concept on the 023, in an attempt to regain some of the separate bump and roll control that had been so taken for granted by teams with active suspension up to 1993. The system was dropped for a number of reasons, to the regret of some engineers within the team. (Tyrrell)

revised for the 1996 FW18.

In 1995 Tyrrell introduced its Hydrolink system, which aimed to make up for the loss of some of active suspension's advantages. It ran for thousands of kilometres on a four poster rig, and improved the handling of the 022 model by curing its tendency to low-speed understeer, but after the 023 car proved a disappointment it became victim of Tyrrell's financial restraints.

Without active suspension it was no longer possible to achieve absolute control of ride height, nor to oppose aerodynamic forces. And while it was simplicity itself with an active car to dial numbers into the computer to make the car stiffer in roll, with a passive car that was impossible, because doing so would affect other parameters. By siting an hydraulic cylinder atop each pushrod, Hydrolink allowed Tyrrell to avoid stiffening the car in roll whenever it sought to stiffen it in bump, by separating the two. Pure vertical movement was taken by one set of springs, pure roll movement on another, with the hydraulic cylinders apportioning the movement.

After the successful test on 022 it was introduced initially at the front of 023 and then later on the rear, but was subsequently dropped during the 1995 season.

'It's one of my constant regrets,' admitted Mike Gascoyne. 'It worked very well on 022, but we took it off 023 when that car wasn't performing particularly well. It transpired that it didn't go any better without it, which suggested that the suspension wasn't part of its problems, and it's one of those things you always mean to go back to, to develop a Mark Two version of. But with our financial situation it's something that has got pushed down the job list, which I personally believe is a great pity.'

While innovation might be too grand a job to describe it, shaped suspension components made an appearance in 1996 when Tyrrell introduced them in Barcelona for the Spanish GP. 'People didn't copy it because we didn't run well there, if we had they'd all have copied it straight away,' said Gascoyne. 'We took it off, then had it back on for Hungary. It made a difference in back-to-back

Aerodynamically-shaped suspension components were introduced by Minardi and Tyrrell in 1995, though in part they date back to the 1960s. By 1997 Tyrrell's 025 featured aerofoil-section wishbones to help clean up airflow, though the FIA had by now moved in to control the excesses of some teams. (Author)

testing at Silverstone, and we were very confident after testing it in the wind-tunnel.'

The full fairing that Tyrrell used in Spain was outlawed by the FIA, which placed restrictions on the chord length as others, such as Minardi, tried to outdo Tyrrell by the end of the season. Tyrrell introduced a revised version which appeared in Argentina in 1997, by which time many other teams had aero-foil-section wishbones. McLaren's, in particular, were stunningly elegant.

'It was really just a matter of people looking at it and deciding on something more aerodynamic than round tube, and gradually they got more elongated until they were aerofoil shaped,' said Jordan's Gary Anderson, the first man to use carbon fibre as a suspension component material. This was on the Jordan 191, his first Formula 1 design which was penned in 1990 in time to make its debut in 1991. 'Others will no doubt say *they* were the first, but I think we got there first. Pushrods need to be very stiff to avoid bending under shock-loading when, for example, a driver goes over a kerb. This driving practice is essential for quick laps at some circuits, such as Argentina or Monza, so with that in mind we came up with carbon fibre pushrods.'

Many cars now also feature carbon fibre upper wishbones, though not necessarily lower wishbones, some of which remain steel. Anderson explained: 'It's the practicalities, really. Making the bottom outboard end of the wishbone, where it drives the pushrod, isn't easy, though we will have them very shortly. It's a question of what's good for you and, really, what do you use carbon for? What's really practical? The pushrods

Carbon fibre suspension components were ushered in by Jordan in 1991 with its 191 chassis. This is the team's 1996 offering, the 196 (below left), which used a carbon fibre pushrod and upper wishbone, while below right is Ferrari's interpretation, the 1997 F310B. (Author)

are easy to manufacture and their stiffness to weight ratio is good, so that's the reason for it. Likewise the upper wishbone is better than a steel one and has good stiffness to weight too. The bottom wishbone's stiffness to weight ratio would also be good, but it's a bit impractical for us at the moment.'

By the beginning of the European season in 1997, Benetton, Williams, Tyrrell, and McLaren used carbon wishbones top and bottom, the rest relying on a mixture of carbon upper and steel lower, or steel top and bottom.

The one thing that has remained a relatively low priority throughout is suspension geometry itself, which has played only a minor role ever since the days of ground effect wing cars in the

1970s and early-1980s. Frank Dernie has never been a fan of suspension geometry as an influence on Formula 1 car behaviour, and held true to his comment from the early 1990s: 'I've never found it to be particularly important.'

Power steering continued to be, however, though the system on Ayrton Senna's Williams was suspected of failure in the aftermath of his fatal accident. The manner in which the Brazilian immediately braked hard enough to scrub 96 kmh (60 mph) off his initial speed of 310 kmh (193 mph) prior to striking the concrete wall at Tamburello, suggested to many observers that he had detected failure in the steering, and Williams is believed to have disconnected the power-assistance on team-mate

As Jean-Christophe Boullion loses the nose wing of his Sauber–Ford during practice for his first GP, at Monaco in 1995, one of the dangers inherent in Formula 1 is apparent as the right front wheel remains attached, though its linkage is clearly damaged. Senna's injuries were inflicted by a wheel attached to a suspension member swinging back into the cockpit, and the FIA subsequently took steps to try to control such situations with greater predictability. (ICN UK Bureau)

Damon Hill's car prior to the restart of that race. As this book was written the Senna trial was still continuing, however, and technical director Patrick Head remained adamant that steering failure was not the cause, and that telemetry had shown steering inputs up until the moment of impact.

Interestingly, Benetton did suffer a confirmed steering failure, at Interlagos in 1995. During practice for the Brazilian GP Michael Schumacher's car plunged off the circuit at the 225 kmh (140 mph) Ferra Dura corner when a small pin sheared in the universal joint that connects the steering column to the smaller section that drops down into the steering rack itself. It was a brand-new pin, of a sort that had been used on all previous Benettons, but a local workshop made up some replacements of more durable material and the problem never recurred.

With modern power-assistance systems the driver can choose to have an almost unlimited degree of assistance, but most teams have found that around 30 per cent is sufficient to assist the driver while still providing him with reasonable feel.

'You've got to have the safety features in there too, so that if anything goes wrong with it, it shuts down,' Anderson said. 'We have a fault detection system. If you've got 70 per cent assistance and the guy is going round a tight corner and it all suddenly shuts down, you could be in trouble because it's going from very light steering to very heavy. The guy's still got to make a reasonable effort to steer so that the difference is not that dramatic and you can actually retain control.

'We use an hydraulic system, naturally, but it is managed electronically. The pump goes on the back of the engine and, in the case of the latest car, is driven by a shaft that mounts into the gearbox. On the 197 when the gearbox is removed the complete hydraulic system

stays as a unit, making it easier and less potentially damaging to split the hydraulic system.'

★ ★ ★

Somewhere in Italy there is a man who can tell you the most intimate things about Formula 1 champions such as Ayrton Senna, Alain Prost, Nelson Piquet, Nigel Mansell, and Michael Schumacher. Little details, such as the thickness and length of their thumbs. He is not the victim of a bizarre new craze, or just short of better things to do; he works for Personal, the company that designs and manufactures steering wheels specifically for Formula 1.

Steering wheels are like tyres. Every car needs them, but nobody really spends much time thinking about them. Yet if the tyres are what transmit a car's messages to the driver, then the steering wheel is the means by which those messages reach his brain, via his hands. Think of steering wheels and tyres in these terms, then remember how badly battered Gerhard Berger's hands were over the bumps of Interlagos during the 1995 Brazilian GP, and suddenly they assume a far greater importance.

All Formula 1 steering wheels are custom made for individual drivers, just as the chassis is tailored to his personal requirements. If you accept that the steering wheel is the most important item on a race car because of its ability to transmit instant messages to the man who controls it, and also that it will transmit road shocks to his hands all through an event, then it makes sense to have one that is made specially for him.

In Formula 1, Ferrari uses Momo wheels, but Personal supplies McLaren, Williams, Benetton, Prost, and other leading teams, while John Barnard's FDD enterprise actually made Berger a new wheel after his Interlagos experience. Though steering wheels might appear to be simple devices, the reality is again complex. For a start, they are not always round. Back in 1972 Tony Southgate used a flat-bottom wheel with his BRM P180, whose cockpit cowling swept back over the driver's hands. More recently other designers have sought to minimize cockpit widths, to obtain the optimum aerodynamic efficiency for the outer shell. This in turn has resulted in smaller wheels, again with flat edges to give the driver sufficient knee room. The cars run at relatively low yaw angles, which means that they can get away with limited steering lock and have such precise steering ratios (about 1.5 turns lock-to-lock) that a driver does not need to twirl the wheel. That in turns means wheels can be very small diameter.

Steering wheels have not only changed shape over the years. 'They have become more and more complex,' said Antonio Conterno, Personal's technical director, 'because now they have all sorts of things on them, such as the paddles to change gear.' Personal does not actually fit these, because they vary from team to team, but supplies the finished wheel with the positions already marked out and electrical connections in place, and the team then simply fits its own mechanisms.

'Each driver likes his own feel to a wheel, his own position for, say, the small indents where he places his thumbs,' Conterno said. Senna, for example, preferred a slightly oval shape rather than a pure circle.

During their fitting drivers hold a dummy wheel with a soft rim, so that an exact replica of that specific shape can then be made to suit their precise tastes, rather as they recline on a bag of expanding foam when the team makes them a seat. 'It used to be very simple,

but now it is becoming very, very complex, because each driver wants his own shape, the right shape,' Conterno said. 'Drivers' thumbs differ in thickness and length, for example, so they need different positions for the switches on the centre of the wheel. These are the sort of things we must take into account. We need to bear in mind always that a steering wheel must fit a driver like a glove; he must never have to think twice about it when he is racing.'

As well as shapes, some drivers also prefer different wheel sizes, and different thicknesses and shape of the rim. Nigel Mansell, for instance, liked a much smaller diameter. 'I looked at his wheel the first time I saw it,' said Mika Hakkinen, with whom Mansell was so fleetingly partnered in his two-race McLaren career, 'and I admit that I laughed. I said to myself: "No way is he going to be able to drive the car flat-out through the first corner at Estoril with a wheel that small!" But he did! Nigel was incredibly strong, and because he liked to use the strength in his wrists, he liked a small wheel.' That was one of the reasons why the McLaren was initially uncomfortable for Mansell, because he liked to wrestle with the smaller wheel and drive with his elbows sticking out and there wasn't room in the cockpit. His 26 cm (10 in) wheel was the smallest Personal has ever made for Formula 1, but the thickness of its rim was greater than most others because of the size of his hands. Most Formula 1 wheels now have a D-shaped section to the rim, rather than a pure circle. Again, this is a matter of driver comfort that has evolved over the years.

Chapter 13

Where angels fear to tread

'The four tyres dictate everything, and unless you are kind to them and don't take too much out of them, you're going to be in trouble. They are the biggest thing, to be honest, the biggest individual component on the car, which give you grip. You must look after them. It's what this is all about.'

Gary Anderson, Technical Director, Jordan

MAX MOSLEY WAS IN full spate, espousing the view in which the FIA had become entrenched and from which no amount of arguing or rhetoric would dissuade it, as the teams prepared for the 1997 Monaco GP and he reiterated yet again his plans for Formula 1's future.

'Although some people dispute this – and no engineer will – the energy of impact if you have a crash is directly proportional to the grip of the tyres,' he began. 'Now some people say if you've got a wide tyre you stop quicker. You do, but you are going faster when you start to have the accident. So your impact is with more energy. Now, if you dispute that, it's rather like saying the earth is flat because it looks flat when you look out the window. But what I have said is a truism. If you reduce the grip of the tyres you do reduce the energy of impact in a crash, everything else being equal.

'The biggest problem we have had over the last 25 years is the steady increase in cornering speeds, which the

best efforts have failed to control. We have constantly changed the aerodynamic characteristics of the cars, we have constantly interfered with horsepower, we have interfered on all sorts of levels with the cars. And despite that there has been an escalation of the speeds so great that some of the great circuits, and some of the great corners of those circuits, have been eliminated. And our view is that this process must stop.'

Mosley expressed the contrite view that tyres were the one factor about which the FIA seemed to have done nothing, though that was not, strictly speaking, true. The width of rear wheels, for example, was reduced from 18 in to 15 in for 1993 in an effort to reduce the amount of rubber on the road and thus to limit cornering speeds. At the time there was the usual outcry from those with vested interests, but one informed observer said: 'You know, they could slow these cars down a whole bunch, and nobody would be any the wiser. Standing watching them you can't tell whether they're cornering at 130 miles an hour or 150, and if the tail is out they're gonna look a whole lot faster even if they're actually going slower!'

That was the American driver Dan Gurney, one of the greatest Formula 1 exponents of the 1960s and still a keen observer of the contemporary scene. He was not alone in his thoughts. The FIA (at that time still the FISA) had been keen to promote better overtaking opportunities, and to reduce grip in the corners, and thus had pushed through the narrower tyres as part of a sweeping package which included reducing the size of the front wings and mounting the rear wings slightly lower to reduce their efficiency. On paper it all sounded very exciting; the sort of thing for which enthusiasts who craved the return of tail-out driving styles had been pleading for years.

At the time Goodyear had a monopoly on Formula 1 tyre supply, having seen off all its opposition, but it was horrified when the changes were first mooted. This was not because the giant American tyre manufacturer is hidebound by vested interests; far from it, for the Akron-based company had long shown itself to be a good friend to the sport. What worried its engineers was that the narrower the tyre, the smaller is the contact patch, the area of tyre surface that actually touches the track. 'That means that more of the car's weight is supported by a smaller area,' said Leo Mehl, at that time Goodyear's director of racing world-wide. 'We are worried that this will lead to greater strain on the sidewalls and more tyre failures. And we are not in the business of indulging in public failures. We would have been happier if we had been consulted more on the form the new regulations would take, so we could have had our say.'

The FISA's premise was simple: by reducing the contact area there would be less grip. Cars might therefore slide around more – and thus look more spectacular – and more opportunities for overtaking would be created not only by the smaller physical size of the cars, but also because the narrower tyres would afford less grip under braking and thus provide a better means of lengthening braking distances than a ban on carbon brakes, which had also been under consideration (see Chapter 10).

Right from the start though, when the new tyres were tested at Estoril in October 1992, the indications were that such aims were unlikely to be realized. At that time the cars using them were around a second slower than their counterparts on 1992 rubber, but then all of the 1993 cars were designed specifically to maximize any advantage in the new regulations. Narrowing the tyres had brought in its train a benefit which went part way towards compensating for the loss of grip. The cross-sectional area of the car was smaller, so there was correspondingly less of it to push through the air. Drag was therefore lower, and speed on the straights increased accordingly.

'The actual frontal area was around a square foot less, which was quite a good thing for us,' said Jordan technical director Gary Anderson. 'At a track like Hockenheim, with its very long straights, that could be worth around six or seven kilometres an hour [three to four miles an hour].'

Within months the new cars were faster than their counterparts, and a fundamental flaw in the pro-sliding argument was exposed. Because they were narrower, the tyres had to be of harder compound, and that was less tolerant of sliding. Everybody quietly forget about their hopes for livelier racing and more overtaking. As happens so often in this highly technical sport, nothing really changed. The expression *plus sa change, plus sa même chose* – the more things change, the more they stay the same – could have been coined specifically for Formula 1.

1994 came and went, taking with it its bitter taste of tragedy and acrimony. 1995 and 1996 proved faster than ever, despite further revisions to the technical regulations which included downsizing engine capacity from 3.5 to 3 litres. Then came 1997, and the tyre war that led to an explosion in lap speeds.

By only the third race – the

This means war! After years of monopoly, Goodyear faced the very strong challenge of Bridgestone from the 1997 season onwards, and suddenly Formula 1 was in the grip of a massive tyre war. Olivier Panis signalled the strength of the Japanese threat by taking third place in the Brazilian GP in his Bridgestone-shod Prost. (ICN UK Bureau)

Argentinean GP – the progress was there for all to see: in 1996 Damon Hill had qualified his super-competitive Williams–Renault on pole position at 1 min 30.346 sec; in 1997 he lapped his markedly less fleet Arrows–Yamaha in 1 min 27.281 sec, three seconds faster. And the Williams–Renaults were quicker still, Jacques Villeneuve lapping his in 1 min 24.473 sec compared to his 1996 best of 1 min 30.907 sec on a circuit that had changed very little.

Gary Anderson dispelled some of the tyre myths, and put things into perspective, when he explained early in 1997: 'The tyres today are relatively too small for the job they are doing, with 700 odd horsepower. Again, because they are too small they've got to get harder in compound to be able to stand the loads, and then because of that you can't drive the tyre. You are driving the grip you've got, and that's 90 per cent effective in a straight line, and as the car gets out of shape it's normal after that that you are going to have an accident. You need something else there other than the downforce.

'You see people spinning, and in reality the car seems to speed up whenever it's spinning. That's really why, because you've actually lost control. You haven't got anything left there to give you a bit of grip.

'I personally believe that the solution would be a wider tyre to allow softer compounds, so that whenever you need them the thing will stop and the guy can drive the tyre grip rather than the car grip.

'It's difficult to know where you draw the line because they want to keep the cornering speeds similar, relatively, because otherwise the circuits are going to have to spend a lot of money on new barriers and gravel traps and they don't want to do that year after year. I think that's quite a good way to do it, just dotting the i's and crossing the t's as the years go by, no big changes just small

Battle lines. Though Goodyear had fewer teams to service with Bridgestone's arrival in 1997, it nevertheless brought as much rubber as it had in previous years to keep its runners on the road. (Author)

ones. But the problem at the moment is that they are focusing on too big changes.'

Peter Wright, the former Lotus engineer credited with the discovery of ground effect in the late-1970s, and now working for the FIA, outlined his theory that with high-grip tyres the amount of energy absorbed is the amount of grip multiplied by the slip angle; and the more grip that the tyre generates the less slip angle it can tolerate without overheating. Which meant that contemporary Formula 1 tyres tended to be relatively non-slideable with low slip angles, hence the need for the drivers to corner their cars as if on rails.

The slick tyres of 1997 were designed to operate at slip angles of little more than 5°. The slip angle is the difference between a car's actual direction of travel and the theoretical line it would describe around a corner given the driver's input at the steering wheel. When front wheel slip angles are greater than those at the rear, the car is understeering, which means that it tends to run wider and not turn into a corner very accurately, though it feels stable on the straight. If the rear slip angles are greater the car tries to spin because it is the back end that tends to run wide, and the driver needs to apply opposite steering lock to control it. This is oversteer, and it is oversteer that is so appealing to spectators since it makes cars appear to dance on the limit of control. Oversteering cars are generally more difficult to control, especially if they turn in as crisply as the Benettons with which Michael Schumacher clinched his World Championships in 1994 and 1995. Most drivers prefer a degree of understeer, since it is the safer condition, but the real aces like nothing more than excellent front-end bite which allows them to position their car with great precision, and then rely on their reflex and skill to cope with whatever action the back-end takes in protest.

The ideal, of course, is more and more to have a neutral handling car, which generates similar slip angles front and rear, for, given the dislike of modern Grand Prix car's tyres for anything over 5°, overheating is the penalty for abuse. Hence the unexciting but practical driving on rails that is all too predominant.

'The four tyres dictate everything,' Anderson underlined, 'and unless you are kind to them and don't take too much out of them, you're going to be in trouble. You must look after them. It's what this is all about.'

When Bridgestone entered Formula 1 at the start of 1997, it had been a long time since there had been a serious tyre war. Goodyear had 344 victories to its credit by the end of 1996, to make it far and away the most successful tyre manufacturer in history. It hadn't faced such a strong challenge since Michelin quit at the end of 1984.

Arrows team owner Tom Walkinshaw was the first to sign with the Japanese company, and spoke for those who predicted a new injection of interest into the sport when he said: 'There probably won't be much in it in half of the races, but the other half could be very dramatic.'

Tyres certainly began to play a more prominent role. Where before Goodyear would decide which control tyre to bring to a specific race, drivers now had a broader choice prior to qualifying. Under new rules the tyre companies were required to bring along two types of dry weather tyre to every race. Competition obliged them to tailor these more to specific circuits, whereas before Goodyear could simply make a limited number of control tyre specifications to suit them all. Not surprisingly, design and development work increased dramatically, as did the importance of testing.

The top teams – Williams, Ferrari, Benetton, McLaren, Jordan, and Sauber – were aligned with Goodyear in 1997, while Arrows, Prost, Stewart, Tyrrell, and Minardi were committed to Bridgestone.

Bridgestone recognized that it started at a disadvantage on certain tracks, given its limited experience, and that it faced a stern challenge. 'Goodyear is a very, very big company,' said Hirohide Hamashima, technical director of Bridgestone Corporation's Motorsports Division. 'And it has a great deal of data on Formula 1. Compared to Goodyear, we are like a baby, with no world-wide motor sport experience. Racing against them, we will learn quickly many things about the fundamental requirements for developing good tyres for Formula 1.'

Under the rules a driver was allowed a total of 36 dry-weather and 28 wet-weather tyres per event. He could try both specifications of dry tyre in free practice, which is held for an hour on Friday morning and another hour in the afternoon, then two three-quarter hour sessions on Saturday morning which are split by half an hour. And since the advent of the tyre war he had much more work to do in deciding which combination best suited his car and his own driving style. Prior to qualifying the team then had to inform the FIA of its choice of tyre specification, based on this running experience, and each driver could then use tyres only of that specification for qualifying and the race. For qualifying itself he could use only 16 tyres of the 28 that he was permitted to use for qualifying, the morning warm-up on race day, and the race itself, and the FIA reserved the right to choose these 16 for him. The front tyres in 1997 measured 25.5 x 9.5–13, meaning that they were of 13-inch internal diameter with a 25.5-inch outer diameter, and 9.5-inch tread width. Rear tyres were sized at 26.0 x 13.0–13. Front tyres weighed around 9 kg (20 lb), rears 11 kg (25 lb).

Formula 1 tyres are constructed along similar lines to road-going radials. Their sidewall stiffness is of paramount importance in determining their influence on steering input, feel, and response, and is a function of the construction design, while the compound determines the overall level of grip. They are tubeless, and are inflated by specially processed air which is converted into nitrogen-rich gas which thus ensures that the tyres retain constant properties. They do not operate in a benign environment, for the temperatures across the tread of a slick could reach 120°C, at operating pressures lower than the usual 30 psi of road cars. Typically, front tyres ran at 20–24psi, rears at 17–19. High temperature build up could increase that pressure by as much as 10 psi, a massive figure when a driver of Schumacher's calibre could accurately tell his engineers when

one of his tyres had half an inch more or less pressure than the other three . . . These tyres were only at their best when operating at optimum temperature, too, which is why they were kept wrapped in pre-heating electric blankets until the car was ready to move. The wets, with their distinctive tread patterns, could wipe away 91 litres (20 gallons) of water a second at high speed, through specially designed drainage channels within the tread pattern.

A typical rain tyre – this is Goodyear's Eagle on Michael Schumacher's Ferrari F310B – can clear up to 91 litres (20 gallons) of water per second at high speed. But while grooved tyres had been associated only with wet weather for almost 25 years, the FIA announced its intention in 1997 to make them mandatory even in the dry for 1998. (Author)

While all this was going on, Mosley had still been pondering fresh ways to exert control over the annual speed escalation. His latest solution came after a conversation with Stirling Moss.

'Stirling started me thinking along these lines,' he admitted, 'when he was talking about historic cars and said that you should never allow historics with treaded tyres and historics with slicks to race at the same time, because the performance gap is so enormous. This set the whole thinking in train. What actually happened was that slicks and aerodynamics came in around the same time, and one has always thought that the enormous climb in performance was due to aerodynamics, but in fact the quantum jump was slicks. I think now that we're on to that, and we shall see.'

Most designers would happily have told him that the fastest way to find three seconds a lap was to bolt on a set of tyres with softer compounds than usual, and Mosley of course knew that all too well himself from the old days of super-soft qualifying tyres, but there is no restraint on hyperbole in Formula 1. What he planned was to re-introduce grooved or treaded tyres for the 1998 season, and effectively to disinvent the slick which had evolved during the 1971 season. By mandating a specific number of circumferential grooves in the tyres, the contact patch would be reduced, and thus the level of grip would also be compromised. Hey presto, cornering speeds would fall.

'If you've got a circuit with a great corner that you want to preserve but can't because of the speed,' he continued, 'you can always have an extra groove. It's not that difficult to do.'

Policing tyre wear appeared to offer potential for argument in the post-race scrutineering bay, but Mosley was adamant that there would not be a problem. 'We are just going to measure the grooves, and if they have worn more than 50 per cent, the car is out. I accept that in the beginning there may be an occasional exclusion. We had exactly the same problem with the plank on the bottom of the monocoques back in 1994.

'The fact is that the engineers and technicians from the tyre companies will make sure their tyres are legal at the end of a race. They have the means to do this, and they will advise the teams accordingly, just as they can tell road car owners how to keep their tyres legal.

'And I think you can assume that we will have the means to avoid a situation where a driver might be told by his team to run on illegal tyres for much of the race, build up a suitable advantage, and then stop for fresh, legal, tyres in the closing stages. Charlie Whiting and Jo Bauer from the FIA will have officials in the pits to check that all the tyres are legal afterwards. It is quite easy to check that, probably by random selection. Methods will be found to prevent all the obvious methods of avoiding compliance. Charlie and Jo are very confident they can do it.'

And the FIA would throw the onus on the teams and drivers to do their homework adequately, particularly on high-wear circuits, so that they monitored the wear rate in free practice on Friday and formed their race strategy accordingly.

'It's exactly like the plank under the car. In the beginning it was a matter of how can we be sure that we don't rub away the plank when we set the car up? And we had one disqualification – Schumacher at Spa in 1994 – and we haven't had a problem since. The teams are very professional, and they'll make damn sure that they don't wear the tyres out. There's no point in running if they're going to do that, and get disqualified.'

At Suzuka in 1994 Damon Hill drove superbly in appalling track conditions to win despite having only three of his Goodyear tyres replaced at his pit stop, and having to rely on a worn fourth tyre when the left rear wheel nut could not be removed. It would be a travesty for such performances in future to be negated by disqualification, when in such an instance a more worn tyre was clearly a handicap and not an advantage. Mosley contended that the FIA had thought of that one, too. 'I think we've got some get-out in the rules if it is evident that some mechanical or set-up problem has caused it . . . In principle we have taken account of all the obvious difficulties. We don't care about flat-spots, for example. And if something has obviously been caused by a defect on the car, then we wouldn't worry.'

Time would tell.

'All of this is very difficult to initiate if you've only got one tyre supplier,' Mosley continued, mounting a hobby horse that many designers believed would fall at the first fence. 'They could simply turn round and say they won't do it. Once you've got two then it becomes possible. You can have a more sensible dialogue.

'One tyre company produced all sorts of argument why grooved tyres wouldn't work, none of which I believed to be valid. Checking this out with engineers, there were some of these arguments that you could actually demonstrate mathematically to be invalid. But there is a great deal of confused thinking. Everybody knows that if a road car has more grip, it is safer. The quicker it stops, the better it goes round corners or avoids obstacles. People extrapolate that to say that it is true of racing cars. In fact, it's the direct opposite. The more grip a racing car has, the more dangerous it is. On the road you have a speed limit which is imposed by law, on a race track you have a speed limit which is a function of how much grip you've got. The energy goes up with the square of the speed, but the really interesting thing is that the energy of the impact in your accident, is directly proportional to the grip of the tyres. So reduce the grip, and you reduce the energy of the impact.

'But if you talk to a racing driver, they feel safer on the higher grip tyres. But of course, when they have a crash it's a bigger one. Generally speaking, when there is an accident in the wet it's not so severe, because they are going slower.

'You can understand it intuitively, very easily, if you imagine a British GP run on packed snow. It would be impossible to hurt yourself because you wouldn't be going fast enough.

'If the tyre thing works as well as I believe it will work, then it's going to be extremely useful because it stops us having to continually make changes to the cars, which are expensive. The latest thing that was going on was what do we do about overtaking and running close? And in the end, after lots of wind-tunnel work and talking to teams, it became clear that within the existing concept of the car it was very difficult for them to run close together, and indeed if they could the teams would have done it already. If somebody had found a way of running close and keeping the downforce, they would have had an advantage. When we first talked to the teams about treaded tyres, we informed them that in the event of such tyres being introduced, we would be able to offer the teams chassis stability.'

Reverting to his theme of looking back to move forwards, Mosley then said: 'What we should have done 20 years ago is start to reduce the platform of the tyre, its basic efficiency, to keep the speeds under control. Had we done that we would not have lost some of the classic corners.'

The proposals, in conjunction with others to reduce the width of the cars from 2 m to 1.8 m ($78^3/_4$ to $70^3/_4$ in approx), met with far from universal acclaim, but the controversy surrounding the suggestion tended to overshadow the existing situation, with the tyre war and the way in which tyre design had created a Grand Prix car that could never live up to the hopes of enthusiasts for sideways motoring.

'I personally think that the concept of grooved tyres will make the tyres harder compound again, and again when they get out of shape there'll be nothing to slow them down,' Gary Anderson lamented. 'It's the same deal we have now. It's all about slowing the cars down. It'll be the same, but worse. If the cornering speeds are reduced then your impact speed should be reduced, but you have nothing to slow you down between losing it and hitting the barrier. You just go on for ever.'

He also laid to rest the idea that grooved tyres might make the cars any more driveable, and decried the part that suggested that the drivers might be able to slide the cars around more and throw them at more spectacular angles:

'People have got to accept that those days are gone. Why is that gonna happen? Again, you're not going to be driving the tyre because the tyre's going to be harder. The aerodynamics don't work when you're out of shape. You can only run the car about 5° in yaw, and the car's moving at that sort of angle all the time and it's not as if you can see it sliding. As the car starts to rotate the downforce is going away, and if you are doing 200 kmh [125 mph] and need x amount of load and you haven't quite got that sort of load and the car starts to slide, you still need that amount to keep the car on the road. It's just deteriorating, so as you get more out of shape so it deteriorates more and you get more out of shape and so on, and you're gonna hit the barrier.

'It's like saying cars go slower in the wet so they won't slide as much and hit the barrier, but they do. You've actually got more chance of avoiding hitting the barrier in the dry because at least you've got some means of control. You can stomp the throttle and use it like a handbrake, Alesi-style, to try and spin the car on the spot. You couldn't do that in the wet. So the cornering speed reduction that they're all talking about isn't necessarily the right thing to go for. I think

you need to have more control after you've lost it.

'You need tyres to slow the cars down, and you cannot do it without them. The softer the compound, the better. I'm a big believer in the bigger tyre and softer compounds.'

Patrick Head smiled at the mention of 5° of yaw being a dangerous angle, and said mischievously: 'You have to get to quite a high degree of yaw before you lose downforce dramatically. The sort of thing that you'd be impressed by! Five degrees? Hmm. Poor old chap!'

But fundamentally he agreed with Anderson. 'I think what it needs is that aerodynamic downforce needs to be reduced. But for some time the tyre performance needs to be left high. You need big wide tyres so that the drivers never think "I must look after this tyre", or "I must never get sideways. Goodness! A little slide. I mustn't do that!" If they have to drive like that then we will get very, very dull racing. And I'm afraid that's what is going to happen.

'The problem is that everybody pontificates about what is going to happen next year, and sometimes we're proved right and sometimes we're proved wrong, but I have to say that having run the car once on grooved tyres with narrow track, I think there is doom and gloom over what the racing is going to be about next year. I think all the FIA is interested in is control. That's all. And the problem is that the tyres are in the Sporting Regulations, which means that at any time that suits them they can take a groove out or add one in, with no notice. That means that you've got the dog on a lead, that's all, and you're just going to change the length of that lead – let it out, pull it in a bit – as it suits you.

'Max keeps coming out with this thing of "Every O-level schoolboy knows . . .", and the fact of the matter is that Max doesn't know. He keeps quoting the O-level schoolboy that does, and I have to say I'd like to see this fellow . . .' Head has been an old hand in the Formula 1 game for a long time (though Williams amassed its 100 GP victories in shorter time than either Ferrari or McLaren achieved theirs), and gave the rueful smile of a man resigned to the whims of others, and well versed in the art of knowing when to fight and when not to, when he added: ''Twas ever thus!'

Ferrari's technical director, Ross Brawn, also entertained reservations: 'Though the concept is that it's a variable that could be changed if the cars got too fast without changing the physical layout of the cars, my feeling is that if each year we have a reduction in the performance of the tyre, then the car that you optimize around that will be different. So there will be a lot of car evolution to go along with the change of tyres. And we are all going off in the dark next year with these treaded tyres; we'll understand them after a while, work out what steering geometry we'll want, what the characteristics are, what else is needed, and that's what will happen because we will have pursued every possible avenue for all possible knowledge to the nth degree. I know the tyre companies aren't very comfortable about it, but I'm sure they will find a solution.'

It was, in many respects, typical Formula 1 *déjà vu*, for Goodyear had been unhappy about the idea of narrowing the tyres for 1993 yet that proceeded without incident. 'They said we can't possibly run with tyres that narrow at the rear,' Brawn chuckled, appreciating the irony, 'but what have we run for the past three years?'

Anderson had another key point to make, regardless of what pattern the tyres had. 'You can be very guilty as a tyre company of playing catch-up, and going in the wrong direction at the wrong time, because the last track dictated something different. The tyres are the biggest thing, to be honest, the biggest individual component on the car, which give you grip.

'The problem is that the tyre companies are going to make better tyres, which is going to decrease the lap times, which is going to upset Max again and they're going to cut more bits of the car off. So it's going to be even harder work.'

Peter Wright was in favour of the grooved tyres, and said: 'I think they looked quite good in the first test at Barcelona. They have harder compounds and make fewer marbles during a race. They were 10 seconds off a 1997 time in their first test, so by the time they're developed they should achieve their aim, which is to keep to 1996 performance levels.'

'Every single time we've done anything to cut downforce the designers have come back and done better than we have,' Mosley lamented, before adding with a chuckle: 'Whereas if you attack the tyres, designers can do what they like. If you've got narrower, treaded tyres, you can have 10,000 bhp and all the downforce you like, you'll have trouble transmitting that power!'

Jacques Villeneuve, who shared that first test in Spain in April 1997 with Williams test driver Jean-Christophe Boullion, did not share his enthusiasm, nor care for it. At that stage the French-Canadian was the leader of the World Championship, and he expressed trenchant views.

'I tried just one set – and it was a joke, basically. It takes all the precision out of the driving and it's like driving a Formula Ford – you know, more horsepower than you've got downforce. You can brake almost as hard at the end of the straight but just before you get into the corner you lose all the feel of the braking and as soon as you turn the wheel then you just have to wait until the corner is over. You cannot do much, because you don't have a clue where the car is going. I think it's ridiculous to drive race cars like that.'

And he continued: 'I don't see how longer braking zones could improve

The 1998 specification treaded tyres were tested early in 1997 by Williams driver Jean-Christophe Boullion, who later threw his own criticism behind that of team leader Jacques Villeneuve by pronouncing them 'dangerous'. Some drivers were alarmed that they had far less grip; the designers were more concerned with having to revise their 1997 design thinking completely to cater for the new tyres' vastly different characteristics. (LAT)

overtaking because if the braking zone is longer it means it's easier to brake at the limit. And once you brake at the limit, if you have more grip you can always try to brake that little bit later. And if you brake too late you can still manage to slow down enough to go round the corner and not go off. So I think it's the wrong thing to do. It's true that the slower you are going into the corner . . .' He paused. 'No, actually, it's not the slower you go round the corner the less likely you will crash, it's the slower you will hit the barrier. So it doesn't matter if you go quicker round the corner if you can slow down more when you spin off.

'You lose a lot of the control of the car, so it's not going to make racing easier. The overtaking has become more difficult, not only because of the cars but I think probably the level of drivers is better than it used to be. The drivers are better prepared physically, mentally, and are more on top of the matter and closer to perfection than they used to be, so that's why it's more difficult to overtake.'

He even hinted at quitting Formula 1. 'I probably won't,' he said, 'but if it becomes boring to drive in Formula 1 then the best racing will probably end up being IndyCars, and that could have a big influence on my decisions. The reason I'm racing is because I enjoy the racing and if that's taken away, just the money side isn't going to be enough to keep me for a long time. For a short period maybe. And I've heard some other drivers saying that as well, that they would probably look at the other side. You need to enjoy it. What's fun this year is the extra grip you have. You really get a rush. Even in Argentina you could get a rush because of the extra speed, and it has become fun.'

He, too, doubted that the new cars would be more spectacular to watch. 'If the car is sliding and you can see that the driver is a passenger because the car has no precision, when you're doing 30 kmh slower, visually it's going to look slower. So, what's the point in having the car sideways if it's visually so much slower that I don't think it's going to be impressive? If that's what you want to see, then just watch Formula Ford.'

Eddie Irvine concurred. 'At the end of the day the way you drive a Formula 1 car quicker is to do it neatly, because they are at their highest efficiency whenever they're going straight. When you're driving sideways you're going slow, so there's gonna be very few guys out there driving round with the tail out because they're going to be going backwards. You're gonna be hurting the tyres and the car won't be working aerodynamically efficiently, so it all comes back to the same thing – aerodynamics.

'Cars in the ITC [the International Touring Car Championship] had tyres as wide as ours but they were a hell of a lot slower. They had a hell of a lot of horsepower but the times they did were nowhere near ours. The racing was better than ours purely because they didn't rely on aerodynamics anything like as much, but at the end of the day the car is always going to be quicker driven neat and tidy. And that's the way we're all able to do it. If you go sideways, it's a mistake. I think to have grooved tyres is ridiculous, to be honest. It's gonna look stupid.'

Villeneuve had another point to make. 'The other thing it's gonna do is, set-up wise, as a driver, now you can do a small change on the car and you can feel it, you can really improve it that way. The

ways the cars are going to be is very numb and there isn't going to be much you're gonna be able to do. Either it's right or wrong and you won't have the fine tuning you have now. I think it's going to take more away from the driver and instead of still being the ultimate sport it is, it's going to become more of a travelling circus.'

Both also suggested another problem. 'If you have an older tyre that has survived,' Villeneuve said, 'it's going to be much quicker at the end of its life because you are not going to roll over the rubber. In qualifying you will probably just go out and do the 12-lap run in one go so you can use up the tyre. It doesn't seem to make sense, does it?'

'You'd have your new tyre and you'd just skim it to get the tread down to the minimum because the deeper the tread is the more unstable the tyre becomes,' Irvine added. 'It's what they used to do in Formula Ford – skim the tyre, get it down to its last legal bit and then go out and run it for the race. It just doesn't add up. I don't understand why the designers, who know as much as the drivers, don't have more say. The ones I talk to seem to agree a lot more with my line of thinking than with the FIA's. The main thing is to get the grip from the rubber and not the aerodynamics.'

'It should change as little possible but I think they should go back to the bigger tyres, the way it used to be,' Villeneuve concluded.

Boullion's comments were somewhat lost in all this, but he said: 'With the grooved tyres the car wanted to slide around so much that it was incredible. Just like being back in a Formula Ford.'

Gerhard Berger was worried that the tyres would look silly, and detract from Formula 1's image, while Johnny Herbert scoffed at suggestions that the grooved rubber would be less susceptible to dirt and dust on the track and might therefore allow drivers to venture more off line in search of overtaking opportunities. 'Dust is dust and dirt is dirt,' he said. 'And if you are the guy on the dust or dirt and you are the guy who has it on his tyres, then you're not going to be able to go as quickly as the guy who is on the better line and who has clean tyres. It's as simple as that.'

Only Damon Hill, of those who had actually tried the tyres, appeared to have any favourable comment. 'It's total nonsense to talk about the car being impossible to drive,' the World Champion said. 'I mean, it has less grip and it just goes slower. It's like driving in the wet; when you take rubber off the road, the car just slides around more. From a performance point of view it's not enjoyable to drive. You don't get a buzz from going flat-out and hanging on through the corners and being impressed by the level of g force, you know? By the same token, you actually have to drive the car on the grooved tyres. Instead of the corners being flat-out, you actually have to slide the car, drift it . . . and play with the throttle. That's my experience of it. I would say I was not as dismayed by the grooved tyres as I thought I was going to be. But when I put my slicks back on, I thoroughly enjoyed myself – because I went faster.'

* * *

Mosley loves to dazzle his audiences with a few historical facts apparently plucked carelessly from memory. At Monaco in 1997 he said: 'Take the example of an old circuit, Brands Hatch, which once hosted Grand Prix races and has not changed fundamentally in 30 years – apart from being slightly slower now. The pole position time at the British GP there in 1968 – which was the last year without aerodynamic aids – was exactly the same as the best time established at the same circuit by a modern Class 2 touring car. The Formula 1 car had 450 bhp, rear-wheel drive, half a ton in weight, and it also had the best driver in the world behind the wheel.

Contrast that with the 2 litre touring car race in 1995, where the pole position was set by a production-based car weighing one ton, 330 bhp, front-wheel drive, and all the limitations imposed by the touring car regulations. The driver, without being too unkind, would probably accept that he wasn't the best in the world, either. But the times were the same. The only possible factor to have made this possible was the tyres.

'If you look at pole position at Monza in 1963, with no aerodynamics, and the last person on the grid there for the F2 race in 1968, you'll find that the F2 person was quicker. That's tyres.'

Without being too unkind, it was possible to drive a coach and horses through this sort of simplistic argument, which took no account of progress in things such as braking efficiency or engine management systems, and rather conveniently overlooked the fact that Graham Hill's pole-winning Lotus 49B did, in fact, have a gigantic overhead wing mounted on the rear axle, not to mention wide nose fins. Or that John Surtees was on pole at Monza in 1963 with a time of 1 min 37.3 sec, compared to the slowest 1968 F2 practice time of 1 min 43.8 sec, set by Robs Lamplough (though Derek Bell's pole time was quicker, at 1 min 33.3 sec).

'The rate of development of tyres has been extraordinary,' Mosley continued. 'And in the end you have to face the fact that if you want to keep the speeds within reason, you've got to do something about the tyres. There will obviously still be a great technical challenge for the tyre manufacturers. The problems which they face are, in fact, more closely linked to those which they face with their production road-going tyres. These huge companies are completely capable of resolving those problems. Meanwhile, we, as a federation, find ourselves in a situation which allows us to react if the tyre companies are too ingenious or clever. We would be able to increase the size of the grooves, or add a groove, as we wish. There would be no limit to any steps that we might wish to take to keep tyre performance under control. And if we start to work closely with the tyre manufacturers, this problem should go away.'

There was sense in this, but it was undermined by the existence of the tyre war in Formula 1. After all, lap times had plummeted, and this simply suggested that though grooved tyres would initially slow things down, such would be the likely pace of development as Goodyear and Bridgestone continued to slug it out – with Michelin rumoured to be joining in too by 1999 – that the same escalation in lap speeds would continue no matter how many grooves there were. And, as one cynic suggested, what did you get but a slick again when you cut enough grooves in a tyre to cover its width?

The majority of people in the paddock subscribed to a wholly different view: that the FIA should allow softer, wider tyres and instead seriously curtail aerodynamics to limit cornering speeds. But that view was steadfastly ignored, and Mosley had a counter-argument ready.

'Having switched to a one-make Formula 3000, we learned a lot about single-seaters and aerodynamics. In making the transfer, we took the opportunity to reduce downforce by 50 per cent, and also – of course, because it is a one-make series – to eliminate all aerodynamic development. The change in lap times was an increase of about two seconds. In other words, if we had had a tyre war in Formula 3000, the cars would have been going quicker, despite the reduction of 50 per cent in downforce. This indicates that the most important element is the tyre.'

Mosley had an even more compelling reason for opting to take the grooved tyre route, and it was eminently simple and practical. He is, after all, a very pragmatic politician. Changing the Technical Regulations was a mammoth task that could not be achieved overnight, even with the new-for-1997 requirement of only 80 per cent agreement between signatories of the Concorde Agreement. But as Head had pointed out, tyres fell under the Sporting Regulations, and thus were within the direct province of Mosley and Ecclestone, who could change them almost at will under the auspices of safety considerations. It was, at a stroke, an inspired means of exerting absolute control over the teams. What did it matter, then, if it appeared, to those who thought control of aerodynamics was probably more important, to be tackling the ever-present problem of escalating speed by holding the wrong end of the cudgel? But what the grooved tyre plan really needed to make it work properly seemed more to be a supply monopoly, similar to those in Formula 3000 and Formula 3 wherein a company would bid for a three-year contract to supply control tyres. But that would never have fitted the FIA's cake-and-eat-it philosophy of controlling Formula 1's technical progress while selling the world an image of unfettered technological development.

Chapter 14

A benign dictator?
– the FIA's view

'If you imagine that you are a Formula 1 team, and you are going to spend many, many millions of dollars on a driver, you've got to be very sure that some other team can't wipe that out by just cheating. There's an awful lot of money at stake.'

Max Mosley, President, FIA

THERE ARE SOME PEOPLE in the Formula 1 paddocks who think that Max Mosley is simply fulfilling his role as president of the *Federation Internationale de l'Automobile* as a stepping stone to greater things within the European Parliament. That this son of the controversial British politician, Sir Oswald Mosley, who was interned during the Second World War for espousing the cause of Adolf Hitler, is merely trying to carve out for himself outside his own country the political career that his father's wartime sympathy and passionate support for Fascism subsequently prevented him from achieving in the land of his birth.

Mosley is an independently wealthy man who delights in explaining that he does not draw a salary from the FIA. (His mother, Diana Guinness, who was interned at Holloway prison at the time of his wartime birth, is one of the celebrated Mitford sisters.) He smiles at such suggestions, and gives self-deprecating, deliberately inconclusive answers. He is often inconsistent, and

history reveals that he has changed his mind on several issues, though the more opposition he meets, the more likely he is to dig his heels in. Cynics point out that, having supported technology to the hilt, he then performed a complete *volte face* that saw him ban its excesses, and later introduce swingeing changes to the new regulations in the wake of the San Marino GP tragedies of 1994, simply because he detected the direction of the prevailing political wind and made sure that he was not facing into it. Again, Mosley smiles at such suggestions, as if to imply that this was indeed quite possible.

But though he once described the key element of his role, tongue in cheek, as being: 'The ability to appear to be a gentleman while being completely self-serving,' his motivations were more in keeping with an attempt to maintain motor sport as an acceptable undertaking. By taking positive action at the right times, he might thus ensure that it did not attract unwanted attention from powerful environmental lobbies seeking a fresh *cause célèbre* into which to sink their protectionist teeth.

Certainly, he cuts a controversial figure, and at times all other parties in Formula 1 – from the drivers to the designers, the team owners, and even the media – have had cause to feel patronized, angered, and even duped. Yet in his own world, Mosley is indeed a consummate politician, and his handling of the aftermath of Imola in 1994 not only successfully defused growing international alarm, but also underlined that while his tongue may be silver, the rest of him can be finely tempered steel when it comes to a fight. During that turmoiled season Flavio Briatore and Tom Walkinshaw of Benetton discovered that to their cost.

At the Spanish GP that year there had been a teams' strike on the first day of practice in protest against sudden revisions to the technical regulations carried through in the name of safety, which meant that Mosley was not obliged to take the circuitous route of seeking 100 per cent unanimity from the teams. There was an acrimonious meeting with Mosley that morning, and at lunch-time Briatore and Walkinshaw had returned to the Benetton motorhome and uttered to the waiting media the fateful words: 'Mosley is finished. We have told him which way up things are, and I think you'll find that from now on he will look after the rest of motor-sport where he has plenty to keep him occupied, and leave running Formula 1 to the teams, who know what they are doing.'

Mosley had succeeded the mercurial Frenchman Jean-Marie Balestre as president of what was then the FISA in October 1991, had been re-elected for five years the following season, and had brandished the big stick whenever necessary in the intervening years. But if Briatore and Walkinshaw really believed that they had won, they were in for an unpleasant lesson in political wrangling that would leave both mewling like nursery infants. And some would suggest

Max Mosley, President of the Federation Internationale de l'Automobile. (LAT)

that, many times over during the remainder of that troubled year, Mosley extracted his pound of flesh from the Benetton carcass.

Looking back, Mosley smiled reflectively at the cathartic moment in which the ground rules, which appear largely to have been respected since, came to be laid down.

'I think that's right. There were one or two people who were a bit over-optimistic in Barcelona,' he said, and to his credit he almost kept a straight face. 'But that's all settled down. Yes, I think on the technical front they realize we are doing an honest and competent job.'

In the initial years of his reign he did not see the FISA's role being to regulate against the sort of runaway success that Williams–Renault had enjoyed in the early 1990s, or which McLaren had achieved throughout 1988 when it won 15 of the 16 races. 'That is entirely a problem for the engineers at McLaren, Ferrari, Benetton, etc. It's not a FISA problem. Our number one priority has to be the safety of the public; number two the safety of the drivers,' he said in 1992. 'There is an argument, however, for us slowing the cars down in the corners; in fact I think it's an overwhelming one. Now that will have the incidental effect of putting up the braking distances, because if you slow the cornering speeds down and you don't do anything else you increase the braking distances. You slightly increase the chances of overtaking, and I think that wouldn't be a bad thing. I think it's too difficult to overtake now. It needs to be possible to overtake. But the present problem at the front of the field is less one of overtaking than of catching Nigel Mansell.'

At that time there were many worries that if electronics were given too much rein the situation might develop wherein the paying public might come to perceive the cars as controlling the drivers, rather than vice versa. 'It's always going to go a bit in that direction,' he countered. 'It's like the difference between a modern fighter 'plane and a Spitfire, or whatever. The fact is that you probably need more qualities to fly a modern fighter than you did a Spitfire in the 'forties.'

When it was suggested that the excitement for spectators had habitually been to see the struggle of the man to control the machine, to do things that ordinary spectators felt they could not, he responded contentiously: 'Yes, but the best driver will still win.' It was a point

that, at times, both Ayrton Senna and Michael Schumacher would strongly disagree with when they found themselves struggling with sub-standard equipment! And when, in 1997, Jacques Villeneuve had obliquely done as Mosley had and suggested that modern pilots were better suited to their role than their forebears, Mosley had reacted with scathing sarcasm.

Williams chief designer Adrian Newey provided a nice postscript to that line of thinking when he said: 'I think the driver's role is shifting slightly, insofar as you no longer have the weekend hero with bags of natural skill who just turns up with his helmet and off he goes. He has to have, not necessarily an understanding of how everything works, but an understanding of how to give good technical feedback. I think talk of the driver's contribution or skill being any less is absolute rubbish. The comparison I like to think of is if you take an F15 pilot and say that it's easy for him with his fly-by-wire controls; when he wants to go hard left he slings the stick over to left and then the computer takes over and sets all the flap and aileron settings to give that hard left turn because there's no mechanical link. I suppose you could argue that therefore some of the pilot's skill is taken away insofar as he doesn't have to do that for himself; but if you suggest that the F15 pilot is less skilled than a Spitfire pilot, he wouldn't really agree with you. It's just shifting emphasis, if you like. But the best driver is still going to be the best driver, basically.'

Reflecting on the situation early in 1997, Mosley said: 'The fundamental thing was that until then you'd had motor sport and ordinary motoring really run along similar lines. I think the split came when we realized that the direction in which road cars were going was not, after all, desirable for motor sport and that we had, in motor sport, to stop all sorts of things that were going to become everyday in road cars. If we didn't do that we would get to the point where a racing driver was really a computer operator, rather than a racing driver, and that would really destroy the whole basis of the sport.

'Although we met a lot of opposition at the time, because people were saying "Why can't I have anti-lock brakes and traction control, I have them on my road car?", I think people realize now that the whole point of motor sport is that you get into a racing car and drive it to the maximum of your ability, and every time you eliminate one element of the skill of doing that, you devalue the sport.

'Of course, it involves enormous difficulty. It's very difficult to write a precise rule how you're going to stop those elements coming in because somebody wants a differential that does, electronically, what it has been doing quite normally for many years mechanically. Questions like that. Various gearchange procedures. They've all got an element of automatic in the sense that they have a press-button gearchange.

'Another thing that we've just done, we've said for 1997 that we will not object to a stall prevention device, so that if a driver spins the electronics stop the engine stalling. That is a driver aid by any sensible definition, but on the other hand it's much safer if he can get the car going and he's not stuck in the middle of the track, both for him and for the marshals.

'But what's happened is that when we bought in the original prohibition there was a lot of opposition from the teams, and we had an elaborate rule about driver aids, saying more or less what they were, and prohibiting them. And one well-known team manager didn't like all these explanations and said could we delete them? Which I was delighted to do. So we ended up with a rule which just said that driver aids are prohibited, and the teams were then going to decide what driver aids were. They were unable, needless to say, to agree, and that left the

FIA in the happy position of itself being able to decide at any moment what a driver aid is. And what happens in real life is that the teams, when they've got some new device, send it in and our technical delegate, Charlie Whiting, says yes or no. And that's been working for three years, and it actually works very well because it saves the team the expense of building something which is then thrown out at scrutineering. And it enables everyone to know where they are. Then we publish to all the teams the things we have said no to, so they don't waste their time, but obviously we don't publish the things we've said yes to because obviously the team might want to keep something like that secret. But we are very, very careful to apply the principles very fairly, and up to now there have been no complaints.

'And, of course, if a team disagreed with our findings they could go to the stewards, because all we are offering is an opinion, it's not legally binding. We, if you like, are the executive and there is a completely separate judiciary, which is the stewards and the FIA Court of Appeal. So if anyone disagreed with us they could turn up with it anyway, Charlie could complain to the stewards, who could find for or against our view. And then one side or the other, us or the team, could appeal to the FIA Court of Appeal, and then that would decide the matter. So far that's never happened.'

And who appoints the stewards? 'I do,' Mosley said, his straight face cracking into a smile which became a laugh. 'But, you see, you appoint people but you don't tell them what to do. And the FIA Court of Appeal is completely independent, that's ordinary lawyers from the big motoring clubs who have nothing to do with the sport at all. I think most people would accept that the stewards are independent, and that they hold the balance between the teams and our technical people.' Some, however, believe that the FIA not only holds all the cards, but actually prints them, since it can choose whether to recognize the ASNs, the local clubs in each country, from which such independent lawyers are chosen.

★ ★ ★

In 1994 there was a great deal of argument on technical matters, and several teams were very unhappy about surrendering technical information, such as source codes, to the FIA. 'I think there were two elements,' Mosley responded. 'One was that the source codes and engine management systems were very often the property of a major manufacturer, and it's not the sort of thing they want to hand around. And secondly, the view back in '93 was that we would never be able to check these things. Some Formula 1 cars now have 300,000 lines of source code; if you take all the programmes, the different little chips they've got, that could be the worst figure. To begin with they said you'll never check it because you'll never be able to get into the codes. But that was easy, I just said if you're not prepared to hand the codes over, don't bother to come to a race. We're not going to let people compete if we can't check what they're competing with. So that argument lasted a few weeks and then they handed over the source codes.

'And then it was whether we had the skills to check them. I think the "launch control" controversy demonstrated that. Benetton had left it in the system. They were not using it, but it was there, and I think the fact that we found it surprised everyone. The significant thing was that when we found that, that was the beginning of the teams accepting that we were capable of doing that, and now I think that our people go and meet their people and these elaborate checks are done, and that works well. With the top teams particularly, we have what we call Option One where we check it all beforehand, and they realize that our people are experts and I think there is a lot of confidence that we are able to check. That is absolutely fundamental, because if you imagine that you are a Formula 1 team, and you are going to spend many, many millions of dollars on a driver, you've got to be very sure that some other team can't wipe that out by just cheating. There's an awful lot of money at stake. But in the paddock now, though one mustn't be complacent, you don't hear the suggestion that other teams are cheating.

'We had the same thing with fuel, and the way we dealt with that initial hiccough at the start of 1995 has built confidence. Again, I don't want to be complacent, but I think the teams have realized that we are very serious about it, and that we do have very good people.' Some would even suggest that, in some cases within the FIA, the poachers have turned gamekeeper.

Whether the teams like it or not, the Mosley administration has always been hands-on. 'That's true. I think there is a danger, if you are in sport's administration, to be seen as old buffers in blazers, and who don't understand the modern sport. We had to take control, because if we didn't something else would have. In the end, had it been right that we weren't able to do it, the teams would have had to find somebody else themselves, they couldn't just have gone on in an anarchic situation. But I think in the end it's worked out quite well.'

Mosley allowed that he was happy enough with the way in which he had handled the overall situation since 1993, and in particular the manner in which the FIA dealt with the aftermath – especially the global politics – of the Senna accident.

'I think it was the only thing to do. There are moments when you have to take the lead, simply because of public opinion. Very often the teams live in their own small world, they don't understand the effect of public opinion on big sponsors, the engine suppliers, the major manufacturers, all these people, and I think it was necessary to do that and the fact that the public reaction is irrational doesn't make any difference. It's no good telling people they are being irrational. You need to defuse such situations. And what many people failed to realize at the time was just how much pressure was growing in certain places for an end to motor sport. There were even questions being asked in the Italian Parliament. Some sort of restorative action was essential.'

Things had found their own level by 1995, and since then the FIA has reached a new conclusion on the vexed subject of containing performance levels, by concentrating on the tyres. In many respects the major surgery had been carried out in the aftermath of Imola in 1994, and only cosmetics were now required, but of course the situation changes every year because such is the technical ingenuity that goes into the cars that the performance increases continually. It is salutary to consider that the 1997 Formula 1 cars, with their 740 bhp, 3 litre engines, were lapping far faster than their counterparts with 1,400 bhp, 1.5 litre turbocharged power units had been a decade earlier.

'What we've got to do now is to prevent the cars getting so much faster every year, so that they present a danger,' Mosley said. 'And as we learn more and more about passive safety, so we build in things like the rear crash test, side impact, better head protection.

'The theory now is that if we can reduce the grip of the tyres, we can keep the performance under control. The teams will find some performance in the chassis, and if it gets excessive we can control it by reducing the size of the tyre's contact patch. And although the tyre companies are not exactly delighted by it, I think they will come to see that it is in fact putting technology more in a road car direction.'

Tyre manufacturers tend to be ignored until and unless something goes wrong, as Goodyear discovered when Nigel Mansell lost the 1986 World Championship because of that dramatic puncture on Dequetteville Terrace at Adelaide, and Mosley also argued that his new philosophy would focus more attention on them. 'It's a new technical challenge for them, there's no doubt about that, and it would mean new compounds and new structures.'

For 1997 the FIA also attempted to contain costs in Formula 1 by reducing testing, although it subsequently backtracked slightly.

'The thing is that things like that have to go through the Formula One Commission,' he said. 'So we said to the Formula One Commission, do you want to do this, this, and this to reduce costs, and they all agreed. Then they all thought about it some more. In the final analysis we think it is a matter for the teams, and we keep urging them to race more and test less, because the irrational person coming from Mars would say that it doesn't make any difference. If you have less testing it's the same for everybody, so why not have, for example, 20 Grands Prix and, for example, five test days, rather than 17 Grands Prix and 20 test days, for the sake of argument. But you have to change the culture. They all think that they are going to gain more from a day's testing than the other teams. In fact it's not true. They might as well stand there shredding hundred dollar bills. But this culture will slowly change. We've changed the rallies, where they used to insist on three weeks for reconnaissance and a three-day rally, and of course you could only do eight rallies a year because it took so much time. Now we're up to 14 rallies and only four days reconnaissance, which is a sensible way of doing it.'

Mosley and the FIA recognize that teams will always spend whatever money they have available, and that only the direction of that investment will change in response to limitations, but said: 'All we can try and do is ensure that a team that has twice as much more doesn't get twice as much performance. The ideal rules would be such that you got to a quite modest level of money and then no matter how much you spent you wouldn't go any quicker. I think the main thing we have to try and do is make sure it doesn't become a money-spending contest, but much more a contest between engineers. The Colin Chapmans and the Keith Duckworths ought to be able to succeed even though they've got less money. As they very much have done historically. And testing is a very, very expensive thing.'

* * *

There was a hint of nostalgia in some of Mosley's comments, but it does not extend to regret that the cars have all come to resemble one another so closely because the rules are so rigid. 'First of all I don't think that can be helped if you want to keep performance under control. But the other thing is, suppose you went completely the other way and just had a box. And said, so long as your car fits into that box and the engine is not more than x litres, do what you like. If you did that, you'd then get another phenomenon, which is the greater the freedom the greater the waste because the greater the freedom the greater the number of possible solutions. People would obviously choose a variety and one would prove to be the best, and if you don't change the rule they would iterate down to the best solution, but at enormous cost because they would throw away all the other stuff. So if you had the box, and the box stayed the same size for 20 years, the cars would all look the same anyway. And if you had the box there would be an enormous expenditure on research and in five or 10 years' time, probably quicker than that, they would all end up with the same thing, having spent a great deal of money. And the cars might look different, but they'd all be the same.'

Mosley's relationship with Formula 1's ultimate powerbroker, Bernie Ecclestone, has long been a source of speculation and wonder. Ecclestone is the vice president of marketing for the FIA, and also president of FOCA, the Formula One Constructors' Association, which was largely made redundant when he and Mosley managed to steamroller through the revisions to the Concorde Agreement for 1997 which, among other things, reduced the need for 100 per cent unanimity on technical decision-making to 80 per cent. It also opened up the purse strings for television revenue. Mosley liked to refer to Ecclestone as 'the Commercial Rights Holder', in allusion to Ecclestone's 15-year contract with the FIA to sell its commercial interests, but few doubt who holds the ultimate power, nor who was instrumental in ensuring that Mosley was duly elected as president of the FISA. The two of them go back a long, long way, to the days when Mosley was FOCA's lawyer and drew up the original Concorde Agreement, which brought peace in the long-running feud between the teams – FOCA – and the governing body – the FISA – during the troubled early-1980s.

It was thus of interest that Ecclestone appeared to strike a note of discord in Argentina early in 1997, then hold out hope for greater stability, when he said: 'I really believe that there is no proof that narrowing the cars down will do whatever we want it to do. I think the FIA are looking into it. If it is wrong and it's not an advantage, for sure everyone will change. But the safety measures for the structures, and things like that, are such now that they're built like tanks and won't need anything further done to them for a few years after that.

'If we had the regulations from five years ago, the grid would be closer, because the have-nots would have caught up. Every time we change something, the guys with the money say "No problem, let's change", and the other guys are struggling. So I think you'll find after 1998 that there will be no need, from a safety aspect, to do anything and I think you'll find the regulations will be fixed for a longer period.'

At this time Patrick Head and Frank Williams were in dispute with the FIA over the terms of the new Concorde Agreement, and in conjunction with McLaren and Tyrrell had refused to sign it, thus forfeiting lucrative television revenues. Each of the renegade teams was threatening to take the FIA to court for alleged restrictive practice, and in the recent past Williams had accused Ecclestone and Mosley of trying to adopt the style of the autocratic NASCAR series for stock cars in America, and of trying to manoeuvre teams into a position where the FIA could dictate everything the way that Bill France Jr did and his legendary late father used to do. Mosley did not demur when it was suggested that benign dictatorship is usually the only thing that ever makes progressive sense, since somewhere along the line one individual should always carry the final can.

'From my point of view nothing's wrong with the idea, except that it takes time,' he said when the idea of changing the Concorde Agreement was mooted yet again in 1996. 'But what I say to them when they say we've got no clear regulations, is that you write them all out, clear regulations, and you all sign them. Or, we'll write them out and you all sign them. But because we can't change the regulations without everybody signing, everybody's got to sign. Nothing would please me more than crystal clear regulations that a child could enforce, and you let the whole thing get on with it. You don't have to think about that, you can think about other things. But they can't do it, because they can never agree . . .'

Bernie Ecclestone, Vice President of Marketing for the FIA, President of FOCA, Rights Holder for the FIA's commercial activities – and the ultimate power-broker of Formula 1. (LAT)

And therein lay the rub that so often militated against change in Formula 1. Hand in glove with that at that time went the call for the Concorde Agreement – the document that bound Formula 1 together in the aftermath of the FISA/FOCA war, yet which had progressively come to hamstring it – to receive a comprehensive and overdue overhaul. If he had had his way Mosley would have changed it immediately, although the irony of unpicking much of the work he had put into it back in the early-1980s was certainly not lost on him. In a way, he had become a victim of his own bygone efficiency.

'I think that the Concorde Agreement had outlived its usefulness,' he said early in 1997. 'And, really, there ought to be a mechanism whereby you consult with everyone, and when you've finished consulting that's it. The FIA takes a decision by whatever means, the Formula One Commission and all the rest of it. But I don't know what they want, because they can't agree unanimously and yet they want to keep the Concorde Agreement.'

NASCAR had been through much of Formula 1's angst in its past, and had had its own unpopular decisions. Whenever they downsized, or changed things so that Ford didn't win and Chevrolet did, or vice versa, they were playing with sizeable corporations which in theory could go ahead with legal action to protect their own interests. Somehow, though, it had never come to that, and NASCAR continued to put on a dramatically popular show. Mosley acknowledged the point. 'I think they've negotiated their way through very cleverly, and if you remember at the end of the 'sixties, beginning of the 'seventies, they stopped the technology and they went down their present route with fixed technology, and all of Detroit said: "That's it, we'll never come back because we want to demonstrate our products to the American public." And now Detroit is as enthusiastic as ever, with the fixed technology.'

In other words, once the storm in Formula 1's teacup abated, everything could be expected to settle down again. As Patrick Head might have said, 'twas ever thus. Until the next crisis stirred everything up again, and ensured that even off-track, Formula 1 never had a dull moment.

The FIA approach thus remained to define the target while encouraging each team to use a high-powered rifle rather than a scatter-gun to try and hit the bull's eye. 'It's probably the most efficient way,' Mosley suggested. 'And I think you do need to change. Cars will look funny when they are 180 cm wide with grooved tyres, but that's part of progress. If they looked the same year after year people would get bored with them. You must remember that this is not a static sport, and some of the things the designers think of are very, very clever. Some of the things they are thinking of doing and want to have ratified, which come in here for assessment, are fascinating. There are a lot of very clever people in Formula 1. And then you have to ask whether they are trying to do the thing which we all know that they mustn't do, which is to replace the driver with a computer, or is it a very clever way of doing what they should be doing, which is making a better racing car? Sometimes it's not obvious . . .'

From time immemorial there has always been a certain element of confrontation between the teams and the sport's governing body, and Mosley is the man tasked with two-stepping his way through the political minefield as he seeks to lead the sport back to the Nirvana it deserted when the question of downforce got so out of hand in the Seventies.

'I'm trying very hard!' he asserted. 'I suppose that the only thing I can claim is that I do understand the problems of running a team. I understand the other side, after my time with March. But of course the difficulty is that there's also conflict between teams because teams are always trying to get a certain advantage. There's always bound to be somebody that's pushing the limits of the regulations somewhere.'

And somebody trying to stop them.

Chapter 15

The designers' view

'Max keeps coming out with this thing of "Every O-level schoolboy knows . . ."
And the fact of the matter is that Max doesn't know, but he keeps quoting the O-
level schoolboy who does. Well, I have to say I'd like to see this fellow . . .'

Patrick Head, Technical Director, Williams

IN MANY WAYS THE disparate roles of the Formula 1 designer and the FIA president are mutually incompatible. Like poacher and gamekeeper, the two frequently find it hard to settle down together. The former is dedicated to using all of his intellect and ability – and his team's budget – to make his cars go faster than they did the previous year. The latter is dedicated to preventing this, and to keeping some sort of restriction on the evolution of performance so that Formula 1 avoids a continuous spiral wherein the cars get quicker and quicker to the point where the circuits must often be modified to keep pace with them. One could almost use the analogy of the FIA as a benign parent trying to keep a precocious child in check, except that the Formula 1 designers are among the most intelligent people one is likely to rub shoulders with, and the FIA is not always benign.

For the most part the designers accept with good grace the need for technological revision to maintain a natural balance, but occasionally there are spats with the governing body such as the one that generated so much acrimony with the banning of electronic 'gizmos' in 1993. And because they are such individuals, and so competitive, it is scant surprise that the boffins rarely appear able to agree amongst themselves on the best course of future action.

Whether the FIA really had got the regulations right for 1997, let alone 1998, was a cause for much debate, and as usual where the technical directors and designers are concerned, there was no shortage of pertinent comment.

* * *

Where some of the less well-heeled teams welcomed the ban on 'gizmos', few of the designers did, for each jealously guards his right to lateral thinking and to push the limits of technology. In some ways it's no different to the reaction of a writer asked not to use big words.

Adrian Newey, who made his name as chief designer for Leyton House before filling a similar role at Williams between

Adrian Newey, the much sought-after design guru who cut his teeth with Leyton House March, made his name with Williams, and now faces a fresh challenge at McLaren. As a rare designer/driver, he also raced a Williams FW16 at the Goodwood Festival of Speed in 1995. (LAT/ICN UK Bureau)

1991 and 1997 and then leaving to join McLaren as technical director, was cautious in his response to the possibility of banning anything.

'As far as the banning of anything goes, the first thing that you have to be very careful about is what you ban. For instance, IndyCars banned semi-automatic transmissions and active suspension . . . It's all down to costs really, which is all very well, but in the coming years there'll be more road cars with active ride and semi-automatics and then you'll have the rather absurd position where road cars will be more sophisticated than racing cars. That's one of the things you've got to be very careful of.'

Ross Brawn, who began his career with Williams and moved via Arrows and Benetton to Ferrari as technical director by 1997, accepted the passing of the electronic era philosophically. 'Well, it's history, isn't it? It was good fun, and it was good fun because we were good at it at Benetton. But I suppose you could say I was wary of it because as a mechanical engineer it meant that the software engineers and the vehicle dynamicists were starting to rule the roost. And I guess in a way that I wasn't so happy about that, because whereas we have a lot of sophisticated analysis equipment now, I can at least understand how a car is working. I can do the changes on an empirical base or a theoretical base, what have you. But active suspension was getting on to a different level. There was a certain level I could understand, and then there was another level of control engineering that was just beyond my experience and understanding. So in some ways, I think we've probably gone in the right direction, for me personally, anyway.'

'I don't really care that they banned all that stuff, because I think it's just the same, you know?' said Gary Anderson, the Jordan technical director, who had previously been in Formula 1 as a mechanic with Brabham and McLaren

Formerly with Williams, Arrows, and Benetton, Ross Brawn now controls the technical side at Ferrari. (Author)

in the 1970s. 'You just have to look at it in a different direction. I would love to have been in a position at that time to have built a fully active, all singing and dancing vehicle, but we had an active front suspension, that was all. We did it as a test kit, and then it got banned, so we were unable to exploit completely our potential understanding of it all.

'When they changed the regulations our way of looking at it had to be that we were a small team, and if we could get

Gary Anderson, a former mechanic with McLaren, who designed his own Formula 3 and Formula SuperVee cars in the early 1980s before switching to IndyCars and then returning to Formula 1 as technical director when Jordan graduated. (Author)

some change made that could hurt the big teams more than us, even though they had more manpower to sort it all out in the end, then in the short-term we could maybe move quicker. But when you give the big teams stability, they'll always move away from the small teams. I don't know where we are at the minute, whether we're a big team or a small team. But we're able to keep the same influence we had as a small team, in that we are able to react pretty quick-

ly but yet have a structure behind us that is strong enough to be a big team.'

Frank Dernie, who designed the Hesketh 308E back in 1977 and then moved in stages via Williams, Lotus, Benetton, and Ligier to become technical director at Arrows, a position he relinquished in mid-1997, still nursed trenchant views about the ban.

'I didn't think it was right then, and I'm still of that opinion!' But he enjoys arguing a situation through, and added: 'On the other hand, we are very unbalanced now. You have a situation where the amount of technology that you could really use in the chassis is extremely limited, whereas the amount you can use in the engine is close to unlimited, as far as electronics are concerned. If you really want to reduce costs, the cost of building a racing car, you could ban anything electronic on the car – no batteries, no alternators, no nothing, just a magneto for the ignition and either carburettors or fuel injectors. Then you'd have no telemetry, that'd save you £150,000 per car; no computers, you'd probably be able to get rid of a third of the travelling people; no data logger, so the driver would come into play much more with his feel and be able to keep things more to himself if he wanted to. It would actually change the motor racing very much, although of course you would actually just spend the budget saving elsewhere. It would be technologically less interesting for a lot of people, but the driver would be much more important again and that would reduce the cost enormously. That's probably a quarter of the money that you spend a year, goes on all of that stuff . . . For the engine people, it's probably more than that.'

★ ★ ★

The question of whether the FIA got the regulations right for 1997, let alone 1998, provoked equally interesting views that suggested that the FIA was moving

Irrepressible, outspoken and garrulous, Frank Dernie's first Formula 1 design was the Hesketh 308E back in 1977. (LAT)

in the opposite direction to anything the designers wanted.

'Well, there hasn't been an absolute wheel-to-wheel ding-dong for the length of a race, but you'd have to say the racing has been closer in 1997 than it was last year, which is really just due to stability,' said Patrick Head, chief technical architect of Williams's staggering achievement of 100 GP victories in less than 20 seasons. 'If you have stability for a length of time, it closes up. If you change the regs in a big way, the teams with the better resources who are able to respond more quickly, and maybe are able to go out testing with something while they are running and developing the car the year before, will inevitably benefit from regulation changes. But we haven't been the ones pushing the new 1998 regulations; that's come from the FIA.

'As for them, I'm not a fan of limiting the speed of the cars by restricting the capability of the tyres, because we've got engines that produce well over 700 bhp and very high degrees of performance from the brakes. Okay, the latter will be cut back a fraction then too, but it is only a fraction. So you've got a lot of capability to give the tyres lots of aggro, from the engine and from the brakes.

'The thing is that if you limit the speed of the car by the capability of the tyre, then in general what it means is that you've got to have drivers who pussyfoot. And by that I mean drivers who drive very smoothly and look after the tyres and don't get the car out of line. And I have to say that I like seeing Grand Prix cars being thrown around. Basically, we should almost go out and

Patrick Head, architect of Williams's staggering record of 100 GP victories within 20 years. (Author)

beg Alain Prost to come back as a driver for 1998, because they will suit him down to the ground! He would be perfect for that kind of car. But Jean-Christophe Boullion said the car was just so boring to drive, and that the limit of it wasn't very high. And before you were well into exploring the limit, if you got up to the area where a not-so-good driver could get to, you could go a lot quicker by going beyond that, but you were just destroying the tyres. And he said that anybody could drive to that level, to the level at which you are starting to damage the tyres. He didn't quite say that I could go out there and do it, but that was his approach!

'The idea that cars will slide around again and be exciting to watch is nonsense. What it does is give the FIA control. If they think the cars are far too fast they can just ask for an extra groove to be put into the tyres. But giving the FIA control over car performance is not necessarily the purpose of what racing is all about.'

'It's difficult to say,' Anderson thought. 'If you look back before Roland Ratzenberger and Ayrton Senna were killed, it was a long time since anybody was really hurt. And we could be sitting in that little time zone right now, and another weekend could highlight something completely different. So I don't think you can ever look at it and say that you've fixed it. You've done something marvellous and nobody's gonna get killed again. What I think the FIA had done by 1997 was address the situation quite well, quite sensibly. The side impact stuff, that means there does have to be a good structure beside you there. We tested the rear impact thing quite well at Silverstone when Giancarlo Fisichella crashed. It did us a good job and saved us quite a lot of money.

'So I think it's all going the right way, but we shouldn't have the big change that is scheduled for 1998. We should address it very carefully and very gently,

and create a change so that, visually, you really can't see a difference. It needs subtle areas defined a bit more. And that means that all your research isn't thrown out the window. To make the cars safer you have to spend the design time in coming up with a concept that will work, and also to spend some time thinking how you will make it better. And while there are massive changes in the regulations, the total effort is going into development and performance. And the niceties of making something a bit better disappear on you. That's not really a very practical solution. It should be a constant thing.

'Safety is safety, though, so where do you draw the line? Accidents can and do happen. Motor racing is dangerous. And if you want to influence the relative perception of the public of the sport, then what's wrong with making it safer?'

Jordan had its 1998 car ready to run in the wind-tunnel as early as April 1997, which Anderson admitted was early for what was still a relatively small team though, effectively, a measure of its growth. But he ran into the age-old problem of definitive regulations: 'We had got it all ready to run, but the next thing we heard was that maybe they were going to let the new 1998 regulations fall by the wayside. That was quite frustrating, because we just didn't know what to build.

'If the regulations went ahead, the drag of the cars would go down because they would be narrower and the frontal area would be less, so of course the cars would be faster in a straight line. But if the car's track was narrower we would need to start again in the wind-tunnel, looking at the influence of the narrower track on airflow along the sides of the car.'

'I think that you have to remember that a lot of the proposed changes came about from a lot of work between the FIA and Technical Working Group,' reminded Brawn. 'And you have to accept that Formula 1 cars, after a period, are going too fast. I think there is a certain risk element in Formula 1, but there is a limit, and I don't think that we should allow the thing to spiral in a way that it exceeds those limits. So it's necessary to have a periodic change in regulations to cut the speed back, and so long as that's done in a controlled and negotiated way, then the teams shouldn't complain. I think there's a reasonable relationship between the teams and the FIA to enable that to happen.'

Anderson, however, wasn't sure that the Technical Working Group enjoyed a great deal of self-determination. 'Basically, you sometimes feel it's a bit of a fad to be honest. It's okay, it is there for discussing things and you can duck and dive a bit. But we're never sure what the brief is, that's the problem. We're never sure where it's coming from. There's this pretty big change coming for 1998 with this narrow track, and there's a lot of people fighting it. And we're trying to plan to get next year's car underway, and we don't know what to build. It could change back in a week's time to something different.'

Dernie wasn't particularly optimistic, either. 'Well, the Technical Working Group operates in a very, very tight framework, because we are only actually authorized to discuss the things we have particularly been asked to discuss. We haven't got an open brief. We are given something specific: please make cars which won't go any quicker next year than they did this; or please make cars with 30 per cent less downforce. But if the way we come up with looks like something certain people don't like, it tends not to happen.' So wings, for example, would have to stay? 'Possibly.'

Back in Barcelona in 1994 Brawn's then employers, Flavio Briatore and Tom Walkinshaw at Benetton, thought that the teams had effectively overthrown FIA President Max Mosley, and that he would thereafter look after the sport outside Formula 1 while the teams determined their own future. They were sadly mistaken, however, as Mosley fought back and outflanked them, and Brawn said in 1997: 'That's all behind us now, and out of that has come a stronger desire to put together regulations in a way that, within reason, suits everyone.'

'I think we've got cars that are much nicer to drive than they were a few years ago,' thought Dernie. 'I think the 1998 rules will give us safer cars, because they will do slower lap times, so if that's the objective, then, yes, they've got the regs right.'

* * *

Twenty years ago every Formula 1 car had its own distinctive, individual look. A Lotus 78, for example, was unlikely to be mistaken for a Ferrari 312T2, a Wolf WR1, a McLaren M26, or an Ensign N177, let alone a Brabham BT45 or a Tyrrell P34. But as the 1990s progressed, Formula 1 cars became so intrinsically similar that, were they to be presented in their natural carbon black colour, it would be difficult to tell one from the other. The truth was that Formula 1 had become just too clever for its own good, to the point where control had to be ever tighter. Ross Brawn reflected on this similarity bred from increasingly restrictive rules which laid down the precise dimensions designers had to acknowledge.

'Well, you can't go backwards, can you? I don't know what the alternatives are. With the knowledge of aerodynamics, all you can fundamentally do is restrict the size of the surfaces that people are using. I mean, if you throw those surfaces open, make them much bigger, give them much more scope, then it's . . . Put it this way. There is a process in Formula 1 of studying what everyone else is doing, to see if it's better or worse than what you are doing, and by that process each team will look at each other and that tends to make it all evolve into a common solution. Sometimes that takes one or two years.

'In the past I don't think teams really had the resources to do that. They tended to have their own path to follow, and looking at others' solutions was just regarded as very time-consuming. You were often better just following your own ideas properly rather than getting distracted by lots of others. Whereas these days there is more capacity for studying what other people are doing, and for looking at other ideas. I mean, the high nose is fairly commonplace now, isn't it? And that's taken two or three years. That's the sort of evolution you get.'

'I personally do believe that the regulations are too definitive these days,' said Dernie, 'but I stress that that is very much a personal view. I would much sooner have more open, freer rules, but that would just be from an I'd-have-more-fun point of view. I think that from a technical point of view you get most enjoyment from having a car that's three seconds a lap faster than everyone else's and just kicking their backsides, but that probably isn't what the FIA's objective is . . . What I would like to see in the rules, and what the FIA would like to see, are probably two very different things from that point of view.'

One might be forgiven for taking the cynical view that the teams annually spend more and more money on technology, just to make cars that are more and more similar . . .

'Because the regulations are so tight, it costs more money to make smaller differences,' Dernie continued, 'so whilst 20 years ago you went to the wind-tunnel six times a year and were disappointed if you didn't come back with 30 per cent more downforce, and it had cost you £200 a day to get it, nowadays you have to spend several orders of magnitude more money than that and if you were to get six per cent a year improvement it would be like Christmas!'

Nick Wirth, chief designer at Benetton, disagreed. 'I don't think the regulations are too restrictive, not at all really. There are still massively more than enough things I can think of that we can do to improve the car, that we just can't work on. What I tried to do in 1997 was to structure the design and development programme very rigidly. So if you went to the design and drawing office in March the engineers would probably have been able to tell you what they would be working on in August, which was very unusual for Benetton. And that was because we'd really started work on the '98 car early. That was just the way I like to work. I like to plan ahead. And I'd still have that facility even though I was engineering Gerhard's car at races. What I had done was to structure the design office; they are more than capable of managing themselves. My role was to catalyse the ideas, to say these are the areas, this is what is important, this is what I want to try and achieve . . . To be very open about it and let them come up with the solution. I didn't want to present them with something fixed. I wanted to oversee, make suggestions, and then let them get on with it. And just make sure that the ideas were coming through for the developments.

'Designing and running a department is all a matter of productivity. What allows you to improve efficiency? What allows you to do more? It's the quality of the people that you have, the way you organize them, and the way information flows through the company. And trying to make sure that you aren't doing the same job twice.

'And the third thing is the technology that you give the people. If you're writing a story and I give you a very good word processor, to come out with a final printed document is going to be quicker than writing it down on a piece of paper or using a typewriter. If I give you good technology, you'll do a better job.

'It's exactly the same with a designer. If you give him the best technology available to design, his productivity will improve. It won't double, because that level of technology isn't there, but if you give him a CAD system that takes half a minute to do something and a couple to do something else, and you integrate that saving of time up over a year, that's hundreds of hours. So if you have a CAD system which is fast, and organize the design and manufacturing process, you are going to give those people more time.'

Wirth was more concerned about where the next generation of Formula 1 designers would come from. 'It's worrying, and it's something we are looking at closely at Benetton. I'm 30 years old, and if you look back at what I've been through, not just in terms of Simtek but my design experience and what I've done, it's very difficult to imagine how somebody would now get a similar amount of experience at my age. In fact, I don't think it's possible. And that is a disadvantage that we need to address if we are to fill my shoes if I eventually move on. I think to be a designer you need to understand everything – aerodynamics, suspension design, composites, stress – there's not one area of the car you could afford to ignore. You need to understand electronics, because when the electronics guys tell you that this box has got to be 240 by 60 cm [8 ft by 2 ft] and have a hundred and sixty kilometre [100 mph] wind blowing over it or else it's going to melt down, you've got to be able to tell them not to be stupid, that they know that's not possible. That they have got to do a better job than that. And they think, "Shit, this guy knows what he's talking about."

'So you've even got to know about electronics. Do we need a wiring loom? Can we use a network, can we do it with fibre optics? You've got to know all the areas, and that's a real worry, because Formula 1 is so specialized. You come in,

Putting behind him the tragedy at Simtek, and the little team's eventual demise, Nick Wirth is now chief designer at Benetton and spearheads the new generation. (Author)

and there are guys working on aerodynamics on such specialized areas, computational fluid dynamics, things like that, and they are brilliant and very clever, but they are my age and they are just focused on one area.'

Harvey Postlethwaite, managing director of engineering at Tyrrell, and a man whose past includes the design of James Hunt's Heskeths and the Ferraris that won the Constructors' Championships in 1982 and 1983, knows precisely what Wirth means. 'That is one of the hardest aspects of the job these days,' he said, 'keeping yourself fully up to speed with all aspects of the technological developments both inside and outside of the sport.'

Harvey Postlethwaite: From Lord Hesketh's eponymous team to Tyrrell, via Ferrari and Sauber, Doctor Harvey P is one of Formula 1's most widely experienced, and respected, technical directors. (LAT)

Wirth has all the bouncy resilience of youth, and continued: 'It's up to you to be dynamic and pushy enough to make the effort to find out, and I try to give myself time to do that. I have all these other things I could do, but I spend a lot of time researching. I try and do what is important. It's very important for someone in my position to be very much up to date with all the latest developments in all areas. I may not be right up on the latest developments in surface finishes, or something like that, but if there is something going on there I'll send someone down to bone up on it and condense it down. It's so important to be well read. If you become totally focused on something and don't look at the world of science and engineering around you, I think you're going to be struggling. The sport doesn't stand still.'

★ ★ ★

John Barnard offered some interesting thoughts on future engine regulations as a means of limiting speeds, bearing in mind little-remembered proposals back in 1993 to revert to a 2.5 litre Formula 1 formula:

'There was quite a lot of push for that. In the FIA's Technical Working Group we have said for a long time now – and we all stand by it – that if you've got to slow cars down, you've got to bring down the horsepower as well. You can't just slow the car all the time, and not the engine. And really, how do you restrict engine power? If you start applying artificial things – restrictors, fuel flow valves – you are going to get all sorts of technical problems. And ultimately I think it's more difficult for the smaller engine people to do a decent job. So how do you do it? My contention is that you have to keep chopping the cubic capacity, in regulated steps and with a reasonable amount of notice.

'The fewer cylinders you have the cheaper it is to build the engine. And forget the arguments from the engine manufacturers. There is no such things as fixed regulations, indefinitely. Forget it, it doesn't happen. We are still racing at circuits such as Monaco, with inherent problems that will never go away. Therefore you have to control the cars and the speeds. They always go faster, they always go round corners quicker, they always generate more power. Slowly but surely these things happen. You've got to regulate it, and one way is to limit engine size.

'When you do that your decisions on what you make inevitably change. You've got 3-litre 10s and eights now, and the old 12s are dead. Let's say you wanted to go to 2.5 litres. You then probably say 12s are completely finished, forget it. A 10 might make it, but an eight starts to look more attractive. Go lower, say to 2 litres, and maybe you reach a point where you say a 10's dead, go for an eight or even a six.'

Though the 2.5 litre proposal failed to materialize into anything further, and drivers have complained throughout the latest 3 litre formula about lack of horsepower, the future might still hold capacity reductions as an ultimate means of limiting the speed spiral.

★ ★ ★

The one thing that no amount of legislation is ever likely to succeed in containing, let alone reducing, is the cost spiral. The FIA attempted to appease the smaller teams when it changed regulations for the 1993 season by restricting tyre width and proposed making wings smaller. In the face of lobbying from the minor teams it kept rear wings the same size instead of reducing them, but obliged teams to mount them lower, thereby achieving the aim of reducing downforce while also achieving a modest cost containment.

Then there was the Ecclestone plan to save costs by limiting testing for 1997 (though most saw this simply as a means of clearing the decks for more races in

Widely regarded as a guru in Formula 1 circles, John Barnard's credits include the introduction of carbon fibre as a chassis manufacturing material, and the creation of semi-automatic transmission. (LAT)

future seasons). 'If it was up to me I'd do it the other way round,' Gary Anderson said. 'I'd make it so that at a race meeting you could do 100 laps on a Friday, all day long, the track would be open from nine o'clock in the morning until six at night. The public could come at any time and see the cars running. That's your test day. And then Saturday becomes the serious day, with qualifying. Something of that nature, where all the safety facilities are there. Then we'd have four Bernie Ecclestone tests a year, or whatever, and that's it.'

Both laudable ideas, but in Formula 1 the dollar will always be king, and there is one certainty: in the sort of technology race now being run: while the biggest budgets may not always be the best, the smaller ones certainly never will be. Frank Dernie spelled out the economic facts of life. 'The cost of Formula 1 is what you've got. It has nothing to do, whatsoever, with the technical regulations. If you had $150 million and you were racing orange carts, then orange carts would cost $150 million a year to run.

'Back in 1994 the money that was not spent on active suspension wasn't handed back to the sponsors on the basis of: "Thanks, chaps, we didn't really need this cash". It was spent on something else. So the technical regulations have got absolutely no influence on the cost of motor racing. The cost of motor racing is what the marketing department manages to persuade sponsors to spend. That is the cost.

'If you want to make the cars cheaper – forgetting the actual cost of the motor racing itself – the best thing to do is to not change the rules. Because the cheapest Formula 1 car that you can make is the one that's exactly the same as the one you made last year. No new moulds, no new research and development. And if you're really stuffed for money, just use the same wings and bits of body-work, the same radiators that you used at the last race. You can't get cheaper than that.

'Every time you change the rules, even if you change them to something that's in principle simpler, it costs a lot of money because it costs a lot of development to re-evaluate what you should be building, plus you've got to throw away all your old bits and make new ones. So until you accept that changing the rules is the biggest cause of escalating costs and stop changing them, you won't make motor racing cheaper.'

And the more clever the designers prove in circumnavigating rules designed to slow them down, the more it's going to be a repetitive cycle. It's called progress.

'It's always been like that,' Dernie concluded. 'Motor racing is all about trying to make your car go quicker.'

Unless you are the FIA, in which case it's all about slowing it down. As long as that is the case, the two will remain uneasy bedfellows, each trying to outwit the other. Which is where we came in . . .

Appendix

The FIA's mandatory crash tests

THE MANDATORY CHASSIS STRUCTURE crash testing introduced by the FIA dates back to 1985, and is intended to provide the utmost means of safeguarding the drivers in the event of foreseeable accidents. Most are conducted, under FIA supervision, at the Cranfield Impact Centre in Bedfordshire, though overseas teams may specify more local sites of a similar standard.

TEST 1
An impact test against a solid barrier (introduced 1985)
This is the head-on collision, the most nerve-wracking for the designer since failure can compromise the entire structure. The purpose is to ensure that the car can adequately protect the driver's ankles and legs.

Test structure
Nose box attached to a complete
  survival cell.

Impact speed
12 m/s.

Mass
780 kg.

Deformation
Limited to the nose box and no damage
  to the fixings of the extinguishers or
  seat belts.

Driver's feet have to be at least
  30 cm from the front of the survival
  cell.

Max mean g
25.

Conditions
Full fire extinguishers fitted.
Fuel tank filled with water.
Dummy, weighing 75 kg, must be fitted
  with seat belts fastened. During the
  impact deceleration in the chest of
  the dummy must not exceed 60g for
  more than 3 m/s.

TEST 2
A static load test on the top of the main roll structure (introduced 1991)
This is designed to assess the ability of the car to withstand inversion without its rollover hoop distorting or breaking under load.

Test structure
Main roll structure attached to a
  complete survival cell.

Test load
72.08 kN, which corresponds to a
  combined load of 57.39 kN vertically,
  42.08 kN longitudinally, and 11.48
  kN laterally.

Deformation

No greater than 50 mm measured along the loading axis and no failure more than 100 mm below the top of the structure measured vertically.

TEST 3
A static load test on the side of the nose (introduced in 1990)

Also known as the 'push-off test', this is designed to make sure that the nose, with its energy-absorbing deformable structure, remains intact during a glancing type of blow, as if the car has struck a barrier at a relatively shallow angle.

Test structure

Nose box attached to a complete survival cell.

Test load

40 kN at a point 55 cm in front of the front wheel axis.

Time

Test load must be held for 30 seconds.

Deformation

No failure of the structure or of any attachment between the nose box and the survival cell.

TEST 4
A static load test on both sides of the survival cell (introduced in 1992)

This is the 'crush' or 'squeeze test', and is designed to ensure that the monocoque chassis will provide adequate protection against side impact. The tests are carried out at various points along the length of the chassis. Gary Anderson tells the story of Jordan mechanics who, driving to Silverstone one morning, came across a damaged racing car monocoque laying in a hedge. It was Formula 1 sized, and it transpired that it was the Life (*née* First) chassis from 1990 which, having failed its crush test, had simply been discarded!

Test structure

Every complete survival cell.

All survival cells must be produced in an identical condition in order that their weights may be compared. The first is weighed and all subsequent units must be within 5% of the initial weight.

Test load

25 kN on the first survival cell, 20 kN on all the subsequent ones.

Test method

A pad measuring 10 cm x 30 cm is placed against both sides of the survival cell and the load applied.

Position

A vertical plane passing through a point mid-way between the front wheel axis and the front roll structure.

Time

Test load must be held for 30 seconds.

Deformation

No permanent deformation greater than 1 mm after the load has been removed. Furthermore, on all subsequent survival cells, the total displacement across the inner surfaces must be no greater than 120% of the displacement measured on the first survival cell at 20 kN.

TEST 5
A static load test on both sides of the survival cell (introduced in 1988)

This is another part of the 'squeeze test', carried out at driver hip level.

Test structure

Every complete survival cell.

All survival cells must be produced in an identical condition in order that their weights may be compared. The first is weighed and all subsequent units must be within 5% of the initial weight.

Test load
30 kN.

Test method
A pad measuring 20 cm diameter is placed against both sides of the survival cell and the load applied.

Position
A vertical plane passing through the anchorage point of the lap seat belts.

Time deformation
Test load must be held for 30 seconds.

Deformation
Maximum displacement of 20 mm and no permanent deformation greater than 1 mm after the load has been removed.

TEST 6
A static load test on both sides of the survival cell (introduced in 1988)
Another part of the 'squeeze test'.

Test structure
Every complete survival cell.
All survival cells must be produced in an identical condition in order that their weights may be compared. The first is weighed and all subsequent units must be within 5% of the initial weight.

Test load
25 kN on the first survival cell, 20 kN on all subsequent ones.

Test method
A pad measuring 10 cm x 30 cm is placed against both sides of the survival cell and the load applied.

Position
A vertical plane passing through the centre of area of the fuel tank side.

Time
Test load must be held for 30 seconds.

Deformation
No permanent deformation greater

than 1 mm after the load has been removed. Furthermore, on all subsequent survival cells, the total displacement across the inner surfaces must be no greater than 120% of the displacement measured on the first survival cell at 20 kN.

TEST 7
A static load on both sides of the survival cell (introduced in 1991)
Another part of the 'squeeze test', designed to assess the ability of the chassis to withstand an impact on the underside.

Test structure
Every complete survival cell.
All survival cells must be produced in an identical condition in order that their weights may be compared. The first is weighed and all subsequent units must be within 5% of the initial weight.

Test load
12.5 kN on the first survival cell, 10 kN on all subsequent ones.

Test method
A pad measuring 20 cm in diameter is placed against the underside of the fuel tank floor and the load applied.

Position
A vertical plane passing through the centre of the area of the fuel tank floor.

Time
Test load must be held for 30 seconds.

Deformation
No permanent deformation greater than 0.5 mm after the load has been removed. Furthermore, on all subsequent survival cells, the total displacement across the inner surfaces must be no greater than 120% of the displacement measured on the first survival cell at 10 kN.

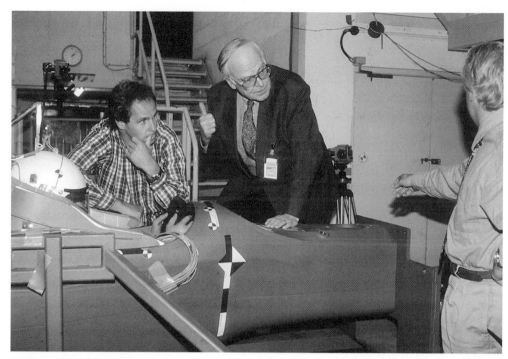

Benetton driver Gerhard Berger and Professor Sid Watkins witness a crash test. (Sutton Motorsport)

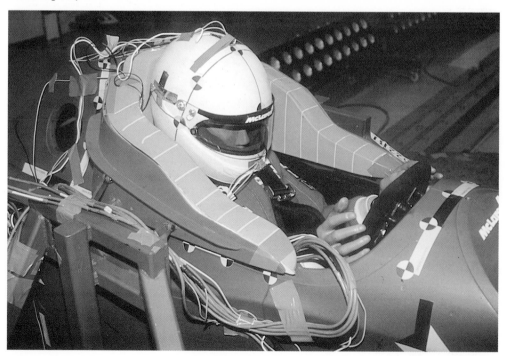

TEST 8
A static load test on both sides of the survival cell (introduced in 1991)
Another part of the 'squeeze test', carried out at the front bulkhead level.

Test structure
Every complete survival cell.

Test load
20 kN.

Test method
A pad measuring 10 cm x 30 cm is placed against both sides of the survival cell and the load applied.

Position
A vertical plane passing through the front wheel axis.

Time
Test load must be held for 30 seconds.

Deformation
No structural failure of the inner skins of the survival cell.

TEST 9
A static load test on both sides of the survival cell (introduced in 1991)
Yet another part of the 'squeeze test'.

Test structure
Every complete survival cell.

Test load
20 kN.

Test method
A pad measuring 10 cm x 30 cm is placed against both sides of the survival cell and the load applied.

Position
A vertical plane passing through the front wheel axis and the seat belt lap strap fixings.

Time
Test load must be held for 30 seconds.

Deformation
No structural failure of the inner skins of the survival cell.

TEST 10
An impact test against a solid barrier (introduced in 1995 and upgraded for 1998)
This is designed to assess ability to withstand side impacts.

Test structure
Side impact absorbing structure attached to both sides of a complete survival cell.

Test load
7 m/s.

Mass
780 kg.

Position
525 mm forward of the rear edge of the cockpit entry template.

Deformation
All deformation must be limited to the impact absorbing structure.
No damage to the survival cell is permissible.
Average deceleration must not exceed 10g.

TEST 11
A static load test on each side of the cockpit rim (introduced in 1996)
Another squeeze test to assess integrity of the cockpit opening.

Test structure
All survival cells must be produced in an identical condition in order that their weights may be compared. The first is weighed and all subsequent units must be within 5% of the initial weight.

Test load
10 kN on the first survival cell, 8 kN on all subsequent ones.

Test method
A pad measuring 10 cm in diameter is placed against each side of the cockpit rim.

Position
200 mm forward of the rear edge of the
  cockpit entry template.

Time
Test load must be held for 30 seconds.

Deformation
No permanent deformation greater
  than 1 mm after the load has been
  removed. Furthermore, on all
  subsequent survival cells, the total
  displacement across the inner
  surfaces must be no greater than
  120% of the displacement measured
  on the first survival cell at 8 kN.

TEST 12
**An impact test against a solid
barrier (introduced in 1997)**
The rear-end equivalent of the head-on
crash test.

Test structure
Rear impact absorbing structure
  attached to the gearbox.

Impact speed
12 m/s.

Mass
780 kg.

Deformation
All deformation must be limited to the
  area behind the rear wheel centre
  line.
Average deceleration must not exceed
  35g and the peak must not exceed
  60g for more than 3 m/s.

Glossary

ABS Anti-lock brakes – a system, similar to traction control, that monitors road wheel speed and reduces brake pressure automatically at the point of wheel lock-up.

Active suspension Computer-controlled suspension which automatically compensates a car's handling during cornering, to maintain optimum aerodynamics.

Airbag An inflatable bag that deploys automatically upon impact to safeguard a car's occupant from injury in an impact.

Airbox The opening at the front of the engine cover designed to encourage admission of ram air into the engine.

Autoclave An oven in which carbon fibre composites are baked to cure them into their intended operational condition.

Barge board A vertical panel situated within the front suspension to influence air flow aft of the front wing. Also called a turning vane.

Buck A wooden structure that duplicates the intended final shape of a component, such as a monocoque chassis, from which the chassis moulds are taken.

CAD Computer-aided design.

CAM Computer-aided manufacture.

Carbon fibre A carbon-impregnated cloth used in chassis manufacture.

Centre of gravity The point on the car through which the forces generated by its weight are said to act.

Centre of pressure The point on the car through which all of the aerodynamic forces may be said to act.

cfd Computational fluid dynamics – a branch of mathematics used to create predictional models for aerodynamic study.

Closed loop A computer circuit in which the system operates automatically.

cvt Continuously variable transmission – a transmission system in which the engine always operates at peak power.

Diffusor The section of the undertray that sweeps up to release the air that has been speeded up during its journey beneath the car.

Downforce The downward pressure generated by the car's motion through the air.

Drag Air resistance to the car's forward motion.

Endplate A vertical surface on the end of a wing, designed to influence airflow.

FIA *Federation Internationale de l'Automobile* – the governing body of world motor sport.

FISA *Federation Internationale de Sport Automobile* – former operating name of the FIA's sporting branch.

Five axis machine A cutting or milling machine capable of operating through a wide variety of angles.

Fly by wire A system wherein there is no mechanical link between components, only electronic, as in Formula 1 car throttle systems.

FOCA Formula One Constructors' Association – the association of Formula 1 teams.

Four poster rig A test rig comprising four posts, which can input forces to areas of a car on test. Used for static assessment of a car's behaviour.

GCU Gearbox control unit – the electronics system which controls the gearbox's shifting action.

G force The force of gravity acting upon a car or driver.

Gizmo Paddock name given to electronic driver aids.

Grenade engine The name given in the past to special engines with a short life expectancy, created purely to produce maximum power for qualifying. They were so close to the edge of mechanical reliability that they frequently self-destructed.

Kevlar A woven material used in racing car chassis and component manufacture.

Lift The pressure of air flowing over or under the car when it is in motion, that tends to try and lift it off the road.

Lift over drag The ratio of downforce (negative lift) to drag. High figures are the best.

Monocoque The name given to a racing car chassis structure in which the body and the chassis are integrated.

Open loop A computer circuit in which the system must be operated manually.

Oversteer The tendency of the rear end of a car to slide wide of the intended line through a corner, due to the rear tyre slip angles being greater than those of the front tyres.

Pitch The tendency of the front or rear of a car to move up and down, independently of each other, in reaction to changes in the road surface or aerodynamic loadings acting upon the car.

Pitch sensitivity Pitch sensitivity is a key to good handling. On a car that has low pitch sensitivity the aerodynamic balance doesn't shift around as the car pitches up and down over bumps, or tends to shift its centre of gravity under acceleration or deceleration.

Plank The rubbing strip of wood – usually Jabroc – fitted longitudinally beneath the floor of a racing car.

Pullrod A suspension component that operates a bottom-mounted spring/damper unit by pulling in response to the movement of the suspension wishbones.

Pushrod A suspension component that operates a top-mounted spring/damper unit by pushing in response to the movement of the suspension wishbones.

RAM Random access memory.

Ride height The height of a car's chassis above the ground plane.

Roll The lateral rolling motion of a car, especially during cornering.

Rollbar A steel bar which acts like a spring in the suspension system to resist a car's tendency to roll during cornering.

Rollover bar A hoop incorporated into the chassis structure immediately behind the driver's seat and also by his legs, designed to offer protection in the event of the car becoming inverted.

Scallop A shaped section of extra bodywork designed to influence airflow.

Seven poster rig A test rig comprising seven posts, which can input forces to areas of a car on test. Used for static assessment of a car's behaviour.

Sidepod Panel on the side of the car housing the water radiators, and an area of deformable structure.

Slip angle The actual angle at which a car corners, compared to the intended angle selected by the driver's positioning of the steering wheel. The angle may differ if the tyre is sliding across the road surface due to speed reducing its level of grip.

Slipstream The suction effect generated by airflow around the back of a car travelling at high speed.

Splitter A horizontal plate designed to separate – or split – airflow, thus directing it to different points of the car.

Strakes Horizontal or vertical plates designed, like endplates, to control airflow over a car body.

Telemetry A system mounted aboard a car, which gathers data electronically during power running, either storing it or transmitting it to the pit.

Traction control A system of electronically monitoring road-wheel speed and, at the onset of wheelspin, reducing engine power to control or obviate it.

Tread The area of the tyre that interfaces with the road. On slicks it is full width, on grooved tyres the area is significantly less.

Understeer The tendency of the front end of a car to slide wide of the intended line through a corner, due to front tyre slip angles being greater than those of the rear tyres.

Undertray The detachable floor of the car.

Wind-tunnel A structure, usually with belt-driven moving ground to simulate a car's motion, in which scale models are tested in fast-flowing air, in order to calculate a car's likely aerodynamic behaviour at full size.

Wing An aerofoil-section horizontal surface designed to create downforce.

Winglet A small extra wing, usually mounted on the bodywork just ahead of the rear wheel.

Yaw The tendency of a car to move laterally away from its intended direction of travel.

Index

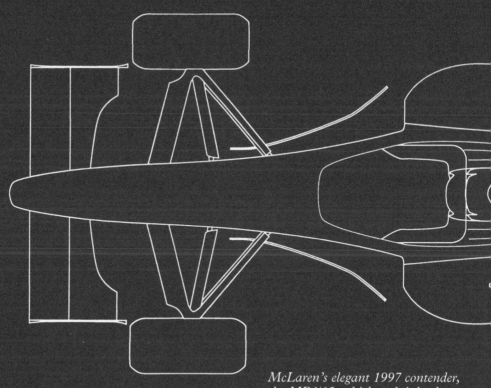

McLaren's elegant 1997 contender, the MP4/12, which took it back into the winner's circle after a three-year drought. (McLaren International)